HERITAGE

HERITAGE is a roman à clef. It was first
published in 1955 in America, and has never
before appeared in this country.

Like Richard Savage, author Anthony West is
the illegitimate son of distinguished and
flamboyant parents, the unhappy product of a
long and tempestuous liaison which ended
admist much bitterness, between Rebecca
West and H. G. Wells. Taken to live with his
mother, albeit grudgingly on her part, the
young Anthony was a bone of contention
caught between these two extrovert celebrities
who brought him into the world without a
thought of what they were doing.

The parallels between fact and fiction are
blatant; the 'secret' of HERITAGE is out – thirty
years after its first appearance and only two
years after the death of that grand old lady of
English letters, Dame Rebecca West. But with
or without historical models the novel is filled
with the breath of life – angry, powerful and
honest it stands not only as a recollection of a
remarkable upbringing but as a brilliantly
inventive work of fiction in its own right.

HERITAGE

'A compulsive read . . . Anthony West is an excellent period scene-painter, with a highly individual gift for a grave-faced brand of comedy-farce'

The Guardian

'What makes the book startling is Anthony West's introduction, as devastating an indictment as any son has written of his mother . . . an extremely well written, vibrant, oddly touching portrait'

Sunday Express

'HERITAGE is an outstanding novel, containing unobtrusively penetrating psychology and an almost Proustian sense of the past . . .'

Financial Times

'Life may have supplied the farce behind it, fuelled it with bitterness, but Mr. West has had the skill to externalise his outrage and make out of it a passionate piece of fiction that would stand alone even if one didn't know the key . . . A fine, gripping read'

Daily Telegraph

'Altogether pleasing'

Sunday Times

About the Author

Anthony West was born on August 4, 1914, in England, and has lived in the United States since 1950. He started out to be a painter and has been successively a dairy farmer, news editor for the BBC, critic and novelist. He has written criticism for the *New Statesman* and the *New Yorker*; a brief critical biography of D. H. Lawrence; and two previous novels, THE VINTAGE and ANOTHER KIND. His most recent publication is a biography of his father H. G. Wells: ASPECTS OF A LIFE.

Heritage

Anthony West

'These are long vendettas,
a peculiar people, neither
forgivers nor forgetters . . .

CORONET BOOKS
Hodder and Stoughton

For Morton Thompson

Copyright © 1955, 1984 by Anthony West

Introduction copyright © 1984 by
Anthony West

First published in the United States of
America in 1955 by Random House

First published in Great Britain in 1984
by Martin Secker & Warburg Ltd

Coronet edition 1985

British Library C.I.P.
West, Anthony
  Heritage.
  I. Title
  813'.54[F]   PR6073.E757

ISBN 0–340–36938–8

Printed and bound in Great Britain for
Hodder and Stoughton Paperbacks, a
division of Hodder and Stoughton Ltd.,
Mill Road, Dunton Green, Sevenoaks,
Kent (Editorial Office: 47 Bedford
Square, London, WC1 3DP by
Richard Clay (The Chaucer Press) Ltd.,
Bungay, Suffolk

Introduction

It is the custom for the author of such a novel as this to introduce it with a disclaimer to the effect that it is fiction and not fact, and that while it is true to its creator's experience it is not the truth about any particular part of that experience. From there it is usual to go on to assure the reader that any resemblances between the invented phantoms who inhabit its pages and any actual persons, living or dead, are purely coincidental. With that business out of the way I will confess that it was not by chance that my narrator-hero came to have Richard Savage for his name, and that the intentional reference it makes, to the early eighteenth-century poet whose mother did her level best to get him hanged, was a mistake. It was a case of taking up a bludgeon to do what a stiletto would have done more neatly. Time softens all things, and I can now also allow that my own mother never went as far with me literally as the Countess of Macclesfield felt able to go with her son. That, however, brings me to the end of the concessions I feel able to make in that quarter. The truth of how things were between my mother and myself was that from the time that I reached the age of puberty, and she came to the point of a final rupture with my father, she was minded to do me what hurt she could, and that she remained set in that determination as long as there was breath in her body to sustain her malice. When I wrote this novel thirty-five years ago I was angry with her. I had lately transplanted myself to the United States to make a fresh start in life, three thousand miles out of her way, but I had found myself pursued by her animosity even at that distance. I had been doubly offended by the steps she had taken to make it difficult for me to make a career for myself in my new country because she had set about the job of queering my pitch with a blatancy that made it plain that she thought me too much of an idiot to notice what she was about. I had the vain hope that if I made it clear to her that I was under no illusions as to the lengths to which she was going to disoblige me, she might tire of her sport and drop it. The calculation, as I should have known, was a fatuous one, and, as I should also have realized, the stupidly-clever idea of using Richard Savage's name had prejudiced whatever chance of success I might have had with the manoeuvre. And then I had also called the book *Heritage*. . . .

The chain of events that led me to pick that title began soon after my mother had come to the parting of the ways with my father. Once it had become clear to her that there were no circumstances in which he would ever think of marrying her she decided to adopt me. The step was explained to me as a prudential one. Unadopted, I would have to make my way through life producing, whenever I had to give formal proof of my identity, a birth certificate that named both my parents, declared my mother's condition at the time of my birth to be that of *spinster*, and so disclosed my bastardy to anyone who saw it: adopted, I would be the possessor of a document recording merely that I was born on such and such a date, and that on another, fourteen years later, legal process had made me the child of a spinster, Cicely Isabel Fairfield, "also known as Rebecca West," with whom I had no recognized previous connection. When I grew up, I was told, I would be able to understand how greatly this improved my condition. It was not pointed out to me at the time that this highly symbolic performance also removed my father from my pedigree, in law if not in fact.

My mother married money not long after my adoption went through, and within a year or so of that happy event she felt called upon to inform my father that he need trouble himself no more to provide for me in his will as her husband, Henry Andrews, was making me his heir. My father later asked me if I knew anything of this, and with a certain complacency I told him that I did, and that he wasn't to worry about me. Henry was *really* rich, and as I understood it I was to come into the bulk of his estate when he died. My father looked at me quizzically for an instant after I had said this, and then let the matter drop, observing that if it were really so I ought to be all right. I recalled his words, and the expression that had been on his face when he uttered them, some years later while I was listening to the reading of his will. Under it I was given the right to take such personal souvenirs of him as I might fancy from the contents of his house, and nothing else. This was not, the document went on to say, because he had anything against me, but because he understood that, unlike his other children, I had substantial expectations from another quarter. When I heard that explanation a flash of intuition informed me that my designation as my step-father's heir had been functional, and that I was not likely to enjoy that status for much longer now that its function had been fulfilled.

My insight was confirmed three years later in the course of a melodramatic scene that was enacted on the front steps of my home in Dorset. Its pretext was an advertisement that had appeared in the two "quality" Sundays on the previous day, in which the publishers of my first novel had announced its forthcoming appearance as one of the titles on their autumn list. Each of the dozen books featured in the advertisement was given the briefest of brief descriptions followed by a snippet of background information about the writer. Of me it was said that I had promise, and that I had begun work on a biography of my father, H. G. Wells. On the morning after this atrocity had run on the book pages of the two papers concerned, my step-father, having proclaimed his coming, drove over from his home near High Wycombe in his Rolls Royce to bring me an ultimatum. He wouldn't come into the house, he explained when he had arrived, because he didn't want to impose himself on me as a guest until he had let me know what he had come to say. It was consequently from a point about half-way up the front steps that he let me have it. He was extremely angry with me for having been so thoughtlessly cruel as to allow my publishers to exploit the dormant scandal of my mother's connection with my father. Its revival had given my mother unimaginable distress. He was prepared to go to any lengths to spare her a repetition of what she had been through in the previous twenty-four hours. He wanted me to understand that unless I was willing to give him my solemn undertaking never to lend myself to the commercial exploitation of this most private of private matters again he would have to think seriously of changing his will. He reminded me that a considerable sum of money was involved, and begged me to do what he asked. I was taken aback by his proposition, and could only tell him that I couldn't possibly do or say anything that might seem to suggest that I had any reason to be ashamed of being the child of either one of my parents. Henry then turned to my wife, Katherine Church, who was standing beside me, to say, with what affected to be a rueful smile, that he deplored my attitude. He hoped, he added, that she would become his ally in the task of persuading me to modify it; it might make it easier for her to do so if she were to consider what the ultimate consequences of my obduracy would necessarily be – the interest that our two children had in his estate as things were would be extinguished along with mine should my conduct force him to change his will. Kitty's response to this was to say "Well *really*, Henry!" and to go indoors, turning her back on him. My step-father lengthened his normally long face considerably, gestured as if to indicate his helplessness in the face of so evident a case of *folie à deux*, told me that he would give me a week to think the matter over, reminded me of the sum that was at risk, and departed. He presently did what he had threatened to do, and that was the end of my expectations.

I was given an even clearer idea of the extent of my mother's passionate desire to do me harm a little while later when I had foolishly involved myself in a sufficiently banal marital difficulty. I fell very hard for a young woman who was as nice as could be, and extremely attractive to me, but who was, literally, a passing stranger.

I made a heavy over-investment of emotion in what should never have been more than an episode, and was soon in a fair way to upsetting my apple cart. My mother gave me every assistance in overturning it. As soon as she became aware that my marriage was going through a rough passage she summoned my wife to London for a lunchtime conference, naming the extremely pleasant, sumptuous, and quiet eating-room at the Green Park end of the Ritz as their meeting place. When she got there Kitty was surprised to find that my step-father was one of the party. She was even more surprised when my mother, after commiserating with her briefly, launched into a presentation of the case for an immediate divorce which had the form of a denunciation of myself and all my works. My mother had, it seemed, been living in dread of the very thing that was happening ever since our marriage. She had never thought that it could last. She had always known that I was utterly irresponsible and – yes – unstable. There was an unaccountable streak of something base in my make up that had made me curiously unreliable even as a child. When it came to a divorce Kitty would have to put herself in the hands of someone really good; if there was the slightest vagueness in the terms of the final settlement she would live to regret it. I was shifty about money matters, and could be relied upon to get at her through the children if I was given any loophole that would allow me to do so . . . At that point Kitty objected that it was early days to be talking about divorce. She was far from sure that it need come to that. As she understood things it was common enough for both men and women who had married young to be overtaken by feelings of sexual restlessness when they felt their middle years closing in on them. She could see that there might be dangers for her in what was happening, but she still felt that far too much was being made of something that was, in her opinion, most unlikely to be the big thing that I was making out of it. She didn't think that there was any chance that it would last. My mother responded to this by exploding with rage. She began by telling Kitty that she was the biggest fool she had ever tried to help out of an appalling situation. I was an utter rotter, and she was an idiot to let me trample all over her. She raised her voice as she launched into a lengthy indictment of my past and present performances. As she ranted on conversation ceased at most of the other tables in the room, and the waiters gave up even the pretence of attending to their duties in favour of standing and staring. Kitty is at a loss to explain how the two men concerted their action, but the scene came to an abrupt end when my step-father and the head waiter, moving together as if they had rehearsed the procedure a dozen times, each took my mother by an arm close to the elbow, plucked her up out of her seat, and carried her from the room, dangling between them. She continued her vilification of her daughter-in-law and myself until the doors of the room closed behind her.

It would be pleasant if I could say that this episode had relieved my mother's feelings and had required no sequel, but that would not be true. The fact is that my mother was never able to forgive Kitty for being generous and understanding where I was concerned, and that the interrupted tirade that was broken off in the Ritz on that memorable occasion was destined to be taken up again, and again, at irregular intervals through the remainder of her life. Each new turn in the melancholy history of my deteriorating relationship with her brought Kitty its fall-out in the form of yet another batch of letters taking up the theme of my vileness and aimed without disguise at extinguishing the last remnants of any residual affection she might have for me. Close to a hundred and thirty of these letters survive. Some of them are brief notes, but the majority are old-fashioned letters of the kind that people used to write before time became as precious as it is today. They are written on both sides of as many as six sheets of eight by ten paper, and their texts can run to better than five hundred words to a side. Some of them contain more than six thousand words. Of the archive as a whole my ex-wife says that it constitutes a fascinating involuntary self-portrait of someone who was treacherous and dishonest, and whose leading passions were money, malice, and meddling. I can agree with that, but for me the pitiful and extraordinary thing about it is that it is *typical*. Katherine Church was not the only recipient of such outpourings – there are at least a dozen archives similar to hers in various hands in England and America, and there may be several more. Some are a good deal larger. Those I am familiar with have it in common that they were built up over periods of years, that they show the same delight in disseminating spiteful slanders and untruths, and that their substance consists of releases of hostility and aggression aimed at specific *bêtes noires* on a private hit-list. One of these collections was in the making as early as the winter of 1922–23, and another, which means rather more to me, covers the period extending from 1924 to 1970, and consists of letters that were addressed to John Gunther. It yields a remarkably complete picture of who my mother's hates were over those years, and contains a more than adequate explanation for the strength of my feelings about that much misunderstood lady. In the days between 1924 and 1928, when my father was the chief of her *bêtes noires*, my mother was having an affair with John. When they first met he was straight from Chicago, and the ultimate in the new school of American foreign correspondents who had learned the reporter's art, so far as they had learned anything, by chasing police cars and hanging around city halls and state capitols. They came to Europe to "cover" it, as ignorant of its history, demography, and economics as they were of its languages. John's physical beauty was as absolute as his innocence: he was six foot two, lean as a rail, golden-haired and golden-skinned, and endowed with marvelously clear blue eyes. He was aflame with enthusiasm for the new world that had been opened to him by his transfer from the windy city to Paris and Vienna. He had the air of being an angel, over-joyed at finding himself a witness to the creation. My mother was thirty-two, he was twenty-three, and I was ten, when the affair began. If he had hung about he might possibly have become a bore, but he came and went unpredictably as the focus of the news shifted in and out of London, and before one had time to be sated with the flawless beauty, the unlimited enthusiasm, and the endless repertory of exciting stories of what was "really" going on wherever he had just come from, he would be gone again. I became very fond of him, and as I grew up he remained high on the list of those people I always looked forward to seeing again. He took a fatherly interest in me and always made me welcome when I showed up on his horizon. When I emigrated to the United States in 1950 the thought that I could count on his friendship when I got there made the move seem a great deal less of a plunge into the void. He was a good friend to me while I was finding my feet, and remained so thereafter. It came as a considerable shock to me to learn after his death that he had been one of those my mother had done her best to turn against me. As soon as she learned of my impending move to New York she began to bombard him with revised versions of her Ritz tirade, warning him that he would be well advised to have nothing whatever to do with me, and building up a formidable case for my untouchability. She could not bear to think that he might be fool enough to befriend me or think well of me. I was not to have anybody's friendship or regard.

I fear that my take grows tedious, and I will only add one more thing to it before I close my case. In the year after John Gunther's death my mother entered into a literary relationship with a certain Gordon N. Ray who has described the resultant book, which deals with her affair with my father and its aftermath, as a collaboration between them. She read, Ray tells us, the successive drafts of his story as he worked them up, corrected his errors of fact, and "filled in the inevitable omissions of a narrative based on fragmentary materials." It is clear from this, I think, that my mother knew of everything that Ray included in his text, and contributed substantially to its content. This means that if she did not actually invent the nasty story in Ray's book that ascribes my existence to a very dirty trick played on her by my father, she at the very least passed it for publication. Ray encapsulates it in the following words: "In an angry moment, when he feared that Rebecca might leave him, Wells intentionally omitted his usual precautions in the hope that pregnancy might bind her to him." I will not speculate as to the strange necessities that have to lie behind the fabrication of this, or as to the purpose that its publication was supposed to serve, and will content myself with saying that in view of the record of which it forms a part, *Heritage* seems to me to be a positively genial and good-humoured work.

Anthony West
September 1983

1

Castlereagh Gardens are to be found in South Kensington, the part of London between the Fulham Road and Kensington Gardens which was taken over from market gardeners and horse copers by the speculative builders in the decade following the Great Exhibition of 1852. The builders replaced the stiff rows of cabbages and Brussels sprouts and the neatly brushed hedges with stiff rows of cliff-faced stucco-fronted houses in a dead Palladian style. Round the corner there lay the friendly inconsequence of old Chelsea, and little proletarian streets with bow-windowed public houses at their ends, but this was an area regularly laid out to express the importance and respectability of its residents, people who knew how to live with dignity.

But the Gardens had gone a long way down hill by the time we went to live there in the early twenties, when I was five or six. In a street just round the corner several houses had been knocked together and turned into a hotel, and although it called itself a family hotel the truth was plain to see—they would let rooms to anyone who had the money to pay. They even had public dances on Saturday nights, and in summer the faint throbbing of their music stole out through a skylight and round the corner into the Square. A committee of residents drafted letters of complaint and talked of legal action each year, but nothing was done. And each year more houses surrounding the Square were turned into flats. When we moved in there were very few left in private hands.

As they had been planned for lavish private lives they did not convert very well and the more I think over our old apartment the odder it seems as a mechanism for living in. We had the old drawing room floor, and the floor above. An elaborate operation had been performed on the old service staircase to make it into our private staircase, and an old boudoir had been divided to make a kitchen and a dining room in a way that produced two rooms as high as they were wide and long. I still remember the odd sense of being the wrong size that the disproportion of the dining room fireplace gave me, planned as it was for a room double the size, and my excitement when I discovered that the elaborate cornice ran straight through the wall and was continued on the other side in the kitchen. It gave me the feeling that we lived in something like a tent or a stage set, which could be struck and rebuilt at will.

From our front windows we could look down into the gardens, a formal Victorian planting with serpentine gravel walks, and rolling lawns broken up by thickets of laurels and evergreen shrubs. The ground floor people had French windows opening onto iron staircases which led straight out into this enclosure, and one spied on them enviously from above as they walked their Sealyhams and Pomeranians, or sat about in deck chairs in kindly weather. They had garden privileges as of right, but we had to apply to the Garden Committee for membership and pay two guineas to get a key to the gate in the speartipped cast iron railings which kept the vulgar out.

We had a key for a couple of years, a cast iron object weigh-

4

ing just over a pound, painted green, and my mother's plan was that I should let myself in whenever I wanted and run wild there for as long as I liked. But she had not read the rules. It was not easy to run wild in Castlereagh Gardens. The rules that began, "All dogs will be kept on leashes in the Gardens," not only prohibited the use of balls, bats, racquets, and kites but also said that "Children and dogs will be accompanied by an adult other than a servant when in the Gardens."

It was in the end more amusing to stand in the window of the drawing room watching the proletarian dogs that squeezed their way through the railings being chased out than to go down there. When I did venture to slip into the holy enclosure by myself it was only to play a kind of hide and seek. Within five or ten minutes from the time I turned the massive key in the lock, no matter how discreetly I behaved, I would feel that I was being watched. Looking along the line of ground floor windows I would find that at one or another of them a shadowy figure was pushing a lace curtain aside with a finger and peeping out anxiously to see whom I was "with." Then in a few minutes an elderly lady would emerge, in stiff-jointed indignation, either to expel me in person or to send the gardener over as her deputy.

After one of these encounters, with a general's widow of sporting instincts who had stalked up behind me to take me by surprise, catching me with my eyes fixed on quite the wrong window from the cover of a clump of sooty Portugal laurels, I went indoors and asked my mother why we lived in such a horrid place. She looked at me with surprise and with a certain irritation: "But darling, it's one of the very nicest parts of London . . . everyone knows that. Most people would love to live here—so close to the parks and the museums."

The parks were a long way off, it seemed to me, far off at the upper end of the monotonous splendors of Queens Gate, and as I knew by experience that nothing would induce my mother to go for a walk in the park or to visit the museums this answer did not satisfy me—it merely added to my curiosity about my mother.

She was not in the least like a Kensington lady, she could not really believe that these sterile gardens, enclosed with cliffs of stucco in which no voices were ever raised, were "one of the very nicest parts of London." I had no very clear ideas about the rest of London. I had only seen parts of it from bus tops on the way to Kew, to Richmond, to the Tower of London, to the Olympia Circus on sightseeing excursions and treats with MacEwan, the Scotch combination of general servant and nursemaid who looked after my mother and myself, but almost all that I had seen seemed alive and amusing in a way that Kensington was not. It did not seem possible that she could pretend that she belonged in these gray streets with these gray people who lived so quietly and with such restraint.

But then the problem, which occupied me more and more, was to know what kind of person she was, what she was, beyond being my mother. She was so many different people that it seemed impossible that she could be any one of them, much less all of them. I knew that she was an actress as well as my mother but that did not explain very much.

Our life together was to me full of mysteries. When I was at home I woke early, as most children do. I would have been happy to be up and doing before the morning lost its freshness, but mornings were always a time of silence and quiet movement on tiptoe, sacred to my mother's professional necessity for sleep when other people were awake. I would play quietly with my toys in my box of a bedroom or read a book, nesting among my rumpled bedclothes, until MacEwan tapped on my door with a fingernail, like a Japanese witch fox, to tell me that breakfast was ready. Then we ate together, whispering a little but not talking much, in the kitchen in the former boudoir, waiting until my mother's bell released the normal volume of human speech. Sometimes it rang before nine-thirty but not often. It usually broke into its jarring whirr between ten and eleven. Years later my mother told me that a famous beauty whose look of youth had been almost miraculously extended into her sixties had given her the secret of her ageless appearance: "Never let them wake you, darling. . . . I've never been called in my life." This secret for preserving an unwrinkled face provided the rule by which we lived through my childhood, an iron rule even though it gave to every day a different starting point.

Once the bell had sounded its summons, MacEwan went into action. Coffee almost as strong as Turkish coffee simmering on the stove was poured into a thick china pot from Normandy that stood warmed and ready beside the percolator, croissants wrapped in a hot cloth were whisked out of the oven and were put on a tray with one huge cup, a single plate, a knife, a pot of butter, honey, and the five daily newspapers. MacEwan swept out of the kitchen with the tray, her starched white apron crackling briskly against her stiff black skirt, almost before the old-fashioned bell had finished jangling at the end of its coiled flat metal spring. I went along behind her, clutching the letters in a bundle, anxiously wondering what Mother's mood was going to be.

If it was bad she would be lying back, sunk into the bed rather than lying on it, with her hair tousled round her like black sea-wrack, her face heavy and lightless, like someone surrendering furiously to an incurable illness and filled with morose hatred for those unstricken. She would mutter a barely civil good morning to MacEwan and wave me away—"Not this morning, Dickie love, Mother's terribly tired." And I would go and be glad to go because there was a sullen ugliness in her face at these times that frightened me, and if I did hesitate a flash of something like hatred would appear and I would be waved off with a gesture of rejection that I found almost too hard to bear on the few occasions when I was fool enough to let myself in for it.

But if the mood was good she would be sitting up smiling, radiant with a warm brown vitality, running a comb through her dark mass of red-black hair, and after joking with us both she would allow me to sit on the end of the bed, opening the letters for her with an onyx-bladed paper knife. It was always a moment of pure delight when I saw her large-mouthed smile on her morning face as I peeped at her round MacEwan's skirts, and knew that I could dart over to the white and gold baroque desk-cum-bureau-cum-dressing table where the onyx-bladed paper knife was to be found among a litter of stockings, chemises, lipsticks, nail files, make-up bottles and jars, unanswered letters, judgment summonses, prompt copies of plays, real jewels, jade and coral brooches, and Indian and Arab bracelets. The knife generally nested between an eighteenth-century green malachite ink stand that served as a paper weight and a square blue china flower tank from Spain which had held, for as far back as I could remember, dark red, and coral red, paper and wax roses.

When I had found the knife I jumped up on the end of the bed and curling up in the yellow silk eiderdown began the fascinating business of opening the letters as neatly as possible while Mother ate her breakfast. She drank the coffee black and ate the croissants more thickly buttered than I have ever seen bread or rolls buttered by anyone else alive. Each little piece of croissant was dipped rapidly in the honey and swept up to her mouth before the sticky gold syrup ran down onto her fingers. Sometimes she popped the pieces into her mouth in time, but as often she did not, and then licked her fingers like a little cat cleaning its paws, putting her tongue a long way out and touching her sticky fingers with its very tip.

While she ate she rolled her eyes sideways and looked at the letters that I laid in front of her. "That's a horrid-looking bill, you can throw that one away. You needn't ever worry about a bill until they send a letter with it." "That looks like

Kip Wiley, put that aside for me to read." "That's some silly little boy who wants a photograph, put it aside on the theatre pile—the people down at the theatre will send him what he wants." "That's a love letter, I'll read that now." If there were enough nice letters and love letters to balance the horrid bills, and if there were no County Court judgment summonses on their cold blue paper, insisting on attention to bills too long disregarded, I would be allowed to stay and read the papers with Mother.

She could not bear to read a newspaper that had been touched by anyone else, and she read them at lightning speed from page one to the back page. As soon as she finished each one she would throw it over to me. "You must learn to read them faster—they aren't worth more than ten minutes each— but if you do know what's in them nobody can make a fool of you."

Sometimes she would draw my attention to particular stories in the news and explain them to me in her own rather special way.

"Did you see that piece about Huey Long? About somebody hitting him in a nightclub. I met him when I was in Washington after the thing I was in in New York folded. He came to dinner in a white suit with tiny thin pink stripes, blue socks with purple stripes, a pink and white tie, a white shirt, and those horrible white and brown shoes. He's a horrible sort of genius. . . ." and then she'd imitate Huey Long.

Or I would tell her that I had read a story about a riot in Paris and she would describe the French police in their flat-topped hats and waterproof capes, and the Parisian mob, and how once she'd seen a charge of mounted police broken up. "Those horrible men had thrown down thousands of children's marbles and the poor horses couldn't keep their footing. . . ." Her nostrils distended with terror and she became a plunging horse with its feet sliding out from under it. Her untidy hair fell over her face, her bare arms made extravagant gestures, and her plain cotton nightdress gave her the air of a gamine of eighteen or nineteen.

She had been everywhere and seen everything, or so it appeared. She pulled out all the contents of her photographic memory as if she were sharing a box of toys with me.

The best times of all were when there was a new murder in the papers, crime reporting in the twenties and early thirties being the strong point of English journalism. She would read the accounts of the investigations and trials in her deep "serious" voice, scamping none of the details.

"Ooh, good, there's a wonderful new mystery—they've found a leg in a parcel caught up a willow tree near the Haw Bridge in Gloucestershire and a body under a floor in Cheltenham . . . listen to this. . . ." And then we'd discuss who was guilty and what was going to happen next: "Of course *he* did it, listen to this appeal he's made to his wife to come out of hiding. Every word of it's bogus, you can tell . . ." and she would read the murderer's desperate piece of lying in a way that brought out all its uneasiness and panic. "They'll find her buried under one of those new chicken houses—you can be sure of that . . . just you wait. Look at the photograph with the detective standing just beside him . . . you can see the detective knows he's killed her. . . ."

She transformed her big baroque bed, flanked by chubby cherubs holding reading lamps that simulated torches, into a little Guignol theatre, and ravished me with pleasures that were not the least less delightful for being thoroughly unhealthy by modern educational standards. But these performances always ended abruptly and unpredictably.

"Well, that's quite enough of that—run along, lamb. I've got a part to study." And then she would spend the rest of the day wrapped in a remoteness that was in its way as frightening as were her moods of anger and discontent. In a

10

pink quilted dressing gown, stained down the front with coffee and carelessly applied make-up, with a stocking or a scarf for a belt, her feet jammed into a slatternly pair of old mules, she would pace up and down the apartment muttering her lines, occasionally letting go with an alternative reading given the full register of her voice.

"It's all been a most dreadful mistake, I never dreamed that you would do this. . . ." "Oh Jamie, Jamie, I can't believe it. . . ." For the most part, while she mouthed these things, she was utterly indifferent to my presence, but occasionally she would become aware of me and her glazed eyes would suddenly gleam with recognition.

"Oh go away—why aren't you out in the park or playing somewhere—why can't you behave like an ordinary child? Why are you always loafing around fugging indoors pestering me . . . MacEwan, MacEwan, take Dickie out for a walk, do something with him . . ." and then she would stalk off into her bedroom.

"What have I done to deserve such a child? . . ."

MacEwan would come on the run and clap me into an overcoat and hat and we would scuttle out breathless into the open air.

"You and that woman will be the death of me yet. . . ."

If it was fine we would walk up Princess Gate to wander in Kensington Gardens for an hour or two and go home at last to a tea of muffins or buttered toast, eaten with whispers in the kitchen. If the weather was wet or cold we would go and sit among the potted palms in the tea rooms of one of the Kensington department stores listening to the melancholy string quartets playing saccharine music, or go to a movie until an hour or two had gone by and the emotional storm was over.

By then the mood would have changed and the exasperation would have a new focus: "Wherever have you been, MacEwan—I've been waiting for you for hours—I can't have you giving up all your time to that child. I haven't a dress that's fit to wear. You've really no excuse for falling down on your job this way. . . ."

These scenes only too often built up in sequence and they would end with dramas in which I had no part. I would hear MacEwan's Scotch burr rumbling against my mother's bell-like declamations.

"It's impossible, I tell you, impossible. I cannot have my entire life disorganized by that child. It's hopeless for me to even try to work in the circumstances. My work's going to pieces—I'm at my wits' end. . . ."

"The poor mite does all he can to keep out of your way, ma'am. I found him playing with his toys under his bed this morning. . . ."

"Yes, that's the sort of thing. Hiding and spying. I can't bear it. . . ."

I hid in my room and effaced myself as far as possible while these discussions followed their inevitable line of development, to the point at which Mother would say, "It's no use, Mac-Ewan, I tell you it's no use—the child must go to Willingham's."

Once this had been said there would be an interlude in which Mr. Willingham was written to and the arrangements were made; a time of heavy tension which MacEwan would ease as best she could by arranging little treats for me—lunches of foods I specially liked, buttered toast at tea, and gifts of boxes of toy soldiers or sets of pasteboard scenery and actors for my "tuppence colored penny plain" toy theatre. Occasionally, at these times of waiting, she would take me in her arms and hold me silently for a minute or two with a look of almost unimaginable sadness on her face. It was a decent Scotch face that never had a touch of make-up on it, and it was not expressive of emotion of any kind at any other time.

MacEwan had another human name, Maggie or Margaret, but nobody had ever heard it or heard her called by it. I was allowed to call her Mackie when she was in good humor, but my mother always called her MacEwan as if she were a man talking to a manservant, and so did everyone who held any sort of intimate or friendly relation with my mother. Naomi Savage's butler in skirts was a joke and legend among the theatre people who came and went in the apartment. Larry Brook, who wrote smart comedies and who at one time was supposed to be a contemporary Congreve, used to invent MacEwan anecdotes: "Naomi's dragon said the divinest thing yesterday. . . ." I heard these stories told at my mother's cocktail parties, at which I was allowed to be present if I kept silent, and they made me wonder because I had never heard MacEwan say anything in the least funny. They made me a little ashamed too, because I knew that often enough, when the frightening blue County Court writs came in and there was no money in the house or in the bank, MacEwan went to her big black handbag with pursed lips to take out cash or her Post Office savings book. She had often helped Mother through such a crisis. We seemed to be either very rich or very poor, but MacEwan always had something, and it was often very badly needed. I never quite understood how Mother had the courage to laugh with Larry Brook and follow up his nonsense with inventions of her own that ended with a peal of laughter. ". . . yes, MacEwan's really too absurd, I don't know why I put up with her. . . ."

The woman who said this, fashionably dressed, impeccably made up, and with beautifully arranged hair, had no movement, no gesture, and no intonation that I ever saw when I was alone with her. She was another person called into being by the entry into the apartment of such people as Larry. I was more frightened of her than of the sullen and silent morning mother because she seemed dispassionate, cold, and only too capable of deciding that she could not "put up with" MacEwan or me or anyone whom the mood suggested that she obliterate. She was often nice to me with the sort of niceness that this personality was capable of, after she had decided to send me to Willingham's. When she heard that there was, and there always was, a vacancy there, and that I would be expected by the next convenient train, she would lull her conscience by taking me to lunch at the Ivy, the smart theatrical restaurant, before packing me off, giving me by the way of congé an exquisite farewell meal that was invariably rounded out by the gift to me of a box of petits fours from Monsieur Abel, the head waiter. It was with a stomach full of Perdrix au Chou and Glâce Jalouse (Rebattet's recipe) that I would be put on an afternoon train at Victoria and sent off into exile in Kent.

The Willinghams were two old troupers who had retired from the profession when Mrs. Willingham's father died and left them his farm near Sandwich. At first picturing themselves in the roles of the old squire and Lady Bountiful, surrounded by a respectful peasantry, they had tried to make a go of the farm as a farm. But they soon came up against realities and were brought down to earth. Actors marry actresses because it is convenient that way, and then lazily or carelessly have children, which, unless they are extremely successful, is not in the least convenient. They have to go on tour, they lead irregular lives, and their ups and downs make it very difficult for them to establish any kind of settled home. Their children are at best a problem and at the worst a curse until they can fend for themselves. The Willinghams, having had a taste of these difficulties, realized, once they had gotten over their first panic at the apparent impossibility of making a farm pay and the endless hard work that it entailed, they could make a much better thing out of running it as a boarding house for actors' children.

They were nice people and they did one very well. There was all the milk a child could drink for the asking, and it was creamy milk too. The eggs were fresh, the bacon was good green home-cured bacon made from the Willinghams' own pigs, and there were plenty of vegetables to eat that came fresh and sweet flavored out of the walled garden at the back of the house. The orchard trees were fun to climb, and, though they were never pruned or sprayed, they produced a great many firm-fleshed apples of the old-fashioned kinds that keep well all through the winter in a twist of newspaper on an attic floor. The barn was full of swinging ropes, rope ladders, and hay to jump on and hide in. Mr. Willingham even kept six or seven safe, pottery little New Forest ponies about the place for us to ride. It was, as everyone who sent a child there could and did say, a wonderful place for children.

The number of the boarders varied from nine to eleven and they were nice enough; the Willinghams were swift to get rid of bullies or troublemakers and I never had any unpleasantness of that kind while I was there. In fact, I remember most of them with affection, particularly Angela Deacon, the fat, friendly, permanent boarder of fourteen or so, who used to take me into her bed and cuddle me on nights when I felt like crying or actually cried to be back with Mackie. She used to tickle me with the ends of her thick black pigtails and tell me stories and she generally succeeded in cheering me up very quickly. Her parents were with a touring company which had somehow lost itself in the Southern Hemisphere and seemed unable to get back to England. They had gone out, full of hope, to play Africa, then Australia and then New Zealand, and Angela had accumulated, as the years of her childhood went slowly by, a very complete collection of illustrated post-cards of the British Dominions and Crown Colonies.

"We should be back in a month or two, meanwhile, darling, remember the old song and keep smiling! It won't be long now, we promise, your loving old daddy and mumsie . . ." Some of Angela's cards were seven years old, but their tone of opti-mism never faltered and Angela believed with an ironclad determination that next week or next month she would be whirled across Kent in Mr. Willingham's car to meet the

P & O or Union Castle liner that would bring her father and mother home. I remember once when I refused to be comforted by her stories of happy reunions and unexpected meetings she fell silent for a little while before she said in a choking voice, "There must be a happy ending, there must, there must . . ." but it was the furthest she ever went towards a breakdown.

On the whole Mr. Willingham did his best to make it a happy place, but he hadn't ever been able to overcome his taste for the easy goodfellowship of the touring companies he had once played with, or his inclination for billiards. Acceptable substitutes for the one, and the other thing itself, were to be found not far off in the little towns of Minster and Sandwich, in the bars of the inns and in their billiard rooms. He spent much of his time there, and judging from the pinkness of his round, open face, which made his walrus-like whiskers seem so brilliantly white, and by the faint smell of liquor that mingled with the scent of tweeds, tobacco, and peppermint throat lozenges that always hung round him, he drank a great deal while in pursuit of his amiable pleasures. He used to return in guilty frame of mind, but we favored that since he purchased absolution for himself so far as he could by visiting the sweetshops before he set out for home. When he came up the drive holding the steering wheel of his little Morris car very tight, and going very slowly, we used to rush out to meet him happily because he was always loaded down with a couple of dozen quarter-pound bags of toffees, boiled sweets, and bars of milk chocolate.

"This is for you because you're good," he would chant as he shared them out. "This is for you because you've got such a funny little mug, this is for you because you've got eyelashes a foot long, this is for you because you fell and skinned your knee yesterday, this is for you because you look like a teddy bear. . . ." It was the sort of thing children love and we loved it—it was like having extra birthdays or an unexpected

16

little Christmas. There was always an odd bag or two of sweetstuff left over too, because Mr. Willingham could never remember just how many children there were under his roof at any given moment; the extra sweets had to be shared out with complicated counting games, half sung in his mellow actor's voice.

"One for puffin', one for stuffin', and one for the gal with the golden hair, one for poodle, one for noodle, and one for the juggins without compare. . . ."

We enjoyed these breaks in our absolute lack of any sort of routine so much that it was hard to understand why, when the first rush of fun and laughter was over, Mr. Willingham often became tearful and was to be heard begging Mrs. Willingham to "forgive your foolish old darling for this once, and believe me, my dear, I do promise with my hand on my heart that it will never happen again."

It seemed wonderful to us and we wanted nothing more than that it should happen again and again. Needless to say, it always did, and needless to say Mrs. Willingham did not seem to mind very much.

Mrs. Willingham had been an ingénue, and an ingénue she had remained, wearing her hair in a girlish long bob, affecting dirndls of bright materials covered with floral patterns and moving with coltish, adolescent gaucherie even though time had brought her an extra hundred pounds or so and a whiteness and pinkness that matched her husband's. She played with us as if we were so many dolls a kind providence had miraculously produced for her, and welcomed us with genuine delight.

It was always she who met us at Minster Halt and every time it was as if something specially nice had happened quite unexpectedly for everybody concerned.

"Why, there you are, you dear little thing," she would say, her china-blue eyes enormous, her eyebrows arched as high as they could be pushed, like croquet hoops, and her arms spread wide. "Gracious, I'd forgotten what a lamb it is, a lamb, a little lamb . . ." She packed the new arrivals into the Morris, or into the Minster taxi if Mr. Willingham was off on one of his sprees, chatting away.

"Angela is still with us, and your friend little Dickie Marchant, and the Morton boys, and Lolly Hughes, oh, there are heaps of your old friends . . . and next week Poppy Lewis— you don't know her but she's a lamb—the prettiest little red-haired thing you ever saw—is having a birthday and we're doing a little ballet in the barn for it and all the older ones are doing a play, and there's been another new calf, and I've never seen so many chicks, the downy silly little things! Dickie, lamb, this is going to be the best time of all. . . ." And one was pulled up under the brim of her flower-loaded straw hat to be given a hug and a great smacking kiss. It didn't seem at all bad to be driving under the arching elms up the lane that led to the Willinghams' farm.

And yet, all the same, when I woke up the next morning in one of the little farm bedrooms, jam-packed with iron bedsteads and sleeping children, to realize that I was not at home, I felt sad, and every night at bedtime at the Willinghams', however good the day had been, I remembered Mackie giving me a last kiss on the platform at Victoria station and muttering, "Don't fash yersel', child, the woman's mood won't last, and you'll be home again soon." It was very important to have that promise in mind, worthless though it so obviously was, just as the promises broken again and again on Angela's postcards were an important saving part of her life. It was impossible to endure existence in this inconsequential Eden unless there were a term to it, and as the days dragged by, turning into weeks, "it isn't going to be much longer." Occasionally, the certainty wore thin and another certainty replaced it. Minster would be one's setting for the rest of one's natural life, there would be no release, and one would grow up with the Willinghams as Angela Deacon was growing up.

These thoughts in spite of the resolute cheerfulness of the place, produced tears and no matter where one hid or how far away one went to have the cry out, the tears, the grief, were detected by Mrs. Willingham's psychological antennae. Before one well knew what was happening her fat comfort was all around one, and one was snuggled into her lap on the blue plush sofa in the front parlor and her tears were mixed with one's own.

"What a silly little pet it is to think it's forgotten! It's the most loved of lambs it is, it is. I know! I know there'll be a letter for it in a day or two . . . but I tell you what, we'll have a pretend birthday tomorrow, with a real cake, and lots of sugar buns all for you because I love you so. . . ." She would write or send a telegram that day to the parent her foster child had cried for and the letter would arrive within the time promised. But hard as she tried to make the place a home and to fill it with love, she fought a losing battle and we were all as glad to go as we were sad to come.

Mackie knew how I felt about the Willinghams' and it was by way of compensation for my being sent there that one surprising day she showed me what my mother did and what an actress was. Mother was out to lunch before playing a matinee and Mackie and I ate in the kitchen before setting out to catch the two-fifteen train to Minster. She had cooked a spring chicken with sweet corn for me as a going-away treat and she was upset when she saw that I couldn't touch it. The scenes during the preceding week had been unusually violent and it was plain to me that the only reason I was being sent away was that I was a nuisance and a distraction about the place. To put it as flatly as I then felt it, I knew that I just wasn't wanted. MacEwan suddenly looked at the clock, looked at me, and came to a decision.

"You'll never understand what all this is about until you see what the woman's up to," she said. "I'll likely lose my place for it but it's better that you should know why you're put upon the way you are than that you should worry your wee heart out. We'll be off to the theatre, and I'll just put you on a later train."

She got me up from the table and started buttoning me into my coat.

"I'm taking you to see your mother act and if there were any sense in things you'd have seen what she was at long since, as I've said time and time again, but there's no talking sense to some people."

MacEwan hurried me off to the theatre, after telephoning a message to Willinghams' saying that I would be coming on a later train. As we climbed into a taxicab on the rank at the corner of Castlereagh Gardens and set out for the Palinode Theatre my heart was beating wildly and I was deliciously excited. I had no idea what to expect, and I was half afraid that I was going to see my mother in some shameful secret activity (why else had she kept it from me for so long), half enormously excited at the thought of seeing the inside of a real theatre at last. . . .

The Palinode was a small enough theatre, built in the eighteen-fifties in the style known to decorators as Louis Quatorze, but as we came into its white lobby, which seemed to have been made of whipped cream, I was enormously impressed. The scarlet carpet, the heavy black doors with their dozens of panes of beveled glass, swinging incessantly as the crowd pressed in to take their seats, the palm trees in brass tubs, the gold-framed mirrors, and the enormous chandeliers all seemed incredibly splendid to me. One of the best things about the place was the painted ceiling.

I looked up at it with excitement and a certain instinctive, prudish horror. A naked woman with the soft white wings of a pigeon was peering down at me through rosy clouds and getting ready to blow a long post horn of the sort formerly carried by the guards on stage coaches. MacEwan had anchored me by a potted palm and threatened me with instant departure for Kent if I moved before she got back with the tickets. I was quite pleased to stay staring upwards, fascinated by the nudity and the mysteries of the painting. To the right of the lady was an old man with a beard and a long roll of paper in one hand and a quill pen in the other; he hovered in the clouds without the aid of wings.

Why did the lady need them if he didn't? On the other side of the lady was a young man with long gold curly hair coming down to his shoulders, strumming on a harp; he had wings, bigger than the trumpet lady's, with black tips to the flight feathers. I speculated on the strength of my memories of the chickens at the Willinghams', perhaps the lady was a plain lady like the way white leghorns were plain hens, and the harp man was like a speckled Sussex. If they laid eggs together, I wondered, would the chicks have black in their feathers or not? And the old man with the pen was probably some sort of Manx angel—I decided they probably were some kind of angels, even though they seemed so bare.

I felt I was being watched and looked around me. Tubby Anderson, the theatre manager, had come into the lobby from his office, following his usual habit of taking a look at the audience before the show, and was staring at me. I knew him at once, I had often seen him at Mother's cocktail parties.

"Hello, youngster, come to see Mummy act?"

"Yes, please, Mr. Anderson, MacEwan's buying the tickets now."

"What the devil's she doing that for? She can have any seat she wants any time. . . . She's only got to ask. . . ." He looked over towards the box office and met MacEwan's eyes as she made her way back towards us.

"What's all this about . . . why are you buying tickets to Naomi's show? . . ."

MacEwan gestured towards me. "Little pitchers . . ." she said mysteriously. "The boy's being packed off to the country again and I'm letting him see his mother act before he goes."

A curious expression crossed Anderson's face. "You mean she doesn't . . ."

"No," said MacEwan, "and she'd better not . . ."

"Poor little blighter," said Anderson. "I'd give you a box if you'd like it—but perhaps you're safer in the dress circle."

"I think we're best out of sight," said MacEwan. "Out of sight, out of mind, and no harm done."

"You know best, I suppose," said Tubby, and stared down into my face with a wondering look. "Have you never seen your mother act before?"

"Oh no, sir. It's terribly exciting."

"Well, I'll be damned," said Tubby. "I'll never make that woman out, never, until my dying day," he said half to himself. "Here, boy." He pulled a handful of change out of his pocket and fished out four half-crowns. "Here's a sort of tip. This is going to be a day to remember."

"I'll look after them for you," said MacEwan, scooping the money out of his hand. "Now thank Mr. Anderson properly."

A look of curiosity came over his face. "Does his father ever . . ." he began.

"Not a word, please," said MacEwan, cutting him off. "We'll be saying good-bye."

I looked back as we started, to smile at him in gratitude, and saw him staring at us.

MacEwan had bought seats off to the side of the front row of the dress circle and as we took our places there I stopped thinking altogether. I was simply a pair of eyes and ears absorbing the theatre. I had never seen so many faces before, rising tier after tier of pink blobs against shadows in the white and gold and scarlet of the house. I listened to the bustle and stir of an unsettled audience for the first time with a strange knotting in the pit of my stomach that I've never forgotten and I turned away from the house to stare up at the dusky gold masks of tragedy and comedy crowning the proscenium arch. I felt the change that instantly came over the

22

murmurous and fidgety crowd as the lights began to dim and I knew by some instinct that it was a good audience. The two gold masks slowly faded into blackness and a bar of light suddenly appeared at the foot of the huge scarlet curtain below them. The knot in my stomach tightened and then abruptly vanished as the front curtains swung apart and the drop curtain behind them, flooded with the magic glow of the footlights, slowly floated up out of sight. Two Roman soldiers stood at the foot of a flight of stairs, splendid in their golden harness and scarlet cloaks, magnificently browned, their helmets held in the crooks of their arms. I gasped at the sight of them and gasped again when I heard a man's voice richly giving out the masculine equivalent of what I had always thought of as my mother's pretend voice, and which had always frightened me as part of some mysterious private game.

"Nay but this dotage of our General's o'erflows the measure; those his goodly eyes that o'er the files and musters of the war . . ."

I grabbed at MacEwan's hand beside me in the dark and clutched it for dear life as I heard her mutter, "It's in the blood, you poor wee beastie, and what else?"

She pressed my hand a few seconds later and whispered, "Now here comes your mother, hold on tight. . . ."

She came on stage in the hieratic headdress of an Egyptian Queen, robed in dark green and blue clouded over with a mist of small gold stars, with Antony all gold and scarlet beside her, and behind them two gigantic Negroes in silver, white, and blue holding crescent-shaped feather fans. Then I heard the voice, richer and softer than I had ever heard it before, familiar and yet wholly unfamiliar, welling out and rolling through the huge cave of blackness around them.

"If it be love indeed, tell me how much . . ."

It was an astonishing and unforgettable revelation and from the moment of that most gloriously contrived entrance—one of the greatest gifts of the race of playwrights to the race of

23

actresses—until the death scene in the monument, I was fascinated and intoxicated.

MacEwan tore me away while Mother and the cast took their curtain calls. Looking back of my shoulder as we hurried up the aisle towards an exit, I saw that Mother and her colleagues were already softening out of their roles and turning into people, smiling everyday smiles in response to the applause which cracked the stylized make-up on their faces, and somehow disowning their Roman and Egyptian clothes by moving in an easier twentieth-century manner. Antony turned to my mother smiling and took her hand, she smiling turned to Caesar and took his, and with linked hands all three bowed towards the house. The noise of the applause, a rising and falling like a mild surf, insulated them within a private silence in which they seemed to resign the power they had so recently been using, to fill the whole auditorium with their voices. They were no longer Kings and Queens, but polite people responding to the compliments of people like themselves.

I remember that I cried in the taxi going to Victoria. It was too much to find that I was still going down to Kent. After so great a discovery, everything should have been changed, and nothing was. I could not explain my feelings to MacEwan and so I took refuge in tears, twisting sideways in my seat to lay my head in her lap unable to explain that there was more of pleasure and excitement behind my tears than pain.

She stroked the back of my head and comforted me in her stern Northern way with harsh words.

"Don't snivel, child, there are more things to cry about in life than going away from home to a farm with ponies to ride, and a crew of young people to play with and that daft Mrs. Willingham to mother you. You'll be laughing at your tears tomorrow. Sit up and keep your chin up. There's my wee man."

She dabbed a little cologne on a handkerchief on my cheeks and round my eyes.

"We'll not let anyone see you've been crying when we get to the station, will we . . ."

She was in a spoiling mood, unusual with her. Before she put me on the train and put me in charge of the guard, she bought me an armful of magazines, the *Sporting and Dramatic,* the *Sketch,* the *Tatler,* and the *Illustrated London News.* It was not at all an unpleasant journey, and the intoxication that had come upon me in the theatre returned to make it go by like a flash.

I remember kneeling on the seat of the empty first-class carriage in which the guard had locked me, watching the lighted windows of the suburban houses sliding by, and, as we passed on into the countryside and the houses thinned out, following the double dance of the telegraph wires and the train lights. The oblong bars of yellow light radiating from the carriage windows now stretched out long and thin as the train ran along an embankment above open fields, now tilted upwards to become short and fat as it clattered through a cutting, flicked upwards to climb hedges or walls or dropped startlingly into a velvety crevasse as the line crossed a road or a stream. In counterpoint to this brisk, jerky, dance of the lights, there was the slower movement of the skein of gleaming wires looped from telegraph pole to telegraph pole, now high above the window, now level with it, and now below it, repeating endlessly their gently curving swoop from pole to pole.

While I watched this ballet, to which the hammering rhythm of the train wheels lent a primitive, African, blood-stirring quality, half hypnotized by excitement, by nervous exhaustion, by the reflections on the window glass, and by the movement outside, my inner eye presented to me again and again the vision of my mother as a Queen.

It was clear to me now that at home she was not a real person at all, that I only knew her when she was in the state of a victrola that was not playing, a radio that was not switched on, a toy shut up in a box or drawer. I played in those days elaborate games with toy soldiers, in which the little lead figures sustained roles as generals, emperors, heroes, assassins, and conspirators for weeks at a time. But I knew that when I was away these personalities ebbed out of them, that they became for MacEwan parts of "my clutter" and were swept up and tipped into shoe boxes to be put away in the toy cupboard as dead things. It occurred to me that the life I shared with my mother was part of her toy-cupboard life, that it was an irrelevant phase of her existence, and that I had that afternoon glimpsed its vital part for the first time. Beyond the orchestra pit in that rich blaze of light behind the proscenium arch, she existed fully and completely, she was there. I could see too, clearly enough, that I did not belong out there, I was no kin to the Queen of Egypt, and if I were to penetrate that magical barrier that divided the audience from the players to demand companionship and attention my demands would appear unreasonable and fantastic.

I imagined, in a waking dream, that MacEwan had taken me to the theatre dressed for the park—in my round flannel child's hat, my winter coat with velveteen revers, and the corduroy gaiters buttoning up at the sides that were the most detestable part of my walks, and led me onto the stage to rebuke my mother for neglecting me. Naomi blasted me with that early-morning gleam of hatred, the Romans stared aghast, and gales of laughter came from the rows of pink faces in the darkened house. Tubby Anderson ran scowling out from the wings and, grabbing me by the shoulder, ran me off stage.

"Does your father . . ." he shouted, grimacing with fury, and shaking me. MacEwan ran up behind him and clapped her hands over his mouth.

I looked up startled into the brick-red face of the guard who smiled down at me. . . . "We're in Minster, Laddiebuck, it's the end of the line for you. Gather up your magazines and I'll hand down your bag."

I stepped out into the cold night air and into the snug little-ness of Minster. The church clock struck the hour, eight or nine perhaps, I forget, though I remember the thin sound of the strokes muffled by a bank of elm trees, the lighted train stretching along the platform like a black and yellow ladder lying on its side, the fishtail gas jets in the square-sided station lamps, and the glinting reflections on the enameled advertisements fixed to the wooden fence at the back of the platform. That was another first in that crowded day—my first arrival at a country station by night.

As I stood shivering a little with my bundle of still unread magazines under my arm, Mrs. Willingham sailed down the platform spreading her arms out wide in the usual way.

"Why there the darling child is—I thought it would never arrive—but bless it here it is—and I'm so glad to see it."

I ran a little way to meet her and gave her back hug for hug as we collided. I wanted to tell her about my discovery of the theatre, about Antony and Cleopatra and of my new happiness at once, but she didn't give me a chance to speak until we were in the Morris and rattling along the dark lanes towards the farm.

Mr. Willingham had come down to meet the train with his wife and they had waited for me in the Bar Parlor of the Railway Arms opposite the station so they were in a mood to respond to my enthusiasm when I did start off talking about Antony and Cleopatra. Mr. Willingham had played Enobarbus once, and to my delight filled the car with a plummy, vocally upholstered reading of the barge speech as soon as I named the play. After hearing the speech for a second time I could parrot it, or a good part of it, and in my excitement burst out with it after him.

"God bless my soul," cried Mr. Willingham. "The divine fire is there, the ichor is in the blood, the boy is doomed, doomed. . . ."

He took one hand off the wheel and patted me on the back.

"Doomed, Mr. Willingham?" I faltered. "Have I done anything wrong?"

"You're frightening the poor child, Hal, you old silly," said Mrs. Willingham.

"Why, you little juggins, I only meant you had it in you to become an actor. I think he will, Flossie, my dear. I'm sure he will." He patted me with warm friendliness.

"He might just as well be a famous writer like his father," said Mrs. Willingham. "Why, lamb, you'll be whatever you want to be if you want hard enough. You're such a bright little thing, really you are."

"My father?" I said, seizing on it, "who is my father? Is he alive? Is he a very famous writer?"

"Why, of course. Don't you know? You silly little thing?" asked Mrs. Willingham. "He . . ."

"Now you've put your foot in it, Flossie," said Mr. Willingham.

He put his arm around me and patted me like a dog. "Flossie's an old rattle," he said. "She doesn't mean half what she says. You mustn't pay any attention to her. She doesn't know anything about your father, I don't believe, no more than you do. Tell me more about that play. Did they do that piece about the music under the ground properly? That used to scare me more than anything else in the theatre. I'll swear that even watching it from the wings has made my hair stand on end. . . . 'T's the God Hercules, whom Antony loved now leaves him . . .' Remember that?"

He prattled on. Mrs. Willingham blew her nose loudly several times until Mr. Willingham told her rather sharply to come off it, and after that we drove on in silence. I wasn't at the farm very long that time, less than a month, but although Mrs. Willingham mothered me to the top of her bent, and arranged more distractions and surprises than ever before, the days seemed to drag interminably. I longed to be back home so that I could catch my mother in such a radiantly good mood that it would be possible to ask her the question the Willinghams couldn't or wouldn't answer. I rehearsed, in my mind, endless scenes in which MacEwan told me the truth I was burning to know.

But when I did go home to London and the apartment, Mother was gone, she was playing Cleopatra in New York with the rest of the company and after that she was to go on to Hollywood to make a movie. It would be an eternity before she returned. I slipped into her room the first morning after my return and stood there for a long time staring about me. MacEwan had set everything to rights and it looked like someone else's bedroom. All the carelessly thrown down clothes were neatly folded away in drawers or hanging in closets. The desk-dressing-table was neat and tidy and the vast bed looked as unused as if it were in a museum.

At each side of its enormous carved head there were a number of photographs grouped closely in a colorful mosaic of small antique picture frames of rubbed gold, boxwood, amboina wood, tortoise shell, and silver. I looked at them with a new curiosity, playwrights, actors, a bemedaled soldier in uniform, a man seated at a piano, the driver of a racing automobile in white crash helmet, a man standing beside a rugged race horse, a child of nine or ten dressed as a Zouave, a man with a lean thoughtful face sitting on a terrace looking over the sea with two dark cypresses behind him and beyond them a vista of white, foreign-looking houses.

I climbed on a chair to look at the little faces, wondering if perhaps one of them was my father. But there was no way of knowing. The smiling or serious faces disclosed no secrets. Their smiles took a deceitful complexion, and those who were not smiling seemed to look guarded and hostile. They were my enemies, hostile guardians of the secret, I decided as I peered narrowly at them, counting the frames. I had heard, somewhere, the title of a Greek play or story whose title seemed to me to be filled with a sinister magic—*The Seven against Thebes*—and, recalling it at that moment, began to plan my own drama, *Fourteen against Richard*.

MacEwan came by the open door and saw me standing there, with my feet on the rose-red and cloth-of-silver Spanish brocade cushion cover.

"Off it, you young limb, and out of there before I fetch you out."

"Mackie," I said, "I'm sure you know, please tell me about my father . . . please, please."

She flushed, standing solidly with the dustpan and brush in her hands, a figure beyond anything practical and unsentimental.

"That would be telling," she said, "and I've promised that I won't. Now come on out of your mother's room, and be off to your toys or books. We'll be away to the park later when I've finished my work."

I jumped down from the chair and ran at her in a black rage, longing consciously for the first time in my life to hurt someone beyond their endurance.

"I hate you, Mackie, I hate you. I hate you more than anything," I screamed and pummeled her stomach and her solid thighs with my fists.

"I hate you. I hate Mother. I hate everybody."

She took me by the shoulders and shook me till my teeth rattled. "I don't wonder at it," she said. "But you've no call to take it out on me. You'll find out all you want to know when your mother wants you to find out, and that's all I can tell you for now."

I subsided with the fury shaken out of me and retired to my room and to the imaginary world of toy soldiers over which I had full control.

Mackie went to the kitchen and wrote a letter, as I afterwards learned, to my mother, saying that she could no longer take the responsibility of looking after me unless the questions

I was asking were answered. I don't know how she put things but it was apparently the wrong way because her letter produced an immediate result. Mother's lawyer, Johnny Wallis, a dark man with a troubled face, came to see us within a week. He had received a cable from America.

"Give MacEwan two months' wages and dismiss. Put Richard in good boys' boarding school. America more wonderful than ever. All love. Naomi."

I don't know what my mother expected that the effect of this message would be or if she had thought of it as having any effect—it might have been a purely automatic gesture, like brushing a fly off one's face almost before conscious of the irritation of its presence. Before I fully realized what was happening Mackie was gone. I had spent an odd ten days as a bewildered guest at the Wallis house and presently, with an outfit of strange new clothes, I was at St. Michael's school for boys.

There is a good deal to be said about such places and their effect on the English character but it would be beside the point. All that I can say is that I have never encountered anything quite so unpleasant in life since. What is to the point is that I very soon made a friend of a short round-faced fair boy called Dulley whose scarlet ears stood out from the side of his head like handles of a jug. He approached me one day as I stood aimless and unhappy at the side of the asphalt playground during the noon break, about a week after I had arrived.

"I say, new bug, what's your name?"

"Savage. What's yours?"

"Dulley. But I've been here a term, you're not allowed to ask me questions. It's some silly custom or something. My father's a journalist, what's yours?"

"I don't know."

"What do you mean, you don't know? Is he dead or are your people divorced?"

"I don't know."

"I say, you aren't illegit, are you? That would be terrific. Didn't you ever ask your mother?"

"No, I don't know why not, but she gets in a bate if you ask her questions she doesn't want to answer."

"I say, that sounds jolly promising. You're probably a missing heir or something, like in books. Is your mother anything special, like a Duchess or anything?"

"I think so. She's an actress. I saw her once. It was marvelous."

Dulley looked alarmed. "You mustn't say marvelous here. Things are wizard or terrific. . . . Savage? Holy Joe, she isn't Naomi Savage, is she? She is, why that's wizardly-terrific."

He looked at me and brushed a lock of yellow hair off his forehead. "All rotting apart, I mean really, it must be fun to have a mother like that. I wish I did. I bet you are illegit, though, actresses do that sort of thing more than anybody. It'll be a terrific thrill finding out who your father is. I bet my father knows."

Every Saturday and Sunday was a visiting day at St. Michael's. Parents could come down and take their children out to lunch and tea if they wanted to and they were allowed to take out one guest of their offspring's choice. Dulley wrote home immediately after this conversation and told his father that I would be his guest on the following Saturday.

"Dear Father, Strange Minor fell on the steps of the san yesterday as he was coming out after getting a dose for being bunged up and broke his arm and fractured his skull. He has concushern. We had the first football match of term on Saturday and played Saint Ermin's they won sixteen to seven. I have a new friend whose mater is Naomi Savage and can he have lunch with us on Saturday. Bring an Ingersoll please, there is a craze for watches this term. Yours with love, Edwin."

He showed me the letter before he mailed it, with a worried look: "You don't mind if I say that, do you? I could have just said you were jolly nice or something and not said anything about your mother, but I thought that would be a sort of thrill for the old man."

I said I didn't mind at all and the letter went off.

St. Michael's stood back from Lamorna Avenue at the end of a brief avenue of gangling lime trees thirty or forty years old. On visiting days schoolboy ritual demanded that one go and sit on the top bar of an iron fence which ran along under this line of trees, to wait for one's parents. That will not sound at all unpleasant to anyone ignorant of the ways of British schools, and visually the sight of fifteen or twenty small boys in blue and yellow caps, blue blazers with brass buttons, and gray flannel shorts, kicking their pink legs and fidgeting in the dapple of the leaf-filtered light was agreeable enough. But the occasion was none the less a social ordeal, productive of a dozen kinds of torment. The cars in which the parents arrived were closely scrutinized and remembered, a boy whose parents arrived in an old or shabby car would be teased mercilessly in the following weeks about his family's poverty. One boy who went to St. Michael's in the same term that I did was known as Birdshit all the time he was there because his mother drove up to face the waiting line of critics in a touring car with a canvas hood on which a gull or some such larger bird had left a white and black trace of its passage.

When the parents arrived the boy had to get off the fence and saunter towards the car with a show of indifference, shaking hands with the people he loved and saying with a blank face:

"Hallo, Father, hallo, Mother . . ."

Woe to him if his mother kissed him or greeted him with a nickname. If that happened he would be greeted by a mob of jeering boys when he came back in the evening to face the cheerless barrack-like common rooms. They would jostle round him covering him with wet kisses.

"Let Mumsie kiss her little oodly, boodly, baby boysie, come and be kissed lambkin, come and be kissed lambkin, let Mumsie kiss its little baby lambkin den. . . ." they would shout in mocking falsetto voices.

Woe, too, to the child whose mother or sister appeared prettily or unusually dressed in anything but the correct bourgeois country uniform of a tweed coat and skirt and showed the slightest sign of being a freak or nonconformist. So one took one's place in the visitors' line with apprehensions that nicely balanced any anticipations of pleasure to come. Dulley's father was on to all this, and careful not to expose his son. He gave a beautifully controlled performance as he brought his open sports car to a stop at our feet, not smiling at the other boys (which would have been criticized as fishing for popularity or, worse, as showing off) and limiting his expression of love for his son to a small wave, a mere lifting of his gauntleted hand a couple of inches from the steering wheel.

"Hallo, Dulley," he said and smiled at me as he shook hands across the low side door. "I don't have to be introduced to you, Town," he said.

"He's Savage," said Dulley. His father flushed. "I'm sorry, Savage, it just slipped out.

"You're so like your father it's funny. You've got Max's eyes and eyebrows—it's amazing. I'd have known you in a crowd. Well, jump in and let's get out of here."

We ran round to the far side of the machine and squashed into the bucket seat beside him, pulling a leather rug with a tickly fur lining up over our knees. We went down to the end of the driveway and turned round the circular patch of grass and tuft of pampas grass in front of the stucco schoolhouse, then drove back past the row of watchful, expressionless faces, and out onto the open road. Dulley, sitting stiff with excitement beside me, nudged me as the car began to gather speed and the blustering wind began to buffet our cheeks.

"I say, that's pretty wizard about it being Town, isn't it? I knew it must be someone terrific. You are a lucky beast, I'd love to have exciting parents like that."

I grinned and opened my mouth to answer, but got a mouthful of wind that choked me as the car accelerated.

I should know more about that second day of discovery than I do, but when I look back I remember only that we had cold salmon, which was new to me, for lunch, and that we had a picnic tea in a hired electric canoe on the Thames, under the banked woods of Cliveden upstream from Boulters Lock and Maidenhead. The polished mahogany of the boat and its maroon cushions piped with yellow cord seemed wonderfully luxurious to me. And nothing had ever pleased me so much before as the flashing, darting life of the river.

We followed a rowing club eight out for practice for some time and I don't suppose that I will ever forget leaning over the throbbing side of the canoe watching the gaily painted oar blades biting into the water at the beginning of each rhythmic powerful stroke that drove the long narrow shell forward so sweetly and easily. It was much easier to think about that sort of thing than about the strange and unexpected discovery that my father was Max Town. He was divided from me by something harder to cross than a mere row of footlights, a barrier of print and a reputation. I had seen his photograph beside feature articles on the League of Nations and similar subjects of political aspect in the daily papers, a darkly foreboding, serious, public face, and I had seen his name on the backs of books. Such a person seemed remote and dead, as far off as Dickens and Thackeray, quite out of the world I inhabited. I trailed a finger in the brown water of the Thames and wondered what he was like when he stepped out of the pages of his books or came out from behind the newspapers.

We slid up to the bank and moored for our picnic under a huge alder. Mr. Dulley produced strawberries from inside a wicker basket, a pot of cream, and a blue Tate and Lyle sugar bag; perhaps it would be enough just to know who my father was without bothering much about what he was. Sooner or later I would find out, somehow or other.

Mr. Dulley had forgotten about spoons. He showed us how to eat the strawberries without. You bit off the tip of the berry, dipped it in the sugar, then into the cream, then popped the white globe into your mouth. I thought of Mother eating croissants and honey and laughed. Life was fun and full of ridiculous small pleasures. It was exciting to have learned in this casual way who my father was and it would be amusing to put him together, piece by piece like a jigsaw puzzle, as I found out more about him. Meanwhile there were more important things to think about—the strawberries and a pair of small dark eyes which kept appearing and disappearing in a cranny among the alder roots. Presently the shape of a water rat gathered round the eyes. It slid out of its burrow and dived into the river with a startling plop to swim away underwater on a course indicated by a line of fat bubbles which drifted slowly off down the greenish-brown stream. It was an afternoon to remember.

2

It only takes a pebble to start an avalanche, and Dulley's father started one with a few idle words a couple of days later. He went to his club for lunch and, as he went upstairs to the dining room, found himself walking beside my father. "Hallo, Max," he said, "this is quite a coincidence. I was having lunch with your son the other day." "Oh, were you? Which one? Freddy or John?" "Neither—the young one, Dickie Savage—he's at the same school as my boy, and they seem to be friends. He's a bright kid. We had a very good afternoon on the river. It's amazing how like you he is; I'd have known him anywhere."

My father said something noncommittal and they went on upstairs to eat. He thought about Mr. Dulley's remarks during his meal, and they stayed in his mind later while he was getting the worst of a political argument with two young Tories in the coffee room. When they left him he found a vent for his irritation: he went over to a desk and dashed off a letter to my mother on the club writing paper.

It was to the effect that I'd been so badly brought up, and

that she'd handled things so stupidly that I'd been boasting about my distinguished parentage at St. Michael's and making capital out of my irregular origin. A journalist had got hold of the story and had been pestering him with sly innuendoes and threats of adverse publicity. This had got to stop. He was exhausted by his recent trip to Russia, and desperately trying to finish a new book. It was intolerable that he should be bothered at such a time. Unless Mother could control her own and my insatiable appetites for notoriety he would have to take legal action to protect himself from this endless probing and prying into his private life. He knew that there were very good boys' schools indeed in Switzerland; one of them, run by two Germans and an Englishman, was an outstanding educational experiment. If my mother would agree to send me there he would make himself responsible for the school fees. As her child I was liable in any case to be highly strung and unstable, it was vital that I should not grow up thinking that I was in any way an unusual or exceptional child. It was in my best interest that I should be put in a school where I would neither be exposed, nor tempted to expose myself, to the activities of mercenary and unscrupulous journalists.

He slipped the letter into an envelope, stamped it, and went out and mailed it in the brassbound club postbox by the porter's lodge. The storm of nervous irritation was over and his spirit was purged. He walked home to his pleasant house on the south side of Regent's Park by way of Manchester Square and Marylebone High Street, dropped in on Frances Edward's bookshop, and browsing there among the stacks forgot the whole thing.

He didn't think of it again for a couple of weeks. On his way back from Russia he had visited East Prussia and had there encountered Lolotte, the Grafin von Essling-Sterling-hoven, who had followed him to England and installed herself in the Regent's Park house shortly after my father had sent off his explosive letter to my mother. She was the daughter of a former German military attaché to the embassy at Constantinople and a very beautiful Phanariot Greek woman he had married. She had inherited an imperious strength from her father, beauty and warmth from her mother, and she brought vivid confusion into Max's life that he very much enjoyed when he felt like playing, and detested when he felt like working. For the first few days of her visit to England he had been in the mood to play, and had very happily given himself up to showing her London and the countryside around it.

She had read all his books, and had a fancy to be taken to all the places he had so vividly described in his early novels. She had brought an enormous white and silver road-racing Mercedes with her, and it amused him to make exotic descents with her on the little semi-suburban market towns and small places where he had lived in his years of poverty as a schoolmaster or which he had visited after that when he was a reporter on the staff of a Sunday paper that specialized in unbelievably precise reports of sex crimes. It amused him enormously to drive her up to smug-looking little shops or commonplace houses which had been the scenes of bizarre crimes. Her reactions delighted him. "But you English are incredible! *Fablehaft!* You mean they all three lived in that little house for a whole year after the murder? It's incredible."

Chance brought them into the neighborhood of Maidenhead one Saturday, and I floated to the top of his mind by some random quirk of association. "D'you know I've got a boy in school somewhere near here, what do you say we look him up and take him out to lunch? Would that amuse you?" "I'd love to, if I see one of your children it will help me to make up my mind if I shall let myself become pregnant or not. I'm sure you make nice babies, Maxie. . . ." "Don't you dare . . ."

I didn't expect any visitor that day, and Dulley didn't expect his father, so we weren't in position on the fence. I was in Drake House common room playing a game with cigarette cards called Nearest the Wall with a boy called Batty Fraser. Standing about three paces from the wall, you flicked ten cards each, alternately, with the quick movement of a nurse shaking down a thermometer, and the boy whose card ended up nearest the wainscot took the pool. Batty had staked some Locomotives of the World that I badly wanted to complete a set against a group of much sought after Champion Breeds of British Dogs. We were both very keen to win and were very intent on our game when one of the House Monitors came in. "I say, Savage, two of the most amazing freaks are out in front asking for you. Brace up and turn out."

Freaks? Had Tubby Anderson, or some of Mother's theatre people taken it into their heads to come down to take me out? I could imagine them standing in the drive waiting for me in camel's-hair coats, belted like dressing gowns, with half the school staring in horror at their brown and white sport shoes. If it was Tubby he would be smoking a cigar and his diamond solitaire ring would be glinting murderously in the sunlight. Though no male parent had ever come to the school wearing a ring, some instinct already implanted in me by the school told me that it would be a fatal thing to do, and as I hurried through Big Hall, through the cloakrooms, grabbing up my cap and coat, and across Master's Hall that faced the front door of the old part of the building, I prayed that it wasn't Tubby. I flew out of the swing doors and stopped dead on the top step as they wheezed shut on their pneumatic hinges behind me. The Grafin's car was fine, in fact its nickel-plated exhaust pipes, the two leather straps holding down the long bonnet, the racing number on the doors, the semi-circular wired racing windshields, and the outside brake and gearshift, all had enormous prestige value. But even though the car was a "come true" beyond question my father and the Grafin had arrived in it, and they would have discounted even the winning car in the Le Mans race, or a record breaker straight from Brooklands track.

My father was walking up and down the driveway talking to the Headmaster about the schools he had seen in Moscow, and the whole topic of progressive education was opening, largely, up. He had brought back from Moscow a black caracul hat, and a long coat reaching almost to the ground with a hint of the Cossack about its waistline and its flared skirt. The Grafin, who was walking on the other side of the Headmaster listening, was wearing a leopardskin coat, a man's polo-necked sweater which made the most of her delicious bosom, and a vivid emerald-green skirt. Her head was cropped almost as short as a boy's, in the extremity of a new fashion, and two heavy gold clips glinted on the lobes of her ears. She saw me first and pointed to me with an arm loaded with Arab bracelets: "Ach, Max, that one's yours all right. He's adorable! But adorable!" I looked away from her in confusion, and met my father's eye. He smiled, half in embarrassment, half in amused delight at my dumbfounded expression, as I recognized him.

I came down the steps and crossed the gravel with dragging feet, thoroughly conscious of the row of craning figures under the lime trees and of a dozen heads peering in defiance of custom over the hedge which screened the side of the house to get a sight of Savage's freaks. I felt like a man going to the scaffold. I thought, though I was far from sure, that I could trust my father—even though he was wearing that frightful hat—but I knew the Grafin was going to do something appalling. I could feel it in my bones.

I was right about my father, he shook hands with me formally enough and conveyed his emotions with a quick squeeze of my shoulder, but the Grafin dropped onto her knees, hugged me to her, and planted a dozen kisses on my cheeks.

"Oh, the *wunderkind*," she cried in German, "he's fantas-

41

tically like you, Max. This is definite, no more contraceptives from now on—I must have a little Essling-Sterlinghoven just like this to take home with me to Germany."

I couldn't understand what she said, but as I wriggled out of her arms I caught sight of the Headmaster's face, flushing scarlet, and I gathered that what she was saying was even worse than it sounded to an ear unused to German.

It was an exciting day. We went to Oxford for lunch, touching ninety-five miles an hour twice on the way. The Grafin attracted a good deal of attention in the dining room of the Randolph Hotel and I was conscious several times during lunch that the people at nearby tables had given up their own conversation in favor of the pleasure of listening to hers. She described a boar hunt on her father's East Prussian estate. She described the Russian invasion in the early stages of World War I. She began to describe the behavior of the Russian troops.

"Great heavens, how old do you think the child is?" cried my father. "Behave, Lolotte. Behave—you really must behave. . . ."

"Do I shock you, Dickee?" she asked. I said no because I thought it would be rude to say yes. "There, you see, you old hypocrite, Dickee understands these things, he is a proper little man—his father's son, and besides he is an actress's boy too. Yah, he understands these things. *Aber, naturlich . . .*"

She rattled on about everything under the sun, and when she wasn't talking my father was, expansively, charmingly and amusingly, steering Lolotte away from sex and procreation, and onto subjects that seemed to him more likely to be interesting to me.

He brought up ancient Britons, and then having made me interested in them decided that we should spend the afternoon looking for the old British road called the Ridgeway—because I was so interested in ancient Britons. The Grafin drove us down the Thames valley to Streatley, and there we turned away west, away from the river, away from Maidenhead, into the high chalk hills. We found the faint grass track up a lane between Compton and Aldworth in the late afternoon, and walked for an hour in the soft evening light on the close-cropped springy turf while my father talked about the beginnings of history in England, about farming, about the civil wars between King and Parliament, and about the early days of flying.

I murmured from time to time that we ought to be getting back, that I was due in at school at six o'clock. "Oh, I'll fix that up—I'll see you don't get into any trouble," he said, waving a friendly arm at the grassy downs. "This is too good to miss for some silly rule or other. Don't you worry."

We sat on the close turf on the high point of the fat round hill above Aldworth, with the gentle tufted landscape of the Thames valley spread out before us, watching the fat sheeplike clouds drifting across the sky on the soft southwest wind. "When I was a reporter on the Reading *Mercury* before I went to London," my father said, "I explored this country. I used to know every inch of it. Every Sunday Ted Bigelow and I would get up at five or so and go off on our bicycles and we'd make a point of going to a new place. That was before the turn of the century, '88, '89, something like that. There weren't any cars about on country roads then, nothing but carts, and traps, and carriages—you were king of the road on a bicycle. There wasn't anything you couldn't pass. You shot by them in silence, you didn't have to have a great roaring rattletrap like Lolotte's to make a show . . . it was fun, good fun, the country pubs were real pubs then and they sold real beer. Good Lord, even the bicycles were different too, the gearing was different—when you went down a hill you had to kick your feet up clear of the pedals so that they could whizz round. . . ."

We had dinner in Henley, and after it, while the Grafin and my father drank coffee and brandy, I tasted hard liquor for the first time in the form of crème de cacao with a float of thick cream on top. When we came out of the Catherine Wheel Hotel the air was cool and fresh, and the early night sky was a luminous dark green. I felt very cozy, drowsy, and well fed, and as soon as I was wrapped up under a rug in the car I dropped off to sleep. My father and the Grafin forgot all about me, and while I lay unaware the big white car swept off down the London road and through Maidenhead at a great pace. It was not until they began to get into the out-skirts of London that something reminded them they had to return me to my school. They swung the car round and drove back again as the moon came up.

It was a little after midnight when we reached St. Michael's, and there was quite a scene with the Headmaster and his wife who were waiting up for us in anger and confu-sion. I was barely awake and I knew very little about it. I only remember my father carrying me into the house, and saying good night to me. "You're a ripping kid, Dick, and we're going to have a lot of good times together from now on." He bent his head down and nuzzled his rough cheek against mine. "Good night, old man, we had a good day, didn't we?"

The Headmaster's wife, stiff with indignation, took him from me and bore me away upstairs. She settled me into bed as if I were a baby in the darkened dormitory, and she, too, kissed me good night. "Poor little mite," she said tenderly, as if something dreadful had happened to me. "Such peo-ple! . . ."

The boy in the next bed, needless to say, was not asleep, only pretending to be, and he watched this tender passage with amazement and delight, and in the morning I found that I had a new school name, "Poor Little Mite," that stayed with me until I left St. Michael's.

But at the time that was the least of my worries. I had a letter from my mother in the middle of that week. I opened the envelope, covered with attractive American stamps, and read it with bewilderment:

"Dear Dickie—I don't know what you've done, you poor little fool, but it's infuriated your father. I suppose I should have told you a long time ago who your father is and what a strange unhappy creature he is, but I couldn't bear to speak about it, and I hoped I wouldn't have to tell you about him until you were old enough to understand these things. He has some idea that you've been telling people at school that you're his son. Some journalist or other who has a boy there has got hold of the story and has been plaguing his life out. I wouldn't bother you with this, and I hope it won't frighten or upset you, and I wouldn't dream of it in the ordinary way. But Tubby writes and tells me that some dreadful German woman has got hold of him and is making him behave in the most odd and demented way just now and I can't tell you how awful it can be for us both if he gets into one of his furies with us. I've tried the best I can to keep you out of his way because he is so strange and unreliable at times, and I do hope you'll be careful not to talk about him in case it should annoy him. Do please try and just keep your mouth shut if anyone asks you impertinent questions. Who your father is is our private business and you don't have to talk about it. I have heard about a wonderful school in Switzerland which might be more fun than St. Michael's. There are lakes and mountains there, and I expect you would slide about on the snow on skis in the winter. Do you think you would like that? I will be back in England at the end of July and we might go to the South of France for the summer holidays. Perhaps you should have swimming lessons before you go, would you ask them to give them to you at the school? All my love, Naomi."

I couldn't make head or tail of it. I read the letter with one hand over a black eye. I had had one tooth knocked out too, in the seventh fight in three days with people who had

45

called my father and the Grafin horrible names. "I say, chaps, do you know what, Savage's father is King of the Gypsies, and the old black crow he goes around with is the Queen. They drive round to the fairs in that white freak car. She tells fortunes, and he does the three-card trick. . . ." "All right, Snow Minor, I'll meet you in the Squash Court after breakfast. . . ." It had been one fight after another after that, and I'd taken some beatings in the name of family honor. What did Mother mean by saying Father was angry with me for talking about *him?* Who had made trouble for whom, anyway? The letter just didn't make sense.

Though I didn't know it then, another letter was in the mail at the time, a request from the Headmaster to Johnny Wallis, who had got me into St. Michael's, asking him to make arrangements for the following term. After mature consideration and a term's trial he had decided that I did not have the kind of background that would enable me to fit in at his school.

The letter gave a rather guarded account of my father's visit, but restrained as it was it upset Johnny. He felt that it was necessary, to avoid any more trouble of the same kind, to write to my father begging him not to go near the school again on any account for my sake. And as my mother's lawyer he wrote to her explaining what had happened, and telling her that he would do all he could to find a suitable school for me to go to in the autumn.

"Candidly, I don't think any school will be able to deal with this kind of thing, and though we ought to do everything we can to stay out of the Courts it may be necessary to get the boy more protection than we can give him unaided. I'm reluctant to advise having him made a ward of the court, but if there's any repetition on his father's part of this irresponsible behavior we should probably take that course. . . ."

He was in an even frame of mind when he wrote the letter, and he had a very clear picture of what he meant. Two quiet-voiced lawyers would go to transact ten or fifteen minutes' business, probably less, with a quiet-voiced judge in chambers, and in due course when the arguments and the papers in the case had been considered the judge would have issued an order making me a Ward in Chancery, a frightening phrase which would have meant nothing worse than that I would have acquired the British Judiciary as a dispassionate extra parent.

But my mother was not in an even frame of mind when she received Johnny's cool and detached note. She was on location, shooting Global Pictures' version of *The Miracle,* and with the temperature in the upper eighties she had spent the day riding a horse out, and out, and once more please, out of the gates of a plaster castle. Every time she had tittuped out under the portcullis and across the drawbridge on her palfrey, in her medieval costume of heavy velvet, she had been plucked out of the saddle and borne off for a short distance by a whiskered bandit who was as hot and sweaty as she was. When she had not been on horseback she had been quarreling with the Hungarian director. He claimed that he was refusing to use stunt riders for the scene because he was trying to make a sincere picture that would have integrity, but she knew very well that he was punishing her for refusing to sleep with him. When she retired to her trailer to rest she found the letter from England waiting for her.

She read it with horror—to her, legal action meant only one thing. She immediately saw herself entering the witness box, as a stir of anticipation swept the courtroom. She could see it all as clearly as if it had already happened. A hostile King's Counsel rose to his feet, and approached her to cross-examine, taking hold of the lapels of his gown and putting his head a little to one side. "Now Miss Savage," he began with an odious courtesy. It would probably be that saturnine brute, John Shaw-Clavering, who loathed women, and was

47

one of Max's best friends. He would make disgraceful use of his private knowledge of her life, blackmailing her with innuendoes that she alone would understand. Those dreadful creatures in the press box, the most degraded men in journalism sank to court reporting as everyone knew, would lap it all up. The judge, probably some crony of Shaw-Clavering's, or a twisted puritan who despised actresses, would covertly do everything he could to harass and torment her. When she left the court to go home she would be faced by batteries of cameras and a staring crowd. The first evening papers would be on the streets, everyone in London would be licking their lips over the headlines, and the salacious, warped stories beneath them. STARTLING NEW EVIDENCE IN TOWN CASE. ACTRESS WEEPS IN WITNESS BOX.

When she stepped out onto the stage that night there would be a tense hush, then the first hiss from the gallery . . . then jeers and catcalls. . . .

She picked up a pen, and the day's exasperations, subtly transformed and refined, began to run onto the paper: "My dear Max. I have no objection to your running around London impersonating Puss in Boots if you must. What you do to your reputation and your dignity is no concern of mine, after all (and I suppose that at your age it is worth doing almost anything to get the flattery and adulation of even a shabby little tart like that Essling-Sterlinghoven girl) but I do feel that you should think seriously about what you are doing when you drag our poor little boy off on your escapades. I suppose you will pretend that it surprises you when I tell you that he's already been expelled from the very decent private school I'd chosen for him because of the exhibition you chose to stage there. I can't tell you what pain and heartbreak it is to me to find that all the years of sacrifice and labor that I've given up to making him a happy normal child are to be thrown away because you take it into your head to make him a plaything for some petite amie you can't think how to amuse. Even if you are utterly indifferent to the child's future I do beg you to think of me; Richard is all I have, and I can't bear to think of what may happen to him if you are going to come and go in his life as cruelly as you came and went in mine. You are such a wonderful creature, and you have such a deadly power to make people believe that you mean what you say, and he's such a defenseless little boy. It will be so easy for you to make him believe that you love him and care for him, and it will be so dreadful for him to find out that you care as little for him as you've cared for the rest of us who've given you our love and devotion. Please, please, promise that if I give in to you and send Richard away to this school in Switzerland you won't pursue him there, to destroy the even pattern of his life all over again. . . ."

Her pen ran on, she covered sheet after sheet of paper in her rounded childish handwriting, and in the end she achieved something memorable. It reached my father at a sufficiently unfortunate moment. For weeks he had had an idea for a new novel taking shape in his head and the time had come when he had wanted to settle down to work on it. But the Grafin Essling-Sterlinghoven had been in his house and neither concentration nor work had been possible. At last he had remonstrated with her, she was being unreasonable, absurd, she must realize that she was interfering with his work. She walked out of the house—and did not return. But her going brought him no peace, and he found it more difficult to get to work than ever. He had no idea where she was, and he found her absence harder to bear than her presence. Every morning he got up at six, following his habit, and made himself tea with the electric kettle and the tea things ready beside his bed, but then instead of going to his desk he roamed round the now dreadfully empty house, missing her, with the unwritten novel itching and burning in the back of his mind. All he had meant to impress on her was that he had to have silence in the house and in his workroom from seven every morning until one o'clock. After that he was ready enough to be all hers. Why couldn't she have understood a simple thing like that? Why could no woman ever understand him?

He heard the letters fall through the slit in the front door into the mail box and went downstairs to fetch them. He came back upstairs ripping open the envelopes with his fingers, and giving their contents a quick glance. An Australian paper wanted an article, a literary committee wanted his support for something, a crank wanted to convince him of the truth of the after life, the suit being made for him at Poole's was ready for a final fitting. There was nothing from Lolotte.

He looked at the envelope with the American stamps on it absently, that couldn't be from her. Wait a minute, though, that's a familiar handwriting. . . . He tore it open and read my mother's letter.

As his eye traveled over the page all his exasperation, perplexity, and unhappiness, found a new focus. Try and keep his son from him, would she? Try to smuggle the boy off to Switzerland out of his way? Something stirred in his memory. Now that he came to think of it, there had been another letter from some shyster lawyer or other along the same lines. He went into his study and rummaged among the letters until Wallis's complaint turned up.

There it was, a coldly formal piece of impertinence. As he considered it the signature seemed to strike a chord—Wallis —Wallis—wait a minute—he knew something about that fellow. Irene Caddle had pointed him out one day at luncheon at Rule's and told him that he was a new beau of Naomi's. A wave of exasperation burst over him. The Grafin had gone, as Naomi had once gone, he was alone. And it was not enough that he was alone and unhappy, he was to be deprived, now, even of the consolation of watching his youngest son grow up, and of the pleasure and comfort of giving him a start in life. He would not stand for it. If Naomi was going to try to harass him with lawyers he would show her that two could play that game.

The vision of old Meopham, the senior partner in Meopham, Lazard, and Lazard, flashed before his eye, easily the most infuriating lawyer, and almost the most infuriating human being, he had ever encountered. Meopham lived like a turtle in a shell, inside a dark suit that had been made for him when he was a young man of apparently twice his present size, and he had the air of having put his head up through his high stiff collar to see how things were coming along outside. He had the accent and the manner of an uneducated man, so that his opponents always underestimated him. On top of that, in all the thirty years that Max had known him he had shown all the signs of doddering senility, trembling hands, weak rheumy eyes, set in a lined yellow face, and quavering voice, so that people pitied him as well as despised him and thus delivered themselves helpless into his hands.

Meopham had handled all the libel suits that had fallen on the Sunday scandal sheet Max had worked for in his reporting days, and he was one of the great artists in the use of legal machinery to bewilder, hamper and frustrate litigants with unassailable cases. He could not only make legal bricks without straw, he could manage almost entirely without clay as well. He was the man for this job, he could be relied on to give yours sincerely J. M. Wallis some surprises.

Max took up the irritating letter and wrote a line under the signature.

"What do you think of this? I know it's late in the day, but isn't there some way we can get a court to establish my right to see the child whenever I want? I'd like to have a voice in planning his education, too. You have a free hand to do your best. Yours as ever, Max."

And if Meopham couldn't do anything it would do no harm to put an end to some of Naomi's nonsense and get things onto a more reasonable footing. His pen began to fly over a sheet of his personal writing paper.

"My dear Naomi, there seems to be some misunderstanding about my visit to St. Michael's which wasn't as whimsical as you've been given to understand. I've been going into the whole question of education lately, and I've been giving a great deal of thought to our son's schooling in consequence. I know I've neglected him in the past, but then a boy doesn't enter the male world until he's eight or so and in the nature of things I couldn't have been much help in the feminine nursery world which has been his sphere until now. I ran down to see him the other day and I can't say that I was at all favorably impressed by the school or its staff. I had a talk with the Headmaster—you seem to have been given a ludicrously one-sided account of our meeting—and I found him wholly unaware of the enormous strides that have been made recently in the teaching of languages and the natural sciences. He seemed quite content to go on cramming boys for examinations in the old uninspired way, and he was stubbornly resistant to new ideas. I spoke pretty strongly about the folly of turning boys out into the twentieth century world with the mental equipment required by the nineteenth century civil service, and I don't think he liked it at all. (I daresay he took out some of his resentment in concocting the malicious account of the interview that has been handed on to you.) I took the Gräfin Essling-Sterlinghoven along with me, incidentally, because she's very much interested in the subject of education, and runs a small model school for the children of her tenants on her estates in East Prussia. But let's leave her out of it, I don't take it upon myself to criticize your choice of companions after all, and I don't think we want to squabble on that level. I don't at least. Be that as it may, I had a long talk with Richard and I was rather upset to find how backward he was. His ideas about history are parochial in the extreme, and he's very vague about math, and geography.

I have a feeling they hadn't got the hang of the way to make the most of his talents at St. Michael's, and I'm not sorry that the time has come for him to move on. I think we should get together and have a serious talk about the boy's future when you get back to England. His prospects are very bright, I think, if he's properly handled, and I think we should be careful to see that he doesn't miss his chances. The next few years, after all, are the vital ones. . . ."

The sweet reasonableness of this letter as an answer to her own disturbed my mother no less than the abrupt turn which it put to a seven years' indifference to my present, my future or even my existence. It made her feel sure that Max was up to something, though she couldn't imagine what. She cabled Wallis, warning him to be on his guard, but the cable arrived when Wallis was off for a week on a friend's yacht, and when he returned to his office it was too late. Meopham, pretending that he had unearthed a plot to smuggle me out of the country, had obtained an injunction restraining my mother or anyone else from taking me out of the British Isles until such time as the court had ruled on the question of my guardianship. The battle had begun.

It dragged on for years. I understood some of its phases at the time, and others only much later.

I enjoyed its beginning. Johnny Wallis came and took me to tea one day at Mr. Justice Bell's chambers in the Temple, a large dark brown room full of dark brown furniture and dark brown portraits of eighteenth- and early nineteenth-century persons who looked as pink-faced and pleasant as the Judge did. Sunlight filtered through a plane tree outside and found its way in at the window, to glint richly on the Judge's silver tea things, the gilt on the bindings of his law books, and on the curly gold frames of the portraits.

I sat on the edge of a Hepplewhite chair and ate a currant bun.

"I hope that's a good bun," said the Judge. "I'm not sure

that I'd rely on my manservant to be an expert when it came to sweet buns—does it have enough currants in it?"

"Oh yes, sir," I said.

"Now where do you suppose those currants come from?"

"A grocer's shop, I suppose, sir," I said.

"I believe they came from Greece," he said. "Did you never hear that?"

I said I had not.

"I used to be very interested in Greece," he said, "in people like Demosthenes, and Socrates, and Alcibiades, and so on. Do they interest you?"

I admitted that I had never heard of them; I disclosed a minute or two later that I did not know anything about the Aeneid, and I could not translate the line he quoted from it. I had not heard of Molière either, or La Fontaine. Johnny Wallis began to look tense. Shakespeare wafted into the conversation, and suddenly while Wallis smiled and the Judge looked amused I was quoting Enobarbus' speech. But after that it appeared that I did not know what the Pharos of Alexandria was, nor where I would expect to find it. I knew it was near the Nile but not much else. Rivers were good things to remember places by, suggested the Judge, offering me another bun. If I went up the Danube I would come to several interesting towns. What was the place that was cut in two by the river and had a name for each part? He couldn't remember—I couldn't remember, either. Buda-Pest, he said, as if he had just remembered it. And then there's another place further upstream where the Hapsburgs had their palaces and all the Austrian waltzes came from. He hummed a bar or two of a Strauss waltz—what was the place called?

Wallis's head was bowed forward and he was looking at me through his eyebrows with a definitely apprehensive expression.

"Well, no matter," said the Judge; "why should you trouble your head over such matters, after all." He smiled

54

charmingly. "I daresay you'd like to see rather more of your father than you have done lately."

"Oh, yes sir," I said.

"Well, perhaps it can be arranged."

Wallis and I went out into the Temple gardens, buttoning up our light summer coats against a hint of autumn in the air.

"I say, he was a nice old man," I said. "He wasn't a bit frightening. I thought a judge would be a very scary old man in a wig, but he was awfully nice."

"You've got a lot to learn, Dickie," said Wallis. He seemed unaccountably depressed. "Let's go and see Charlie Chaplin," he said suddenly as we came out onto the Strand with its jam of scarlet buses, black taxis and private cars, "I could do with some cheering up before I face your mother."

As we sat and watched *The Gold Rush* I enjoyed myself very much; I did not realize that I had been given an examination and had failed it, or that Meopham and my father had won a round from Wallis and my mother. Nor would I have been at all depressed if I had known it, because the immediate effect of the tea party was that the court laid down, among other things relating to my schooling, that my father must have reasonable access to me, and defined reasonable access in terms that allowed for my going to stay with him for visits of some duration. My father spent a great deal of his time in those days at his apartment in Paris, so that my world underwent an exciting enlargement in consequence of this arrangement.

I had often seen the boat trains for Folkstone and Dover flashing through Ashford Junction without slackening speed, when I was on my way down to Minster, and had peered out of the windows of the slow local train standing at the branch line platform, at the faces of the people in the Pullmans, wondering what it would be like to go abroad. Now it was my turn to peer out of the Pullman to catch a glimpse of the familiar local train with its green carriages standing waiting to begin its sedate progress up the branch line towards Canterbury, Minster and Ramsgate, and I wondered if any dimly seen face inside it was that of a child going to the Willinghams'. I learned what it was like to stand in the bow of a boat waiting to catch a first glimpse of a new country, and then on later journeys the thrill of searching for familiar landmarks across a narrowing strip of pale green sea, looking first for Cap Griz Nez to rise up over the horizon and, as soon as I could distinguish the houses in Sangatte, hurrying across to the other rail to catch sight of the clock tower of the Hotel de Ville in Calais rising up out of the flat expanse of the ugly town. At the Gare Maritime after the excitement of going ashore in a babble of French, there was the almost greater excitement of seeing, drawn up alongside the Paris *rapide,* the rows of dark blue sleeping cars of the Train Bleu which would travel all through the night towards the Mediterranean, and of the Orient Express which would roll on across Europe until it came to the gateway of Asia at Constantinople. I was at the entry to another world, one in which anything might happen, and in which everything was different.

Max would meet me under the huge glass tent of the Gare du Nord in Paris, and would sweep me off to the apartment overlooking the Parc Monceau through streets filled with a blaze of unfamiliar color, high-pitched sound, and rapid movement. At the apartment I would be handed over to Marie, my father's rosy-faced but white-haired Burgundian maid, whom I recognized on sight as a spiritual kinswoman of MacEwan. She would carry me off at once to plunge me into a hot bath in a bathroom in which everything had a flavor of the exotic. Its faucets were unlike English taps, and the waste, operated by a little porcelain-coated lever, was as unlike the familiar English rubber plug on a chain as anything could be. Afterwards I would have supper at a low table in front of the sofa in the salon, sitting wrapped in a bathrobe of white toweling, while my father, ready to go out for the evening, in dinner jacket or white tie and tails, sat talking to me, telling me what he had seen on a recent trip to Morocco, or about his flight back from Prague in an open-cockpit airplane, or some such new adventure. Then as an eighteenth-century Vulcan, surrounded by Graces, on the mantelpiece let his hammer fall eight times on a gilded bell made in the shape of a shield which rested on top of the anvil-shaped clock, he would depart and Marie would take me off to the guest room. I would lie awake in its heavily elegant Empire bed for a space, listening to the noises of the Parisian traffic outside, and looking about me in the faint light thrown into the room by the street lamps at the silver and white paneling, at the prettily patterned *toile de jouy* curtains, and at the pleasant directoire chairs and tables, which gracefully paid their frivolous tributes to the arts of Greece and the Roman Republic. I would think how delightful it would be to live like this always.

In the morning Marie would bring me a breakfast of the kind I had so often seen my mother enjoying, with the difference that the coffee was mixed with hot milk, and served not in a cup but in a porringer. While I sat up in bed sipping the coffee, which she had sweetened with half a dozen lumps of sugar, she would lay out my clothes, and talk to me, rolling her R's in the Burgundian fashion, drawing me out in order to tease me about my English accent and the strange way the English did things. As I was breakfasting and dressing, my father would be finishing his day's work, shortened to a bare three hours in honor of my visit, and at ten o'clock he would appear, bouncing with energy to tell me what plans he had made for the day.

"A quiet day today, I think. I've got tickets for a show I think you'll like tonight, and I don't want to tire you. . . ."

But it never was a quiet day. Every day there was something new and exciting to do, and everything we did was made to seem amusing. Even meals, which I had thought of as a serious part of keeping alive rather than as a pleasure, were made into fun.

"You know on a sunny day like this we ought to see if we can get someone to feed us out in the open, under some trees, with flowers to look at and a lake to keep us cool. Let's see if we can find something like that in the Bois. What do you say?" Off we would go in the Voisin convertible with its silver hawk on the bonnet, and presently the Pavillon d'Armenonville would be unearthed as if it was a surprise that had been especially arranged for us. Or after a morning spent in some such unexpected corner of the Tuileries as the Musée de la Marine, with its wonderful and endless collection of ship models, he would say, "I feel stuffy after all that poking about indoors, I'd like to have lunch in a treetop. Let's go and look for a tree house with a good kitchen." I would find myself eating at L'Ermitage at Robinson, on one of the platforms run out into the treetops from a clifftop from which one looked down upon a bosky bourgeois paradise of absurd little villas, and across to the Parc de Seaux and the wide sweep of southern Paris which lay beyond.

For a week or ten days Max would give up all his time and his energy to playing with me, treating the city as if it was a fair which had been set up for our amusement. And then, all too suddenly, the days had flown away, and I would find myself on the boat train again, rushing away from Dover through the Kent countryside, so snug, so cozy, and so small in scale.

As it grew dark the attendant would produce the Southern Railway tea, served in a square dark-green pot, and slices of pound cake, which was the final and absolute proof that I was back home. The London suburbs would close in on the railroad track, trapping it at last between somber rows of terrace houses, and then with a sullen hissing the train would come to a stop in Victoria Station. The adventure was over. A solidly driven London taxi, so unlike a volatile, darting, and impetuous French cab, would drive me through increasingly familiar streets, and at last I would find myself staring up at the gaunt stucco façade of the Kensington house, and at the windows of our apartment.

When I entered the corridor hall it would seem narrower than ever, my room, the little dining room, and the tiny kitchen, more boxlike, and the drawing room, for all its size, more crowded and jumbled. I knew, now, that the Aubusson on the floor was a late one, and not good even of its date. I could see that the pieces of furniture, in spite of the pretty loose covers, and the small cigarette boxes of rare woods, and the ornaments, the Spanish figures, and miniature Japanese No masks, that distracted one from their outlines were second rate even when of good period. They spoke of economy and small domestic prudences, and of bargains. I sensed that I had come back to a narrower, less lavish world than that which I had visited.

Unpacking in my room I could cling to Paris, and to my father's expansive way of living, for a few moments. My father always arranged that the maid should slip a few surprises into my suitcase, luxurious replacements for such of my clothes as had seemed to him to look worn or shabby, and a gift like an Italian leather wallet, a pair of fleece-lined bedroom slippers from Hermès, or an envelope with an astonishingly large check in it. And there was generally some delicacy, made by Marie, and slipped in on her own account, tucked away somewhere. When the excitement of these discoveries had worn off I would find myself sitting in the little armchair that had been demoted from my mother's room when two of its springs had gone, looking at the carpet which had been dyed dark plum from a much lighter color, and at my natural elm bed and chest of drawers from Heal's cottage-furniture department. I would count the gray days which remained of the holidays and which would be spent in this town of Aerated Bread Company Tea shops, Lyons Corner Houses, and excessively ordinary sights and sounds. The Plaza-Athénée, the Korniloff, the Pavillon de l'Élysée, and the whole way of life of which they were part seemed to belong on another planet.

I would try to preserve links with that way by small maneuvers, by trying to insist on keeping up breakfast à la Marie. But Mother's maids were not co-operative to maintaining affectations on my part which they only tolerated, and then grudgingly, in my mother because she was a star whose picture got into the papers. In a few days I would be back on cornflakes, bacon and eggs, and coffee in a teacup.

Marie once gave me a bowl with a flowered pattern of the kind which I drank from with such delight while she gossipped with me, but Stoneham, my mother's maid at the time, could never be induced to put a drop of anything to drink into it. "It's for porridge, Master Richard, and I won't do such a ridiculous thing," she said when I tried to get her to let me use it for my coffee. "Anyone who isn't mental can see it's a bowl, not a cup." She hid it when I went back to school, and I never succeeded in finding it again.

My mother did not notice my growing discontent with our old way of life for some time, she was in any case preoccupied by her professional concerns, and above that, since she had not wanted me to set up a relationship with my father she averted her mind from the whole subject, never asking me anything about him, or about what I had seen or done on my visits to him. Occasionally, if I used a French word, partly out of naïve snobbery, and partly to provoke her into recognizing that I had been abroad, she would snap.

"You're really getting absurdly affected, you'll end up by making yourself quite ridiculous if you talk like that—like those idiotic Roumanians who pretend that they've forgotten their own language." I would feel crushed and hurt, and Mother would exploit the situation remorselessly.

"Besides, you know, you've picked up a vulgar accent—I suppose you've been talking to some servant or other—and you give yourself away, it's the way you roll your R's. If you want to speak good French I can get you a tutor and you can really work at it. . . ."

That was not what I wanted at all, and I sulked, so that the whole question of France passed out of our talk to become the vivid element in my dreams and fantasies. I would mope about the apartment with my hands in my pockets longing to be back, hatefully bored, spending long hours of sunlit mornings and bright afternoons indoors listening to Radio Paris, or playing French records on the victrola.

Enlightenment came to my mother suddenly, as soon as she turned her quick mind to the subject which she had for so long evaded. On her way out to lunch she passed the drawing room door, and saw me sprawled on the sofa reading a French novel.

"Why aren't you out? Why are you always fugging indoors? How can you bear to be inside on a lovely day like this?"

She came in and stood over me in a spasm of irritation.

"Why don't you ever do anything like other children?" She twitched the book out of my hands. "Reading Cocteau at your age—I really don't know what your father thinks he's doing to you. . . ."

"I'm fourteen, what's so wrong about reading a book if I want to—and besides there isn't anything to do in London."

She didn't reply at once, but stared at me for a few seconds with her nostrils a little dilated, and her eyes curiously enlarged. She had suddenly seen in an interior vision exactly what my father thought he was doing to me, charming me away from her, making me dissatisfied and discontented with the kind of life she had arranged for me, teaching me to look towards him for everything that made life enjoyable or attractive, subtly preparing for the day when I would break away from her and turn to him.

She ruffled my hair with a surprisingly tender expression softening her face.

"I suppose you don't have a very good time here, poor lamb. I'm so tied up with the theatre that I find it very hard to get away to do things I want to do with you. It's just as horrid for me as it is for you. . . ."

I looked at her carefully, wondering at this abrupt change of front. My ear detected that hint of music in her voice that showed that she was thinking of the effect of her words and not speaking entirely naturally. There was a slightly glazed look in her eyes too that I had learned over the years to recognize, and which showed that she was playing, not looking at the person she was speaking to but seeing herself on a miniature stage within her mind acting out a scene, in this case a scene of tenderness with her only son who misunderstood her.

I made a sharp movement to break onto the stage of this tiny private theatre, knowing that it would remove the glazed look from her eyes and bring her back into the room with me and off that inner stage.

Her eyes cleared and she smiled her irresistible gamine smile, she became the naughty child who sometimes read the papers with me, and stopped being the wronged mother.

"I'd forgotten how fast you've been growing up," she said. "You've grown out of toys, and walks in the park. I'll have to think of something."

She turned to the mirror to adjust the diamond clip in her red woollen toque, and began to leave me in contemplation of herself and her own exquisite tigerish loveliness; she would be looking her best when she came into the Ivy and walked down the triangular room towards Larry Brook's table. All the non-theatre people there would lift their heads a little and stare while pretending not to, people were such fools about the theatre.

And the answer to her problem came to her at once. The glamour of the theatre would balance the glamour of Max's prosperity, and of "abroad." She turned to me with a smile, the smile of the bright, gay person of the cocktail parties, the person who made the marginal members of Larry's crowd say, "Naomi's really one of the chaps, Naomi's a pal, and I mean that, darling. . . ."

She settled her skirt over her hips with a swift patting movement of her hands, a sign that something was definitely settled in her mind.

"Why don't you come down to the theatre this afternoon and watch the rehearsal? It might be fun for you. Go to the stage door and tell Shepherd who you are, I'll leave word with him to let you in. I hope you'll come, lamb, I really do." She darted a look at her watch. "I must run . . ." and she was gone.

Stoneham gave me my lunch as soon as she was out of the house, and I ate the tasteless food indifferently, reading between mouthfuls from *Le Grand Écart*, which was propped up in front of my plate. It would be fun to get in with a set who lived like that, it might happen in Paris, it could never happen in London. As soon as I was old enough I would go to France and live with my father, and then . . .

"Are you going to be all day, Master Richard? I want to get the washing up done so that I can get out. It's not everybody who wants to stuff indoors all day."

I looked up at Stoneham's bleak thin-lipped face peering round the door.

"Oh, all right, just a minute."

Her face withdrew. "Some people have no consideration," she muttered as the door closed.

When I had finished an acid dish of stewed plums and custard I went up to my room, and threw the book down on the bed, remembering resentfully just how Mother had said come down to the theatre. It was simply a dodge to get me out, and she was going to be there anyway so it was an amusement that wouldn't be any trouble to her. It wasn't a bit like the sort of thing Max thought of and arranged. I was in half a mind not to go, or to take myself to the War Museum or out to Kew Gardens instead in order to irritate her into taking more notice of my existence, but still, it would be something to talk about when I went back to school, so I decided to go.

I sauntered out and took a bus to the theatre district. It took me out of the London of parks and leafy squares into the seedy neighborhood of Piccadilly Circus and Leicester Square, and the narrow warren-like back streets behind them. I got off and found my way to the stage door of the theatre, a hole in a towering brick wall festooned with pipes and iron fire escapes which hung over an alley leading out of Gerrard Lane.

An old man with a dirty yellow walrus mustache and a mottled face like a carnival mask sat inside the open door in a glass box, picking his nose and reading the racing edition of the *Evening Standard*.

"You get on aht of it," he said without looking up, and continuing to probe into his right nostril with his little finger, "we don't allow no autograph 'unters to 'ang around 'ere."

I looked in at the cement staircase leading up to a pair of battered swing doors, at the stained and smeared buff walls of the entry, dirtier and dingier than anything I had ever seen. SILENCE. NO SPITTING. NO SMOKING, said a notice on the wall.

"Please, my mother said . . ." The man blew through his mustache and turned his protruding eyes in my direction.

"What do I care what your fuggin mother said. You fug off before I come arter yer. . . ."

64

I turned to go, angrily. Mother hadn't even bothered to tell him I was coming. I'd come all the way up here to find that she'd forgotten me as soon as she'd left the house, it was just like her. I went out into the dingy alley again. I would go straight to Mr. Justice Bell in the Temple to tell him how awful things were, and he would say that I could go and live with Max in France all the time.

"Hi you," shouted the walrus mustache, peering out of its box, "you ain't Savage's kid is you, because if you is, you is ter go in." I went back.

"You should of tole me, 'stead of sneakin' off like that. You go in them doors and ask some'n or other to show you the way out front. You ain't to go on stage until yer mother comes an' gets yer, see?"

I went up the concrete steps and in at the swing doors, and an electrician showed me the way through into the darkened house with its twelve hundred empty seats.

"Sit where you like, the whole kit and caboodle's yours fer the askin'."

He left me in the twilight. I took a seat in the front of the dress circle and stared down at my mother and the little group of people in street clothes standing chatting idly on the underlit stage mysteriously scattered with cheap bent wood chairs. Four men in their shirtsleeves were arguing over something in the fourth row of the orchestra seats. I recognized Larry Brook by the way he kept running his hand over the back of his head, but I didn't know the others.

In bitter disappointment I listened to the faint murmuring of their talk and remembered the blaze and glory of *Antony and Cleopatra*. What was going on? Larry straightened up suddenly and called out, "We'll do that again—as it stands, just once more please. From 'Not if I can help it,' Mortimer's exit and Naomi's entrance. And let's not gabble it this time. Let's have the timing." The group on the stage broke up and organized itself into a pattern. My mother, who had been standing in a relaxed easy position, took a few strides across the stage and stopped near one of the chairs. As she stood there I had a curious impression that she gained a few inches in height, and her face, which had been a pink blob, suddenly took on features and an expression of great happiness, it was as if she was a light which had suddenly been turned on. And when I turned from her to the other actors I saw that they had all, to a greater or lesser extent, illumined themselves in the same way. And then for ten minutes the stage and the theatre were filled with words and movement, with the almost incomprehensible fragment of a play which none the less held me spellbound until its flow was rudely broken into by the man sitting beside Larry.

"No! No! No!" He cried as if in agony, waving a sheet of paper over his head. "Break there, please. Larry, it really won't do. Those two lines have to come out. . . ."

The actors suddenly became people again, and the scripts which were in their hands and which had become invisible suddenly reappeared. Their bodies softened and their faces, turned towards the interrupter, ceased to bear any relation to the words they had been speaking and became small pink blobs with the faintest hint of curiosity about them. My mother sank into a chair and, kicking off a shoe, began to knead her instep. Larry and the interrupter began arguing again while the cast slowly drifted out of their pattern and clotted into three whispering groups.

"Well, all right then," said Larry in a petulant voice, as the interrupter rose to his feet, "have it your own way."

"Now don't sulk, we all concede that you're the genius of the age, you just happen in this single instance to have loused up a perfectly good scene with two perfectly stinking remarks that don't make sense, can't be read even by geniuses like our darling Naomi and Sam, and don't matter a damn to the play. . . ."

"You're producing the thing, I suppose that gives you the right to wipe your boots on it if you choose."

"I choose," replied the producer, cooing the word. Larry walked away from him up the center aisle lighting a cigarette with three matches in the perfectly still air.

"Now, my dears," said the producer, calling to the actors with the same hissing geniality in which he had spoken to Larry, "take your pens and pencils in your hot little hands and draw a firm line through those two deplorable speeches that we've been arguing about for so long. And now let's run through this scene again while our Mr. Brook retires to the dress circle and works off his wicked temper."

He turned to wave at Larry with an exaggerated flapping of his hand, and a faint "gertcha," floated out from the darkness behind him in the shadowy pit.

"Now to business," he said in a brisker voice and the same relighting of the actors took place as they once more took their positions.

While I watched the little figures on the stage Larry Brook came down the gangway and without noticing me slumped into a seat not far off. Looking along the curve of the empty front row I could just see his face, and I was surprised by it. I'd always seen him looking professionally boyish and cheerful at parties, and now lit faintly from below, he looked lined and worried. A part of his lower lip was tucked in under a tooth and his hands were locked together nervously. He stared tensely downward at the actors until the point where the two cut lines had been was gone by, then he lay back in his seat and taking a pen from his pocket scratched them out. As he sat there, now following the scene purely automatically, he became aware that he was being watched and looking round quickly saw me. For a second an expression of annoyance, almost of malevolence, crossed his face, and then he recognized me.

"Hallo, Dickie," he said. He came over, pulling his face muscles to attention as he came so that when he reached me he had become the boy wonder once more, all youthful charm.

"I didn't know you had a taste for this sort of punishment. It's hell, isn't it?"

"I think it's terrific."

"Well, you wouldn't if you had another three weeks of it ahead of you. There's no torture like pulling a play into its final shape. By the time this thing goes up to Birmingham for the tryout I'll be an old, old man."

He looked down at the stage. "It's fun seeing the stuff I've written slowly turning into that thing down there, and it's extraordinary to see a character you've imagined being turned into a real person by your mother. She has the most amazing way of sensing the whole of what you've seen in your mind and bringing it to life in front of you. She's the kind of actress playwrights dream about. She works like a dog . . ."

It was indeed a wonderful thing to watch, and I spent day after day in the dark and silent upper part of the theatre staring down at the transformation that took place on the bare boards in front of the naked back wall of the theatre. One by one the awkward lines were weeded out, dead patches were removed, and clarifications of obscurities written in. The relation of each scene to the main line of development became clear, until the whole of Larry's story was visible as a balanced unity. As I came to understand the way the theatre puts flesh onto the bones of a play I got to know the theatre people. Warmed by my wholehearted admiration Larry became a friend, I met and was tolerated by the producer, and even Kenning, the quiet-voiced, beautifully dressed businessman who was the god who called this whole self-contained universe of pretense into being, would nod and smile as he went past me on his mysterious occasions. The scenery arrived. the props, and at last the costumes. In the end I sat in my

68

usual place watching the piece as a whole declaring itself in its completeness in that magic pool of light, a play at last.

In those weeks of work my mother changed too. She had ceased to be my mother, she was no kinswoman of the Queen of Egypt I had once seen, she was the wife of the Governor of a British Colony suddenly swept off her feet and head over heels in love with a visitor to her husband's domain. She was altogether and entirely a well-bred conventional woman who had never done what she wanted, and never known how much she could want, a woman as strange to me as she was unlike the Naomi who was my mother. Behind her was a complete life history, schooling at Cheltenham, hunt balls, London coming-out parties, a long marriage spent in furthering a dull but sweet and reliable husband's career, a march through an emotional desert in which she had never realized the capacity of her heart.

The play was not, to tell the truth, a very good one. In his middle period Larry Brook was turning away from comedy and trying to write a better emotional tragedy than *The Three Sisters,* a thing which it was not in his power to do, but he had contrived an exceptionally moving middlebrow tearjerker.

My mother knew, I think, that it was not a very good play —but it was not her function to criticize plays, it was her function to be what they called on her to be. And I saw that she fulfilled her function, and even went beyond it by giving the Governor's wife a reality which did not lie in her original lines.

For the first time I realized that she too was a creative artist in her way, that she was in some sort the equal of Max, although her inventions died nightly as the theatre lights went out and could not be put in bookcases alongside his fifty novels, and his volumes of short stories.

When I went back to school after that holiday I did not

dream so much about returning to France to live, I thought instead about the theatre, and of learning how to use the whole elaborate apparatus that was concealed behind the proscenium arch. I would become a stage manager, like Ibsen, and I would work at it until the theatre was a machine that I knew better than I knew myself, and then I would write play after play that used its capacities to the utmost. I would add a new chapter to the history of the stage, it would be Shakespeare, Ibsen, Shaw, and Savage.

As I formulated these ambitions I discovered that I had inherited my mother's gift, though I did not make the discovery by reasoning about it. I started to write plays. I would rough out a plot, fit the characters with names, and visualize the settings in my imagination. I might get as far as the dialogue for Scene One, Act I, or even into Scene Two, writing in the back of a school exercise book, or on a lined pad such as my father used for his first drafts, on the dining table at home. My imagination would run ahead of me.

The play was finished. Kenning and Archer, the professional management team who had my mother under contract, had read it. Kenning came from behind his desk as I was shown into his office in the Adelphi, smiling his slightly twisted ironic smile, and holding out his hard, firm hand in greeting.

"We're tremendously excited about this play of yours, Richard, it's the real right thing beyond any question. We're going to do it this autumn. . . ." I sat in the stalls watching the rehearsals in the center of the little group of executives, brilliantly improvising new lines when called on to do so, and coaching the actors with suggestions that won the admiration of the producer, who quickly realized that he was my subordinate rather than a collaborator.

I read the criticisms after the opening, the critics had seen the point of the play, and recognized its force. But that was not enough, and my imagination jumped forward. The critics were recognizing the force and compelling power of my fifth or sixth play, and were beginning to use the word genius. Kenning came to visit me at my small house in Paris and I gave him lunch. As we drank our coffee and smoked our cigars he begged me to let him have my next play and I told him that in spite of the offers I was getting from other managements, and from New York, I was loyal to Kenning and Archer.

My first-night curtain speeches were famous for their wit, I had a big following in Berlin, Vienna, and New York, and I had learned to smile easily into the flicker of flash-lamps as I got off trains and liners. But though I was successful I was uncorrupted by my success, I was humble in the theatre and continually learning more about its possibilities.

I made a young actress my protégée and taught her all I had learned until she was an even greater actress than my mother. When she reached the height of her powers I wrote my most perfect play for her. The first night was an epiphany rather than a triumph. Bartlett, the most venomous and embittered of the critics, fought his way to me after the final curtain, and I saw as he came near me that there were tears in his eyes. He pressed my hand in silence and turned away.

I read Bartlett's notice in the Sunday *Times* with curiosity: "Last Friday night was one of the great moments in the history of the English stage, one in which a great playwright and a great actress simultaneously achieved maturity and full command of their medium. It is hard to believe that there can ever have been . . ."

I woke from one of these reveries to find myself sitting facing Larry Brook in a tea shop in Knightsbridge. He was drinking his second cup and staring thoughtfully at me over its rim.

"Well, where have you been, and who have you been?" he

said as I blinked at him. "You know, I met you on the street, and you just didn't know me, and when I spoke to you you didn't hear me. When I first caught sight of you you looked so like dear Naomi that it gave me quite a turn—drink some tea and tell me all about it."

"All about what?"

"Whatever the dream was—whatever the trouble is . . . I don't know."

He wasn't talking in his smart voice, he sounded rather ordinary and rather nice.

"I don't suppose you can put it into words right off without thinking about it, my dear boy, but when I find you wandering along the street looking as if you were hypnotized, I'm bound to think something must be wrong. What were you? A soldier? An enormously important statesman? Or an actor worshipped by thousands of idiotic fans?"

"How did you know?" I asked.

"I don't know your mother and work with her for nothing." He smiled again, a little sourly, looking down into his cup.

"I've no right to talk to you like this, but somebody ought to. I'm not saying your mother isn't a very wonderful woman, but she has a weakness. She gets hold of some story that interests her or amuses her, and she turns it into a story about herself. Somebody in the story attracts her and she becomes that other person. Sometimes she prefers the stories she makes up about herself to the facts. I'm not calling her a liar mind you. . . . It's like someone who has a wardrobe full of beautiful clothes, some are prettier than others and she prefers to wear them. That's all it amounts to."

"It's like being able to choose who you are, instead of having to be who you are," I said.

Larry looked at me sharply. "That's it. You seem to know how it works." He poured himself another cup of tea, and shifted uneasily on the uncomfortable wheelback chair. "I'd forgotten what ghastly places tea rooms are," he said. "Where do you suppose they find these dreadful thin-legged chairs and tables, and these frightfully cheerful little chintzes—I suppose there must be tea room suppliers—like the people who supply bars with beer mugs and brass rails . . . .and all those poor sad-looking girls with names like Prudence and Unity, in those unspeakable aprons? 'From Beckenham, from Bromley, from far off Potters Bar.' "

I looked at him, at his monkey-like wise face, which seemed so shrewd and knowing.

"Larry, Mr. Brook," I said. "Why is everything about us so odd? . . ."

His hand flew to his tie and he darted an alarmed look at me, and down at his clothes. "Odd, my dear boy? . . ."

"No, I don't mean anything about you, I mean about us, me, my father, my mother. Why does Mother always try to pretend Father doesn't exist? Why don't they ever see each other, or talk about each other? Why didn't my father ever come near me until I was nearly ten years old? What is it all supposed to be about?"

Larry looked at me in astonishment, and I looked back at him with almost as much surprise, the questions seemed so obvious now that they were in words, and I was amazed that I had never found words for them before or thought to put them to anyone. That I had suddenly put them across a tea table to Larry, rather than to anyone else, was much less surprising than anything else at the time to me, though it was clearly enough a shock to him.

While I sat half-elated at having discovered the cause of the vague ill-defined malaise which had been growing heavier and heavier on my mind for so long, and half-horrified to find what it was, he looked at me, playing with one finger with his other hand as if he were twisting a ring on it, and once or twice he opened his mouth and drew breath as if he were going to say something before he actually spoke.

"These things are difficult to explain to anyone, and they're almost impossible to explain in your case because, if you won't be hurt by my saying it, you're still a child. I know you feel immensely grown up because you've been feeling interested in girls for a year or two, and because you've been wearing long pants with your school suits for the last term or two. But there's an awful lot to learn still. I've been trying to find out ever since I was your age, and I haven't made out an awful lot, you've probably noticed it in my plays. When it comes down to it there are things I don't understand about people, and it shows when you get my stuff out on the stage. . . ." A hurt, bewildered look crossed his face momentarily and was chased away by his unbelievable charm-school smile.

"If I could answer your questions I'd be terrific, Ibsen wouldn't be in it, or Chekhov. You know what was wrong with my last play, or perhaps you don't. I wanted to show them an intensely respectable woman suddenly picked up and swept away by an intensely unrespectable storm of emotion— and I couldn't do it because I just didn't really know how that kind of woman lives. You see, I'm a competent playwright, not a genius. Now, your mother—she's a genius. She saw what I was trying to do, and she knew all about that kind of woman. She's been to Cheltenham, where my woman was supposed to have come from, a couple of times—with touring companies in the old days—and I suppose she'd seen that kind of life out of the windows of trains and taxis. And after she was successful she met that kind of person now and again at weekend parties and dinners—I don't know how she did it but out of that she made a complete picture of herself as one of those women, brought up in a nice home, genteelly educated, nicely married, and shaped by a regular, steady, pattern of living. She lived that life in her mind, from birth to death. She had that life all ready in her wardrobe, and when she read my play it was there waiting for her to put on. Your father's the same, you must have read his books. You know what he's like—you must be

74

able to see him in his books. Some people get cross with him because he always comes into them—but he's always in a new life even if you can recognize his dark brown eyes and so forth, when he describes the hero. He makes up a complete story about himself. He gossips—or rather he listens to gossip. He'll sit and listen to anyone for hours if they'll really tell him all about their troubles, he drinks it in, all the endless little details about how they felt, and what they wanted, and what actually happened. He hasn't got the time to live the hundreds of lives he needs for his books so he sucks up other people's lives, and then he goes off and dreams himself through the stories he's been told. I used to get on very well with him, we used to see a great deal of each other at one time. It lasted for a couple of years—then he suddenly dropped me. He's found out all he wanted to know about me—he wanted me to be the successful young playwright in that book of his, *Man's Estate* —or rather it was the other way round, when he'd "got" me, *Man's Estate* took shape round what he knew about me and one or two other people. It's more about Max if he had lived my life than it is about me, really. While I was going around with him he took me to play a game he plays—he calls it the Road Back Game—in some awful place in Kent—Reculver? No, Birchington, that was it, a second-rate resort that's a little more refined than Ramsgate or Margate. I'd never been there before, nor had he. We wandered round it all day inventing a bogus childhood for ourselves. We picked out houses to be born in, located the day school we went to when we were small, the sweetshop where we spent our pocket money, the private schools we went to when we were old enough to become boarders—everything, down to the stores our mothers bought their clothes at, the grocers, and the butchers, there wasn't a detail missing. And all the time we were doing it Max was inventing characters to round out the story, a little Frenchwoman who lived in the high street over Steele and Ardeny's, the nicest pastry shop, and did sewing for our mothers and gossipped so terribly, the parson our mothers liked and our fathers disliked, boys we liked at school and boys we hated. I had tremendous fun, and I put a great deal into the game in my small way. I wasn't brought up in Birchington of course, but in Beckenham, which is a place very like it, though it isn't by the sea, so I could see when Max went wrong—which wasn't very often—and I'd pull him up when he did. He always listened when I objected, and then he'd work in my corrections. I remember one thing—he described the big square blocks of red Lifebuoy soap, and the smell of carbolic that comes off them, as part of coming home after school on winter afternoons and getting ready for tea. I knew that he was wrong about that—that kind of soap belongs in a sink, not a handbasin, and in a working-class house, not a middle-class one. A boy of the kind we were supposed to be would have washed his hands in a downstairs lavatory that the servants didn't use, and he would have found a cake of that half-transparent brown stuff, Pears' Coal Tar Soap, there. Max took it all in. The hero in *Man's Estate* was a boy in a place like Birchington—it's called Rathbourne in the book—and when he discovers that his father drinks he's washing his hands in the downstairs lavatory after he's come back from school one day. He looks out of the little side window over the handbasin while he's washing his hands for tea and he sees his father being helped out of a cab by a grinning cab driver. I forget how the semi-transparent cake of brown soap comes into it, but it's there. . . ."

Larry stopped and tried to pour himself some more tea but the pot was dry.

"They never have big enough pots," he said absently, waving towards the waitress. "We'd adore another pot if we could have one," he said, flashing all his charm at her. I sat and looked at him while he ate a small sugared cake, it was all very interesting but it didn't seem to have much to do with my questions. I supposed that he had slipped away, as all grown-up people slipped away when one tried to find out anything at all important. Perhaps I would have to find Johnny Wallis and have a talk with him. He had been around a good deal lately, and had been being very friendly in a fatherly sort of way. The tea came and Larry drank a cup with the same absent air that he had brought to consuming the pink and white cake.

"You see they're both so wonderful at making up stories on the strength of a few facts that they don't very often pay much attention to the humdrum sort of stories that most people live out from fact to fact after they've been born, or fallen in love, or married. They met, they fell in love, and they both made up wonderful stories about what the rest of their lives were going to be, and what the other person was like. And when they started living together they found how different the stories were, and how badly they fitted into each other's stories. They felt they'd been terribly deceived, they were angry, and bitterly hurt. If you ever write you'll realize how infuriating it would be to find that your characters were rearranging your stories behind your back. They're always hurting themselves like that, your mother more than your father, though he does it too. Generally there's a quick cure—they scrap the old story and rewrite another one that puts it right out of their minds."

Larry paused again and fiddled with his cup as if he was reading a fortune in the tea leaves.

"All I can see is a thing like a squashed parrot," he murmured. I looked into my cup and saw something like an Indian and another thing rather like a ship.

"You don't believe in telling fortunes, do you?" I said.

"No—well, that is, yes," said Larry, "though I don't mean tea leaves, and crystals or anything like that. I mean I can tell your fortune up to a point. You see, when your father and mother scrapped the stories they'd written about each other and set out to write new ones they couldn't scrap you. No

matter how much rewriting they did you were still there—
oh, I can see the difficulty of it, clearly enough, though I don't
suppose you can. I've written things and seen they were no
good and thrown them out. I can't imagine what it would
be like if one of the characters out of those plays refused to
disappear, but hung round, developing his own traits, and
making more and more insistent demands for a place in my
work. It would be ghastly, and I'd be furious."

He paused again and eyed me. "I'm not being very kind to
you, I'm afraid—but I'm being honest with you because I
like you. I'll tell you your fortune—you're going to be miserable for a few years because you're going to try to force your
way into your parents' stories about themselves—it can't be
done. You won't have any sort of happiness until you give
it up. . . ." He leaned forward, looking down at his neatly
manicured hands. "If you've got their gift for making stories,
for God's own sake keep it out of your life. Whenever you
find yourself making a story about yourself instead of living
with the facts fight your way back into the daylight. It's the
only thing to do. . . . I shouldn't have said all this, I know,
it's busybodyish and awful of me. But you looked so lost on
the street just now, so Goddamned defenseless that it brought
out the rescue worker in me." He laughed, and I found myself laughing with him. "You will forgive me, won't you? It's
just that I do terribly like to see my friends being tidy and
happy with their lives. . . ."

I recalled that my mother had given me a warning about
Larry Brook a year or two before.

"He's the kindest boy, and I'm terribly glad he's being
nice to you, but there's a reason—only I can't explain what
it is now, you'll understand when you're older—why you
ought to be a little careful not to be too friendly with him. I
shouldn't ever go up to his apartment if I were you, not unless I'm with you, or there are other people there. People say

the most awful things—even when they don't mean anything
—and Larry says things that lead to misunderstandings—he
can't help it, poor lamb—it's just the way he is—so you will
be careful, won't you?"

Perhaps he was a storyteller too, and perhaps the story
that he was weaving round me and my parents was part of
the danger that I had to be mindful of in his presence. I was
young and inexperienced and I had no way of telling if that
was the danger, or something else.

We parted outside the tea shop. Larry jumped into a taxi
and went off to his bright, glittering, enviable life, while I
walked home.

It was getting dark, and the streets were full of the stir
and bustle of Christmas time. I walked along the north side
of the Brompton Road looking in at the shop windows and
watching the flow and movement of the other side of the
street. The side I was on was mostly given up to antique
shops in those days, and its opposite shore, so to speak, domi-
nated by one of the larger department stores, was the one
given up to hurry and rush. The northern pavement was
wide, and about halfway from the curb to the shopfronts, a
couple of broad steps which ran the length of the street formed
a raised terrace. I walked slowly along it looking down across
the stream of traffic to the other pavement, thinking how odd
it was that the eighteen inch difference in level gave one such
a sense of detachment and separation. I was like a spectator
looking on at a show. Its theme was Christmas, and all the
men and women flitting to and fro in front of the bright windows filled with Christmas trees, holly garlands, brightly colored ornaments, and expensive gewgaws could be fitted into
a Dickensian seasonal story. All the men and women hurrying in and out of the stores were buying gifts, to please each
other, and to show their affection for their friends. They
would soon all be carrying their parcels and bundles off to

warm, cozy, Cratchit-like nests of good cheer. What were they really doing, I wondered, and where were they really going and would I be any better off for knowing the truth?

I often wandered along the north side of that street, between the incense-scented baroque splendors of the Brompton Oratory and the Regency stucco front of Tatterstall's Auction stables, on my way to visit a friend of mine. The Oratory often hummed excitingly with chanted Latin, and Tatterstall's with its associations with the world of point to points, hunting, gentleman riders, jockeys, the turf, and sporting prints had a romance of its own; a romance added to by the fact that it faced a triangular plot of land, planted with plane trees, which was said to have been a burial pit during the Great Plague of London, and for that reason untouchable. Between the two extremes, of the life devoted to God, and the life devoted to horses, at each end of the street, stretched a row of shops holding every kind of treasure—from great classic marble heads from eighteenth-century Italian gardens, wrought-iron screens from Catalonian churches, fireplaces from vanished houses, to delicate furniture from every country in Europe, Benin bronzes, Chinese scroll paintings, ship models, and porcelains from all over the world—almost everything imaginable that was curious or beautiful.

It was an interest in toy soldiers and miniature weapons which first took me there. As I rode past on a bus top I saw a set of miniature field artillery, two field guns with caissons, in one of the windows. I hurried back from the next stop and went in hopefully to ask the price. When I showed my disappointment at the revelation of the value that collectors put on such things, Mr. Wykesman, the kindly Jewish owner of the shop, consoled me and won my friendship by showing me the other military items in his stock, the banners of long disbanded and dispersed regiments, old cartridge pouches, sabretaches, swords, poignards, horsepistols, muskets, and other fragments of warlike gear. To my eyes his finest thing was a cavalry helmet ornamented with a Medusa's head and a plume of scarlet feathers. Mr. Wykesman laughed at me when I picked it out. He told me that it had been the uniform head-dress of a volunteer yeomanry squadron formed in a southern market town in the years when Napoleon was threatening to invade England, a unit which had never fired a shot in battle.

"Some pot-bellied corn chandler or country magistrate who dreamed of being Alcibiades strutted about in it for a year or two," said Mr. Wykesman, "and then it went up into an attic. That's the way it is with war and weapons, the more fun the stuff is the less it has to do with the real thing."

He showed me a beautiful suit of Spanish armor, chased and inlaid with curling designs.

"There's a pretty bit of nonsense, I'll sell it as easily as anything to some collector. It's a tournament suit, and I doubt if it was ever worn except in a dress parade—it was made long after people had stopped fighting seriously in armor, just for show."

He led me to his desk at the back of the shop and showed me a round thing like a saucepan without a handle that he had been using as an ash tray.

"Now there—there you've got a real fighting man's helmet, the real thing. Some tough German mercenary wore it under his wide-brimmed hat all through the Thirty Years' War as like as not . . . but that's one I won't sell till dooms-day. Nobody's interested in the real thing because it doesn't match up with their ideas."

He gazed about his shop with the dark eyes and his habitual expression of amusement.

"Nobody likes the truth. They all come in here looking for stuff to dress up their lives with—genuine antiques that'll give them status of people of taste—they're scared to buy new stuff because it would give away what their taste actually was. As for weapon collectors, bankers, stockbrokers, commercial artists—I don't know what—they come in here with some dream of being feudal lords or young Lochinvars. The only kind of man who never comes in here bothering me for old muskets and so forth is a soldier. . . . Not one in ten, not one in a hundred, comes in here with an eye for the really beautiful stuff. . . ."

He took me over to a glass-fronted bookcase which was serving him as a china cabinet, and showed me a row of Korean bowls, standing in the shadowy depths of the great brown mahogany museum-piece.

"There you see—" he took one of the bowls out and handed it to me, "that's a green, isn't it, a wonderful color, and look at the shape of it—all light and grace—and once, seven hundred years ago, it was just a lump of clay. It's worth thirty shillings—and that great lump of brown wood, glass and gilding it sits on is worth a thousand pounds. Somebody will come in one of these days and buy it. It'll sit in his rooms saying look what a rich man I am, I've got one of the four bookcases made in 1764 to the order of Lord Havicourt by Samuel Billings of Longacre. I'm rich and I've got good taste too, because everything Billings designed is in guaranteed good taste, the Burlington Magazine says so, and so does Apollo . . . and the fool who buys it will be amused that old Wykesman keeps his Korean pots in such a wonderful thing. . . ."

I very often went down to see Mr. Wykesman on winter afternoons, to sit gossiping with him beside the fire which he kept going in the snuggery in the back part of the shop where he sat waiting for customers. He told me anecdotes about the sales at country houses and town houses where he bought his precious things, and other anecdotes about his clients and the strange commissions they sometimes gave him.

As he talked I recognized that his shop was a prop room, like that under the stage of the Palinode Theatre; his long lines of precious things were in temporary retirement. They were the dismantled scenery of every kind of drama, waiting their turn to be fetched out and used in new shows.

I walked towards Mr. Wykesman's shop thinking over what Larry had said, and it occurred to me for the first time that my mother might not be an altogether happy woman. I had thought till then that in the process of growing up people discovered the answers to all the questions that troubled the young, and came with maturity to a stage of serene self-command in which everything seemed simple and easy. And for the first time it had been revealed to me that I was a problem for her to deal with in the course of her march towards some goal of which I had no idea. I knew that she wished to be, and worked to be, the greatest actress of her day, and I knew that she was my mother; it had not occurred to me that she might have another goal, beyond that.

When one is young one thinks along primitive lines; I was at the stage in which one makes propitiatory offerings in the way that savage tribesmen lay cockerels and baskets of fruit on the altars of the gods. I decided I would give my mother a really nice Christmas present, so I went into Mr. Wykesman's shop and after talking with him a little while bought two of his sea-green Korean bowls.

I found my mother waiting for me in the drawing room, sitting on the sofa with a letter from my father on the low lacquered table inlaid with mother of pearl in front of her. Her manner as she made me sit beside her, and as she stroked my hair, with a fond caressing hand, was affectionate in a way which, combined with the letter, made me uneasy.

"Dickie, are you counting terribly much on Christmas here with me? I hope you aren't—because your father has taken it into his head to want you to come over to him. I think it's crazy of him to uproot you suddenly like this only a week before Christmas—but he's written to me begging for you to come—he's never given you a Christmas—he seems to want to before you're too grown up to enjoy it. He's such a baby—he loves giving people parcels to open, and arranging surprises. I won't say anything one way or the other about whether you ought to go or not, but he's obviously thought about it a lot, and he rather begs for you in a sweet way. Would you very much hate to go? I know that Essling-Sterlinghoven woman he lives with is pretty tiresome, but it would be a wonderful thing for him if you could bear it. It'll be sad for me, and I'll miss you, but I have you all the time after all, and it doesn't seem fair of me to hold onto you when it seems to mean so much to him. . . ."

When she had gone through the motions of letting me decide whether or not I would accept Max's invitation she became a great deal brisker and gayer, and a good deal more natural. She was the gamine rather than the tender mother when she told me that she'd known all along that I wouldn't be able to resist the idea of Christmas with Max and that she was so sure of it that she'd already got the tickets and seat reservations for the journey. It was with the gesture of a naughty little girl that she produced the envelope from the travel agency containing these things: "You see, I had them ready—just in case."

I looked at the tickets and saw that they were marked for a longer journey than I had expected, beyond Paris, and that I was to ride through the night in the Blue Train, southwards, clear across France to Cannes. I looked at her in surprise, murmuring, "But these are . . ."

"Oh yes, that's part of the fun of it for Max. He's got a house he's terribly proud of down at Antibes—he's dying to show it you—I expect it will be lovely, and the journey will be fun too. You'll wake up somewhere beyond Arles, and by the time you've dressed and breakfasted you'll be looking out at the Mediterranean. I wish I could go with you. . . ."

I interrupted her. "They're for tomorrow morning—I'll

probably have to leave before you're up. I'd better give you my Christmas present tonight. I'll fetch it now."

I went into the hall and brought in Mr. Wykesman's square box, handling it carefully as I remembered the dealer's long fingers caressing the bowls.

"What a divine green," she said, glancing at them as she lifted them out of the tissue paper, "they'll make wonderful ash trays. There . . ." She put one down on the lacquered table. "Oh no, that green fights with that mother of pearl." She looked swiftly around her. "Where shall we put them . . . I know." She got up and took it around to a bookshelf on the far side of the room.

"There. Now, bless you, darling—I've got to run. And I expect you've lots of packing to do. Thank you for the bowls, they're adorable." She gathered up my father's letter with a swift gesture and put it in her bag.

"Kiss me, there's a love. I know you'll have a happy time with Max. Good night. . . ."

She swirled out of the room, leaving behind the dying fragrance of her delicious scent. I stood looking across the room at the bowls standing on the bookshelf, wondering if they had succeeded or failed as an offering. I turned away from them, and tried to console myself with the thought that within forty-eight hours I would be looking at the Mediterranean, the sea of Greeks, and Romans, galleys and Corsairs. But though I tried to take pleasure in the idea, it meant more than anything else that I would be spending the first Christmas within my memory away from Castlereagh Gardens.

My mother was not awake when I left to catch the boat train on the following morning, and for the first time I felt depressed as I crossed the Channel. I was going into exile, leaving behind the theatre and things I was attached to, for an interlude taken out of the proper natural flow of life.

My father met me at the station in Cannes, friendly and

smiling, but with a certain reserve which puzzled me. He didn't drive straight over to his house at Antibes, but took me to lunch at a small restaurant in Cannes itself where we ate in unusual constraint. When coffee came I was in the grip of a feeling of awkwardness which I had never felt with Max before. I had become aware during the meal that he was furiously angry.

My second glass of Traminer was untouched in front of me when I reached out for my coffee cup.

"Don't do that—finish your wine first—" said Max, almost snapping at me. Then modifying his tone he said, "You see, once you've tasted the coffee the wine will seem sour. . . . I'm sorry to be ill tempered, but I'm in the middle of a lot of things just now—I'm finishing a book—and, well, there are other complications. Your visit isn't as convenient as it could be. Of course I like having you around—but some times are more convenient than others, and this isn't one of the better times . . . I'm sorry, but there it is. . . ."

I looked at him with surprise and disappointment.

"I could go home if you like—I only came because Mother told me you'd begged her to let me spend Christmas with you. . . ."

My father was lighting a cigar, staring at me over a match flame which now flared up and now died down as he drew on the cigar. He abruptly flicked the match out and put the cigar down.

"She . . . told . . . you . . ." His face was red with anger, then his eyes twinkled and he burst into a laugh. "Oh, it isn't possible . . . Naomi's the devil . . ." He fell back in his chair, laughing until the tears rolled down his cheeks. "How could she have thought she was going to get away with that one. . . ." he said, and began to laugh again. "She's incredible."

I wondered for a moment if he was out of his mind. There

seemed nothing funny in my mother's telling me that he had wanted me to spend Christmas with him.

"Well, let this be a lesson to you," he said at last wiping his eyes, "when you've learnt to understand your mother you'll know more about women than anybody who ever lived." He searched for his pocketbook and drew a letter out of it. "This is cheating really, but we're playing a game that hasn't any rules. Listen to this. . . .

" 'Dear Max. I know you're a very busy man, and very much wrapped up in your affairs, but I think you should occasionally give a thought to other people's interests. I don't know if you've ever thought that Dickie always visits you when you happen to feel like having him, and I don't suppose that you've ever thought that there are other times when he very much longs to be with you. I was talking to him the other day, just after his birthday, and he said to me that he wondered why he'd never had anything like a birthday or Christmas with you. I said you were a very busy man, and he said rather sadly that the fathers of the other boys he knew were very busy too, but they had time to make nice Christmases and birthdays all the same. I put it to you that you really ought to make the effort this year and give him a really good Christmas. He's a funny dreamy boy and he's getting into the awkward age of asking questions that go very deeply into things and I'm rather worried about the adjustment he's going to make to life. I really feel that it would make a tremendous difference to him if you could have him this Christmas. . . .' "

While my father read this letter the sense of going into exile which had obsessed me all through the long journey from London returned with redoubled force. The train had stopped somewhere near Lyons in the middle of the night, and I had awakened to hear the shrill sound of a French locomotive whistle echoing weirdly across a wide plain like a warning cry from a spirit giving me a last chance to go back before I entered an enchanted land. I seemed to hear its mournful cry again as I listened to the disingenuous phrases of the letter, but this time it announced that it was too late to withdraw from whatever mysterious enterprise I had embarked upon.

I looked away from my father, across a *place* planted with a quincunx of trees to the harbor crowded with elegant yachts whose white, black and green hulls and yellow varnished masts gleamed in the wine-like winter sunshine, and to the old town whose mound of reddish roofs was crowned with a square church tower; a strange place, filled with strange people, of whom I knew nothing. But then, so was Castlereagh Gardens, and my home. I looked away from the alien town to my father's face and met his eyes. He gave me a look full of complicity and understanding to which I replied with a grin.

"Well, that makes us allies, fellow victims," he said, all friendliness and geniality again.

I was flattered and excited, I recognized that I was being invited by one adult to make a party against another on level terms and took my first step forward into that world of lies, treachery, deceit, and fierce emotions that lay beyond childhood. The pretenses that fathers and mothers loved each other and their children as a matter of course could now be abandoned, the fathers loved the fathers, the mothers the mothers, the children looked after themselves, and occasionally their interests coincided, the important thing was not to be caught up in one's own lies, or to be fooled by anyone else's.

My father blew out a thin jet of cobalt-blue cigar smoke and his expression became thoughtful.

"I feel pretty badly about what's happened to you in these last few years," he said, "but believe me it wasn't altogether my fault. Your mother's a very difficult woman at times—she's like a cat—she can't bring herself to do anything the simple ordinary way. She always has to go round a thing and round it, and then up to it sideways—it makes life difficult for those who are close to her. She couldn't understand me for always wanting things to be straightforward. When I do a thing I put down my cards face upwards, that's what I want to do, that's the way I'm going to do it. I like things to be simple. Your mother couldn't stand that . . . but let's forget these far-off unhappy things. What's happened can't be helped. We'd best try to make a go of things as they are. . . ."

He tapped two inches of ash off the end of his cigar into an ash tray, and sighed.

"You got on pretty well with Lolotte, didn't you? At any rate she likes you, and I hope you'll get on with her. She's staying with me just now. Don't let her way of saying things to shock people upset you—she can't help doing it and she doesn't mean any harm by it. Every now and then she says things that get me rattled—you may think we're quarreling, but it's all in fun really. I'm just telling you this now so that you won't be surprised by the way she behaves. She's a handful, but I'm very fond of her. We've tried parting once or twice, but as soon as we get away we find we can't live apart." He looked at his wrist watch. "She's having lunch with a friend in town, she's going to meet us here and then we're going to drive out to the farm. I expect she'll be here in about a quarter of an hour—she's a quarter of an hour late now and half an hour is her usual amount of leeway." Exasperation gleamed in his eyes for a moment. "I've argued with her about it time and time and time again, but she just can't keep an appointment. . . . I know what, though, we'll show her we're men of spirit. There's a record shop just down the street where they have Spanish music—wonderful stuff—we'll go and get you some and when we come back she'll be waiting for us."

The record shop was next to a fish market, outside which

was a tub of spiky sea urchins, brown, pale yellow and red, and it produced *sardanas* that astonished me and delighted me with their odd combination of Arab and Spanish rhythms and assonances. Max bought me a dozen records, telling me while he did so all about the Arab kingdoms in Spain, about Granada, and the great mosque at Seville. The minutes ran by very pleasantly, and when we came back to the restaurant the Grafin Essling-Sterlinghoven was waiting for us, sitting with a little white dog in her lap. She looked very German in a black leather coat under which she was wearing a white woollen dress. She was a little thinner than when I had last seen her, and a little more beautiful.

"Dickie," she said, "see how abominably your father treats me—I wait for him where he tells me to wait, patiently, like a dog. When you get back home you can tell your mother how he humiliates me—that is what he wishes—she will snigger at me as all these waiters are sniggering at me—tell her he treats me like a kept woman, or a parcel that he can pick up and set down as he pleases—tell her my life is one long round of such humiliations. . . ."

"Oh, damn," said my father, with his voice rising to a squeak, "you know very well . . ."

"There now, he curses me in front of his son. . . ." She raised her eyes to heaven, like a martyr. "One lives a hard life when one sacrifices oneself to the caprices of a genius . . . there now I have teased you enough, poor Maxie. I am bad, I was late, you may beat me tonight if you wish. Meanwhile take the dog so that I can hug Dickie. . . ." She took my hands and stared at me with a strange intensity, eying me from top to toe. "You have grown. You are tall—taller than your father already—you are turning into a man—what hideous clothes you English make your children wear. . . ."

"It's the school uniform," I said weakly.

"It is gray and horrible," she said. "We will go and buy you French clothes and you can pretend you are a *lycéen* and not an English schoolboy. I will pretend you are my son while you are here—the son I should have made Max give me."

In spite of Max's objections she bore me off and presently I was dressed up in a fantastic French imitation of English sports clothes, with a wonderfully fluffy tweed jacket, and monstrous brogues with soles nearly an inch and a half thick. I resisted a beret, and she gave way unwillingly.

"You are only fifteen, and you are already hidebound. It is a terrible thing to be English—terrible. Wear it just for a moment to see. You will look dashing and handsome, I promise you."

Standing in front of the haberdasher's triple mirror in my outrageous get-up—*tout ce qu'il a de plus sportsman,* as the assistant said—I felt thoroughly ashamed of myself. Max standing in the background could hardly bear to look at me, and I could hardly bear to look at myself in the glass. Lolotte popped the beret on my head—"There, you see, you will be irresistible—I cannot resist you. I must kiss you now." I stiffened as she embraced me, and looked over her shoulder into the mirror into the grinning face of the tailor. Lolotte recoiled.

"Do you always turn to wood when a woman kisses you —you are not like your father. . . ." I blushed, and was ashamed of blushing, of having blood, of being alive. "I see, I see, I understand." She held up her hands in astonishment. "You are a virgin—you are afraid of girls! Max, it is incredible how Naomi has brought up this son of yours. . . ."

"Lolotte!" cried my father.

". . . he is gauche, he does not know what to do with his hands, he cannot speak, he has no experience. . . ."

"Lolotte!"

"How can you bear it that that woman should let your son become such a hobbledehoy. . . ."

Other assistants in the store, other customers edged up to watch the strange spectacle. I was as red as a beetroot, Max was much the same color, Lolotte was lecturing us at the top of her voice on the monstrous consequences of my virginity. When she saw that the French in the shop were missing something of what she was saying, she began to speak their language and raised her voice somewhat so that they should miss nothing. I stood with burning cheeks, incapable of saying a word, incapable of movement, like an allegorical figure representing shame. Max at last pushed a handful of money into the shopman's grasp and propelled us both out of the shop by main force, Lolotte still talking over a shoulder to the bystanders who followed us out onto the pavement with delight and amazement on their faces.

As we drove out to Les Orangers in the Voisin I sat in the back and Lolotte and Max argued furiously in the front seat. ". . . incredible piece of idiotic vulgarity . . ."

"Vulgarity—you dare to talk to me of vulgarity—you are a man of the people, a proletarian—you know nothing about how to give a boy a decent upbringing. You . . ."

"Don't talk to me about decency, after that exhibition. You don't know the first thing about decency. . . ."

"You hypocrite. You, you who sleep with me in all the hotels in Europe, and parade me as your mistress wherever you go—you lecture me on decency and propriety. . . ."

I cowered in the back seat near to tears. Lolotte was mad, my father was mad, and how could my mother have betrayed me into the hands of this pair of lunatics for my Christmas holidays.

". . . I shall leave, I shall go tomorrow—there are men in the world who appreciate a woman who is a woman. . . ."

"Fine, that suits me—it couldn't suit me better . . . I'll be glad to have a little peace and quiet in my home. . . ."

A dead silence fell in the front of the car. The white dog sitting on the cushions beside me licked my hand furtively and looked up at me with beseeching eyes. I caressed it and it gently wagged its tail.

The tension did not diminish as we drove out of Cannes into the hills behind it, and we got out of the car at the end of the dirt road which led up to it in an uneasy silence. I liked the look of Les Orangers, an old farmhouse standing among olive trees on a terraced hillside, but I could not take it in under the circumstances. Lolotte showed me to my room as if she were anxious to get rid of me, and having thrust me in through its doorway ran off to resume her quarrel with Max. A few seconds after she had gone I heard her voice raised almost to a shout in another part of the house, and my father's angry squeaking rising shrilly against it.

I threw myself on the bed in an agony of grief. My mother was a liar, my father a buffoon who lived with a madwoman —what was to become of me? The storm in the other part of the house raged on, and then a silence fell. Boredom ousted my distress. I began to explore my room, liking its heavy simplified baroque Provençal furniture, and the cheerful red and white material of the curtains and chair covers. A fire of olive wood burning quietly in the wide fireplace filled the air with an agreeable spicy scent, and there was a comfortable armchair in front of it. When I looked out of the window I saw the sea gleaming above the silvery heads of the olive trees in the wide sweep of Cannes bay, and a little way off shore the low lines of Iles des Lerins on whose rocky shore Paganini was buried because no priest would let him rest in consecrated ground. To the west the steep slopes of the Esterel mountains were already black against the afternoon sky. It was after all, compared with Castlereagh Gardens, not such a bad place to be.

There was a snuffling and subdued whining at the door and when I opened it the bright-eyed white dog was there, smiling at me in the fashion of small dogs with its pink tongue hanging out. I thought he might show me round the place and tiptoed down the stairs with him, hoping we would not meet anyone. The gardens were pleasantly laid out round a big square water tank, and beyond them there was the aromatic olive orchard terraced like an enormous flight of steps. The little dog ran off ahead of me along a path which climbed up the hillside among the olive trees and I followed him, scrambling up the rough steps in the stone faces of the terraces in his wake, until presently we came out on a cart track. The dog paused, looking up and down, and then looking down began to bark in a cheerful way. My father and Lolotte came in sight walking arm in arm, her head was resting on his shoulder and they were deep in whispered conversation. Lolotte waved to me when she saw me, and my father smiled broadly. The dog ran towards them with its tail waving frantically, bounding along in an ecstasy which made it seem as if it were trying to fly. Everything was, after all, going to be all right, however incomprehensible.

That evening there was a dinner party at Les Orangers, as perplexing as the other events of the day, though wholly unlike them. Lolotte appeared at it in the role of a gracious hostess, courteous, and ripplingly conversational in the most conventional way as she played up to my father, who presided over the whole thing as a solemn man of affairs. I watched the faces of the guests as they drank martinis before dinner, while they ate their way through the five-course meal, and afterwards when the women had left the table and the men were left to their brandy and cigars, waiting to catch the slight look of irony, of amused contempt, that showed that they knew they were at the table of a buffoon whose woman dragged him into one fantastic public humiliation after another. They eyed him appraisingly, but seriously, and when there was laughter they were laughing with him and not at him. When the talk turned to grave political matters over the brandy they listened to his opinions, and it became clear to me that they respected him. ". . . as I see it this lunatic French policy of punishing Germany, and humiliating it, is just beginning to make itself felt. The democratic Germany that we all had such hopes of after the war is finished—the

French burked it—they did everything they could to prove it wasn't a reality and now it isn't. The country's drifting into something much worse than we've seen yet. Oh, I know those old boys, the military clique, were pretty bad, but they were nothing to this Brown Shirt crowd—I went to a meeting in Leipzig a couple of months ago and I listened to a lunatic dervish—a fellow called Hitler—the crowd lapped it up, and his rowdies marched through the streets as if they owned them—that's the man who's going to take over Germany in a year or two—and when he does, then you'll see something. I tell you the Europe we've known all our lives is breaking up. That Russian thing was only a beginning, those weren't Asiatic horrors—they're the horrors of a new time. . . ."

The English member of Parliament who had been a cabinet minister looked thoughtful, but not amused. So did the Hungarian economist. I looked away from them to the immense bulk of the Atabeg Suleiman, deputy prime minister of Turkey and mysteriously one of the richest men in the world, who was drawing invisible symbols on the tablecloth with his finger tips.

"I feel just like you, Max," he said with the faintest hint of a foreign accent. "It seems to me that we are coming to the end of the period of armistice, and that jockeying for favorable opening positions in a new war has begun. But my feeling is that this man Mussolini's the danger. . . ."

"Mussolini's only an actor," said Max, "playing at Caesar. This man Hitler will lead him by the nose before long—wherever he wants to. Mussolini can't do anything if the Americans cut his money off, but, when Hitler gets hold of Krupps and the Ruhr he'll be able to set the world dancing to any tune he chooses to call. . . ."

"But, Max," said the cabinet minister, "don't you think . . ." My father brushed him aside. I sat smoking my first cigar with curiosity, and almost with enjoyment, drinking it all in. The talk drifted off in the direction of anecdotes about Mussolini, Diego Rivera, De Valera, and the new race of strong men who were plaguing Europe. It was conversation of a kind that I had never listened to before and I was excited: under Max's wing I was entering a world of vast extent in which the affairs of the theatre seemed very small beer.

I went to sleep happily, quite forgetting the humiliating public announcement of my virginity which I had thought of a few hours before as a blow from which I would never recover, forgetting too the blow which Max had dealt me by reading, and as a capital joke, my mother's letter.

The next two days were pleasant ones. The olive orchard behind Les Orangers ran up to the summit of a small hill, which was a plateau some fourteen or fifteen acres in extent planted with white jasmine and lavender, grown for the scent manufactured in Grasse. From this level piece of ground one looked over a gentle valley partly given over to flower-growing for the same purpose, and partly given over to olive trees. Beyond that the foothills of the Alpes Maritimes covered with pine forests rose up until they merged with the snowy crests of the main mountain ridge some thirty or forty miles away. I wandered happily through the valley guided by the little white dog, who took me to call on all his friends in the neighborhood, the curly-tailed mongrels of the shopkeepers in the village of St. Vicaire-les-Toits, the *chien de race* who was assistant to the gatekeeper of the Château des Ursins, the rug-like watchdogs chained up outside barrels on the nearby farms. It was no more than civil to pass the time of day with the owners of the dogs on these visits, so that I became familiar for the first time with the twanging nasal singsong of Provençal speech, and with its abundance of reflexives. When I told one of the farmers that at home I lived in a town, he remarked, pulling at his handlebar mustaches, that *"ang se mangje bieng dang les villes, ang m'a dit qu'ils mangje de la viangde tous les jours. . . ."* His "one eats oneself well" seemed to me to go as far as one could go with reflexives and gave me a quite special pleasure, so did the fact that the man himself, nut-brown, gnarled like the stem of an old olive tree, smelling of sweat, and with fingernails of greenish black, made most of his money out of roses, going through his fields every morning before the dew was off the freshly opened buds, cutting them before the heat of the sun should have sucked out their sweetness. In the season he took half a ton of half-opened roses to the factory every day before noon, shooting their loveliness out of burlap bags into bins at the unloading platform.

My father seemed uneasy when I said at lunch that I had met this man, and asked, anxiously, what he had said about him.

"He didn't say much," I said, "he just looked at me and said, *'ah, vous, vous estes le fils du patron, ça se voit. . . .'* that's all." I suppressed the fact that he had gone on to say, *"C'est pas votre mère, la Boche la haute, hein?"* and Max said with a scowl, "Marchand's a scoundrel, the less you have to do with him the better. . . ." Lolotte laughed.

"Poor Maxie, Marchand robbed him outrageously over this place, he'll never forgive him. It was all to do with the water tank—" she pointed down into the garden. "It was a persecution. We bought the house. The builders came and put it to rights—inside it was a pigsty when we bought it. No bathrooms, nothing, the wagons kept in here where we are eating, hens and horses in a stable where the kitchen and the drawing room are. The room above here looking over the water tank we made Max's workroom. Nothing will disturb him there—he will look out across the hills to the sea, and he will work, work, work, in the divine silence. The builders finish and move away. We move in. Max starts to work. We have three days of peace, Max smiles happily. And then—what is this? A troop of women with baskets of laundry file in through the garden gate and settle by the water tank. They talk, they sing, they slap the laundry on the stone parapet round the tank. Max rushes out. What is this, it is his garden, his water tank, what are they doing here? The ladies say they are those of the Farm La Haye des Rochers, the tank is the place where they do their laundry, they have done it there for time immemorial. Max will have none of it, he has bought Les Orangers, and all that is changed now. The next day they are back, with a gendarme, and their notary with papers. There is a *servitude* on Les Orangers, people of La Haye des Rochers have a legally established right to do their washing in the basin in the forecourt of the farm called Les Orangers. Twice a week they come there, chattering and singing. Max is frantic. Will they sell their rights? No, but they will sell La Haye des Rochers for a good sum. Max is furious and will not buy. They come again and again with their baskets. At last in exasperation he buys. We have another farm. We have peace though—for ten days. Then one morning as Max works he looks up from his papers, another troop of women with their baskets of laundry are filing into the garden. Max rushes out, no, no, the question of *servitudes* is all settled now that he owns La Haye des Rochers. But no, monsieur, we are not of La Haye des Rochers, we are from La Garderie on the other side. They have a *servitude,* too. We go through the same process. After that it is the turn of the people of Les Putiers, down the hill from La Garderie, and we buy them out also. Then it is all over, the affair of *les blanchisseuses,* we are free of the laundrywomen. We lay out a lawn round the tank, and plant up the garden. Then one day there is Marchand when Max looks up from his papers, standing by while his two Percherons suck up water out of the tank. Yes, Marchand has a *servitude* too, whenever he wants he can water animals in the basin. When we have bought out Marchand—he sells his *servitude,* not his farm—we discover that all the people of La Haye des Rochers, of La Garderie, of Les Putiers, are his brothers and cousins. They have been trying to sell out for years, since the price of olives went down after the war, so they could raise the money to make a fresh start in the north where farming is easier. Marchand showed them the way to do it, by this legal blackmail. And at the last, when he wanted to change his cart and his Percherons for a new Renault truck, he joined the game. They are grasping, these peasants, they treat people the way they treat their thin soil, squeezing it for the last penny. And their lawyers and notaries who get fat skimming cream off water . . ."

She threw up her hands. "Marchand and his friends put us through the wringer—we were trusting and idiotic, and they made royal fools of us. . . ."

My father was laughing now. "It's all water over the dam," he said. "I should have known better, but I didn't. It's odd though, when it annoys me to remember *l'affaire Marchand* Lolotte finds it funny—and when I'm amused by it it infuriates Lolotte."

"It maddens me to see you being so good-humored about these avaricious peasants," said Lolotte savagely, "that's all. I am an aristocrat. My forefathers knew how to deal with such people—when they misbehaved we hanged them, or cropped their ears and put them in the pillory. . . ."

My father turned to me. "Which side are you on in the French Revolution?" he said. "Are you a Roundhead or a Cavalier? You take sides when you read novels and stories about all that, don't you?"

"I am sure he is a King's man like any decent person; aren't you, Dickie?" said Lolotte.

I shook my head. It was curious, I had never really thought about it before, but in history lessons at school, and when I was reading books about the French Revolution and the Civil Wars in England, I had always been on the side of the people against the Kings. I had always wanted them to catch the Scarlet Pimpernel, and ridden in the ranks of the New Model Army—never with Prince Rupert and the Cavaliers.

"That's right," said Max. "Don't fool yourself like Lolotte.

She really comes from a long line of Greek merchants who preyed on their Turkish masters, it makes her feel better to pretend that she's one of the last pillars of the ancient regime. . . ."

"The Essling-Sterlinghovens are noble," screamed Lolotte. "You boor . . . they are in the Almanach de Gotha. They were living in a castle when your family were living in mud huts. . . ."

"They were bandits in the Middle Ages, and Kings rewarded them for butchering other Kings' subjects by giving them stolen lands," said Max.

"You are impossible," cried Lolotte, "but impossible, blood and breeding mean nothing to you—you belong with the little people—you are a mongrel like Marchand. You are irredeemable."

My father winked at me. "Maybe I am," he said, and then he looked thoughtful. "I don't suppose Naomi has told you very much about me, Dickie, I forget if I ever told her much of my start in life. If I did I don't suppose she would pass it on to you."

There was a curiously sardonic look on his face, and for a moment he looked cruel.

"You're tall, Dickie, you're bigger than I am already. I was stunted by the time I was your age. I had rickets when I was small, and when I was growing I slept in a little bed that I couldn't stretch out in—a cot really. Four of us slept in one room— It had a window but I don't believe it opened—I can't remember ever seeing it open at any rate. My brothers Jack and Ted slept together in an iron bedstead on one side of the room, Harry slept in a camp bed on the other side, and my cot was under the window. I was lucky to have a bed to myself, I suppose. My sisters Emily, Flossie, and poor Amy only had one bed between the three of them. It was a big double bed in the next room to ours—a mingy little room —there was just room to squeeze past it and the truckle bed

Granny Walsh—mother's mother—slept in. I was glad I didn't have to sleep in with them—Granny Walsh was senile, prematurely, and out of her mind a good deal of the time. My father worked as a farmhand, from five in the morning till five in the afternoon for eighteen shillings a week. My mother was supposed to feed us and clothe us all out of that. None of us children ever had anything new to wear—when Jack grew out of things Ted got them, and when Ted was done with them, Harry had his turn, and then they came down to me. By the time I got them there was more patched and darned onto them than there was left of the original garment —and the boots we wore—Gawd! You'd be ashamed to put them on your feet. And the food we ate! Breakfast was Indian tea, and bread with a skim of jam on it. We'd take a baked potato and a bit of hard cheese to eat at school in the lunch break, and then we'd have Indian tea and bread and scrape for the last meal of the day. Sundays we had meat, bacon boiled with beans and cabbage, or a roast of pork. The Vicar used to pitch into my father for neglecting his garden, they had beautiful walled gardens up at the vicarage. He called my father feckless. 'Good fresh vegetables would put some color into the cheeks of those pasty-faced children of yours,' he used to say. It didn't seem to strike him that my father mightn't have the heart for much gardening after his twelve-hour day in the fields, and Mother hadn't the strength after she'd been in childbed nine times—oh yes, two of us were born dead, and one—another girl—died before she was six months old— Mother said it was God's mercy—and I suppose it was. Anyway, by the time Father had raised potatoes to last the year round, and set out cabbages, he was about through with gardening." Max swallowed hard, and crumbled the remains of his roll into little pellets. . . . "We were pushed out into jobs as soon as we could get them. I went out to be a carter's boy when I was ten, at nine shillings a week. I paid my mother five shillings a week board, and clothed myself and amused myself with the four shillings left over. I had to be on the job at seven, and I left off at five, whatever the weather. I saved up two shillings every week—no matter what. By the time I was twelve and a half I had five pounds and I was plucking up my courage to run away. Ted was twenty them. He ran away to Canada—we never heard from him again. He knew where I hid my money and he stole it before he went. He left a note saying he'd send it back when he'd made his fortune . . . gaw—how I hated him for that, with a bitterness you'll never know. I was growing then and hungry all the time—I'd set snares for rabbits on my way home from work. Sometimes when I caught them I'd take them home and Mother would make rabbit pie—meat in the middle of the week, luxury—I can still remember the look of that pale pink meat in a pie that was two-thirds potato—sometimes I'd cheat and cook the rabbit all for myself in a can on a fire of trash wood over by the hedge when I was working a field. I meant to run away as soon as I had five pounds saved again. . . ." Max began to throw the pellets of bread lying on the tablecloth in front of him over the edge of the terrace, one by one with an abrupt jerky movement. "I knew I had to get out soon. If I stayed too long I'd never get away—I'd be trapped like my father. Jack had joined the regular army—he was off in India somewhere—he didn't write very often. He'd escaped. Ted was gone. Amy was tubercular. Emily was married to a farmhand in the village and was having her first baby. Flossie was working at home nursing Granny Walsh, and helping Mother, who was getting too weak for the rough work, at the cooking, the cleaning, and the darning. Father was getting more and more crippled with arthritis. It was a matter of time before he was fired from his job in the dairy. He'd get the sack just as soon as his hands got too bad for him to keep on with the milking. . . . When he was out of a job Harry or I would be keeping the family out of our wages. I knew it was in Harry's mind to vanish like Ted, he'd spoken of Canada once or twice when we were alone together, and I knew that he'd made some discreet inquiries about Australia. We watched each other like hawks for the first signs. He was easier in his mind than I was because he knew I couldn't have saved up passage money—but there were people who advertised in the *Western Gazette*—a weekly—the only newspaper that came into the house—offering passages to the colonies to men and youths who would sign on for long-term contracts. He used to stare at me when I read the paper to see if I was looking for these ads, and he always tried to come with me if I went into town Saturday nights. He'd stick like glue until we were safe home again. He had got work with a jobbing carpenter and builder's decorator, and I knew it was because he wanted to have a trade before he went overseas. I watched him to see if he was buying clothes or any tools that looked like part of an outfit. I was determined that I'd be off at the first move he made. I wasn't going to be caught." My father paused, biting his lip. "That was long before the old-age pensions came in, the old people were just a drag and a burden then. Their children could choose between sending them to the workhouse or living in squalor—they didn't have much chance to save on those wages—not enough to live on for very long—not much more than the burial money that they couldn't bear to be without. Their great dread was of being buried by the parish. We used to long to see Granny Walsh dead and out of the way, but she got a baby's robust health when she slipped back into senility and it seemed as if she'd live forever. I wouldn't have minded keeping Father and Mother so much, but there was Amy lying about, getting more and more helpless, and there was Granny Walsh moaning and snuffling to herself, and the four of them together were such a load to have to take up right at the beginning of life that I couldn't bear it. I knew it was a finisher, or it would have been. . . . I would have spent a lifetime under that rotting thatch, in those miserable little rooms, I wouldn't have lived at all. . . ."

His face was set in a fixed stare, I could see that he no longer saw the French valley and the pine woods beyond the olive grove. I guessed that he saw the silent, reproachful faces of his parents, and the shadowed pallor of the face of the dying Amy.

"I suppose they were bitterly hurt when I went away, without a word. But how could I have said a word? My father would have looked at me. My mother would have cried, so would Amy. And Harry would have beaten me to a pulp —and gone himself. . . . I'd thought it out, but I left sooner than I meant to, in anger, but not with them. We'd been carting mangolds all day, in a light drizzle that turned into a steady drenching rain in the last half hour before knocking off. I was going home. I had an old hat of my father's on my head—it wasn't waterproof but the brim took a lot of the wet out clear of my collar and my ears, and it was better than nothing. I was wearing a cape made out of old corn sacks by way of a waterproof—I couldn't run to oilskins. The hat was sodden, the sacks were sodden, the wet was working through to my skin. Trimming the leaf off mangolds and throwing them up into a cart is heavy work, and I was dead beat. I heard a trap coming up the lane behind me and I didn't look round or take my hands out of my pockets. I was too tired to care who it was. As the trap came up alongside me a pony whip whistled down onto my shoulders. It stung I can tell you—I knew just where it went on my back. I looked up, and there was my boss, Mr. Alveston, grinning at me like a dog under the shelter of a trap umbrella, looking very smart in his raglan coat and brown bowler hat: 'There's a lesson for you, Town, my boy,' he said, 'maybe that'll teach you to tip your hat to your betters another time.' I knew what he wanted. I took my hands out of my pocket and touched the brim of my hat with my right hand as I was meant to. My mother, bless her heart, had taught me how to do it—she called it minding my betters—I had to do it to the Vicar, to Lord Eastbury from up the valley, to anyone who came by in a carriage, or rode by on a horse, to anyone who looked like gentry, and to the farmers, of course. 'There, that's better,' said Mr. Alveston grinning all over his face. He whipped up his pony and drove on. I stood looking after him and when he was out of sight I took off my hat and jumped on it. I was mad with anger. I ran away the next Saturday, before I'd paid Mother my week's board—she always remembered that until her dying day—I went into Salisbury with Harry and slipped away from him while he was drinking with some other boys from the village in a public house in the Shambles, not far from the Butter Cross. I ran down to the station and hid in a waiting room until the next London train came in. When it pulled out I was on it—I couldn't believe my luck—right up to the last minute I thought Harry was going to appear to haul me out and drag me back home. . . ." His expression changed, it unglazed, and the warmth returned to it. "You know the noise trains make when they're running along fast, te tum te tum, te tum te tum, it's always got words to me: 'Max Town has got away, Max Town has got away. . . .' That was what the train said all the way to London that time, that's what every train has said ever since. . . ."

He broke off, and looked down across the garden to the dirt road leading up to the house. The postman was wheeling his bicycle up the road, whistling, with his faded kepi on the back of his head. He waved when he saw us looking down at him and, leaning his machine against a tree, turned off the drive and shambled up through the garden in his dusty boots, pulling his cap off and taking a telegram from inside its greasy band as he came. As he came onto the terrace he saluted Max and myself with a mock-military flourish and handed the pale green envelope to Lolotte. She opened it and gave an extravagant cry of surprise.

"It's from my niece Ermine—she can get away to spend Christmas with us. . . ."

"Oh blast," said Max. "How am I to get any work done if you fill the place with your relatives? We'll give LeNormand a reply—tell your precious Ermine that the house is full—that we can't put her up. . . ."

"It's too late," said Lolotte, quickly, "she's on her way. The telegram says she arrives in Cannes tonight. . . ."

"Oh, very well—I suppose it can't be helped. It's all right, LeNormand, there's no answer Have a glass of wine before you go."

LeNormand drank his *petit verre* at a gulp, smacked his lips, bowed to us all and departed.

After he had gone there was a brief silence.

"Just what are you up to, Lolotte?" said Max, looking at her head with his head slightly on one side. She looked demure.

"But nothing, Max—nothing, it's just that I am fond of Ermine, and I wanted to have the poor girl with me for Christmas—it is a small pleasure for me—please don't deny it. You have your Richard—why shouldn't I have my Ermine? I am fond of my family even though I pretend not to be."

"Well, you might have let me know—at least," said Max, "still it can't be helped now—and anyway she'll be company for Dickie."

"That's what I was thinking of," said Lolotte with dovelike innocence. Half an hour later we drove down into Cannes to do our Christmas shopping, and to meet Ermine.

I liked Ermine from the minute that I saw her walking out of the station with Lolotte. She gave me a warm grin and showed a mouthful of little white teeth, and looked me in the eyes with a friendly, conspiratorial expression. She was a tall fair girl, with a snub nose, and a big mouth. My first impression was that she was ugly, but by the time I was shaking hands with her I realized that she was pretty in an unfamiliar way. She spoke English with a German accent which was a great deal stronger than Lolotte's, and which was oddly exciting. She was two or three years older than I, but the disparity in our ages seemed to make very little difference. I had always found that girls just that much older than myself were very difficult to deal with, there was something curiously guarded about them, and they moved with a physical awareness of themselves which I found embarrassing and disturbing. Ermine handled her long arms and legs with a free self-assurance that somehow gave me an easy self-confidence. As we talked in the back of the car on the way up to Les Orangers as if we had known each other for a long time, some secret amusement was bubbling up inside her, and it made everything we said seem funny. Just before we got to the turn off she said, "Richard, I want to tell you a secret, put your head close to mine."

I leaned towards her, she cupped her hands round her mouth and whispered into my ear. A heavy lock of her hair fell across her hands and lay against my cheek. It felt soft and smelt sweet and good. There was something very agreeable too about the feel of the sides of her hands against my neck and my cheekbone. The car lurched slightly and she dropped one hand onto my shoulder.

"I think I'm going to like this Christmas very much," she said, and she blew gently into my ear. The movement of the car as we turned into the road up to Les Orangers flung us apart. Something made me look up at the rear-view mirror at that instant and I saw one of Max's eyes framed in it staring into mine. Beside me Ermine was laughing wildly as if she had told me an outrageous joke, I remained transfixed by my father's glare and felt myself blushing scarlet. I was ashamed, but I had no idea why.

It was two days before Christmas. As I lay in bed that night I wondered what sort of presents I would get, and I worried a little because I had nothing for Ermine. I wished that I had thought to get something for her while we were shopping in Cannes, something really nice.

There was an odd flavor to the day after Ermine's arrival. There was a tension in the air involving my father, Lolotte, and the girl which centered strangely on myself. I couldn't make it out. On the morning of Christmas Eve Ermine suggested that we explore and we walked over to the silent and abandoned farm buildings of La Garderie. When we were halfway there my father came hurrying up behind us.

"I didn't feel like working. I thought I'd come along with you." He was badly out of breath, as if he'd run to catch us up. I was surprised that he should have interrupted his morning's work, but pleased. He talked amusingly about the neighborhood, the Roman remains near by, the Saracen pirates who used to raid the district in the Middle Ages, and about Mirabeau, who came from Grasse. I was always interested when he talked about history, and I was sad to see that Ermine listened to him with impatience and looked sulky as he trotted along beside us on his short legs.

At lunch Lolotte drew Ermine out and she talked gaily and amusingly about her family and her life in Germany. Max sat at the end of the table in an unusual silence, with his head leaning forward so that his eyebrows almost masked his eyes. He watched Ermine most of the time, but every now and then he gave a quick searching look at me or at Lolotte. I couldn't make it out.

After lunch we sat drinking our coffee in an awkward silence until Ermine said, "Aunt Lolotte, may I take the Mercedes this afternoon? I want to go down into Nice. Richard will drive with me and see that I don't go too fast."

"Of course," said Lolotte.

"It's ridiculous," said Max, "you can't dream of turning those two children loose with that racing car. They'll kill themselves. I'll drive you in the Voisin, if you really want to go."

Ermine gave a quick look at Lolotte and shrugged her shoulders.

"You're being absurd, Max," cried Lolotte. "Ermine is nearly eighteen, she has been driving for years. I would let her drive me anywhere. She's driven the Mercedes hundreds of miles—it's perfectly all right."

"That's all very well, but Naomi would never forgive me if anything happened to Dickie," said Max. "I can't take the responsibility. I'm afraid it's out of the question."

"Naomi! That woman wouldn't care if . . ."

"Now Lolotte, I won't have you abusing Naomi—you've promised—remember . . ."

A furious argument broke out. Ermine got to her feet. "I've got a headache, I think I'll go and lie down." She disappeared. A few seconds later Lolotte followed her. "I'll get the child some aspirin."

My father and I sat in silence for a time, and then he too got up and stalked indoors. The afternoon was very still and silent, I felt angry and humiliated. I had been treated as a child in public, and I knew that it would have been fun to go into Nice with Ermine. I heard Lolotte laugh inside the house, and Ermine laughed with her. I felt that they were laughing at me.

I left the terrace and walked over to La Garderie. There was a big fig tree sprawling over its grange roof that looked as if it would be easy to climb, and I made my way up into its silver-gray branches. I found that the red tiles of the roof were warm from the sun when I got up to that level and I sat on them feeling comforted. Les Orangers down the slope, half-hidden by the olives, dwarfed by the long line of the Alpes Maritimes which towered over the hills behind it, looked like a doll's house. The still air was gently scented by the breath of the pine trees that hemmed in La Garderie's few acres of terraced ground, and it was pleasant to feel the heat of the sun on one's back while looking up at the dazzling white snow on the mountains.

Max, a small bustling figure, came walking out along the cart track leading up the hill, calling to me: "Richard, oh, Richard, Richard . . ." In aggravation I lay down, flattening myself against the tiles, pretty sure that he wouldn't see me. He passed by, calling me again and again, and the silence returned.

A poem came into my head and I tried to put it into shape. "I am time's prisoner, but my sentence has a term, I will be free, my manhood shall confirm . . ." Confirm what? Term was a hard word to rhyme to—firm, affirm, there wasn't much. The beginning definitely had to be saved: "I am time's prisoner . . ."

Three sparrows brawled over some morsel a little way from me. I raised myself on my elbows and watched them while the empty minutes drained by. They suddenly lifted themselves into the air and carried their dispute off and away through the crystal silence.

I looked around to see what had alarmed them. Ermine's wide mouth smiled at me over the edge of the roof through the branches of the fig tree. She climbed onto the tiles and sat down beside me, brushing the hair out of her eyes. "I saw you from my window and I thought I'd come up and join you."

"I didn't see you coming."

"I came round the back of the hill—Max's down by Le Putier—still searching for you. I was dodging him. That's why I came the long way."

She giggled. She was wearing the shortest shorts I had

ever seen, and I noticed that her legs were covered with an almost invisible sheen of tiny gold hairs. She took a grass stem out of her mouth and tickled my ear with it.

"It's funny, Richard, but I feel as if I'd known you for a long time. It's nice when you feel somebody is sympathetic, isn't it?"

I didn't want to stare at her legs, but I couldn't help it. She stretched them out. "I've got pretty legs, haven't I?"

I felt myself blushing scarlet. "Yes," I muttered. She giggled again. "You said that just as if you were under water, yeughle. You've never kissed a girl, have you?"

I remembered Angela, the sad-eyed girl who had mothered me at the Willinghams', I had kissed her once or twice and with intense feeling, but somehow I was aware that Ermine was not talking about that kind of thing. I shook my head.

"Well, try, you've got to begin sometime."

The enormous sky arched over the roof seemed like a huge staring eye fixed upon me, I felt horribly self-conscious as I gave her a swift peck on the cheek. "That's no good, that's definitely beginner's stuff," she said. "No marks for technique, and none for effort. Now I'll show you."

It was, after a first uneasy second in which I felt I was suffocating, very enjoyable.

"There," said Ermine, "now you try." I tried. "Much better. But next time hold me as if you meant it. I won't fall apart. Women don't like to be touched uncertainly. You mustn't let them feel you are unsure of yourself. Here endeth the first lesson."

She sat with crossed legs looking at me. "Let's have a cigarette."

"I don't smoke," I said.

"You should," she said, "it looks *mondaine,* and besides, it makes all sorts of things easier. You know, you put your heads close together over a match, and so forth and so on. . . ."

She blew a thin jet of smoke out of her nose. "Half the battle at this stage in life is looking experienced, even if you aren't. You know, when you look at my legs and feel excited you shouldn't show it. You ought to look at them like a connoisseur. Drop your eyelids a little, and look at them slowly —like this." Her eyes traveled dreamily over me. "Men's bodies are nice," she said. "I adore their backs and hips. What part of my body do you like?"

"I like all of you," I muttered, feeling myself blushing again.

"No, no, that's not good enough. That's an evasion. It's like the way you touched me, an uncertainty. You've got to bluff, and behave as if you knew all about it. You should say something like 'You have an adorable bosom,' or 'You have a delicious little *derrière.*' You must say something chic and flattering. Try again."

I sat like a pudding with my eyes cast down, I didn't dare to look at her. She reached out and with a firm hand lifted my chin and for a second or two looked into my eyes.

"What the devil are you two doing up there?" Max was standing in the yard of La Garderie staring up at us, looking hot and cross. "That roof is as rotten as a pear. Do you want to break your necks? Come down at once. I've been looking for you everywhere, Richard, didn't you hear me calling you?"

"No," I said over my shoulder, halfway down the fig tree, "I didn't hear anything."

When I was on the ground I looked up at Ermine climbing down. She did have a very nice firm behind, and under her boy's shirt you could see that her long straight back ran into her hips very cleanly. I had never looked at a woman that way before. I had looked at the photographs of show girls and acrobatic dancers in the magazines, in a furtive way when I thought that I was alone, but never at a person. Seven or eight feet from the ground Ermine turned, rounding the tree. "I'm going to jump; give me a hand, Richard."

I stepped forward and she jumped down into my arms, resting her hands on my shoulders. We held the pose for a second or two longer than was, strictly speaking, necessary. She looked over my shoulder at Max with a curious expression.

"Lolotte wants you down at the house," he said. She ran off, with her golden hair flying, and we walked after her in silence along the dusty road dappled with the delicate tracery of shadow cast by the olive trees.

"You're growing fast, Dickie," said Max. "You're in a hurry to be a man. I know. I felt it at your age. But don't try to force things. I was in too much of a hurry and I hurt myself. Don't make the same mistake. You've all the time in the world ahead of you."

I had no idea what he was talking about, so I said nothing. We walked on, our footfalls scarcely making a sound in the soft powdered dust of the cart track.

"If you start . . . to live . . . too soon, the way I did, you get some funny ideas about life. You get an idea that women can give you something that you can only give yourself. Because you don't realize that, you go from woman to woman looking for it. Each one is a disappointment, and you move on. Take it slow, and wait until the right woman comes along when you're good and ready for her. Flirting and playing the fool doesn't do you any good in the long run. I've found that out."

I began to understand, I had done wrong in kissing Ermine on the roof. He patted my shoulder.

"I don't want to be a spoil sport, I'm just passing on the fruit of some bitter experience to you for your own good. There, I think I've made myself pretty clear, that's enough of that."

He brightened. "I thought I'd take you into Grasse, we can

get some scent as a Christmas present for young Ermine. Grasse is a jolly place, when you get to know it."

We whirled off in the Voisin, the men by themselves. We bought a huge bottle of Rose-Geranium for Ermine, and some little eighteenth-century toys in an antique shop. We bought blood oranges on the branch with the small ruddy fruit glowing among long pointed evergreen leaves for Christmas decorations. We visited the birthplace of Mirabeau. We visited the Musée Fragonard. As the dangerous hours flowed away Max talked about the memoirs of St.-Simon, and the Revolution. He was in the mood to suggest that Fragonard's delicate improprieties were a part of the corruption that bred the Revolution, and he drew a powerful moral lesson from the dark tempest of Mirabeau's life. I was impressed, but several times I found my thoughts wandering off to Ermine. Max seemed to be overvaluing that kiss, after all we were just friends and it had all been in fun.

Emerging from the Musée Fragonard and climbing up worn stone steps we came out onto the Mall where we had parked the Voisin. It was growing late, and a cold wind was blowing off the mountains towards the sea. They were lighting a charcoal brazier among the café tables under the trees on the far side of the Mall, and the lights in the shops were coming on. Not much of the day was left. We drove home, contented, with our parcels.

After dinner we played a ridiculous game, Racing Demon, a competitive Patience which rapidly became a competition in cheating. I had played with Max once or twice before and had always been badly beaten because I had stuck blindly to the rules. This time I saw that Max was cheating, that Lolotte was cheating, and Ermine too. When I won my first game all pretenses broke down, and we abandoned the game, helpless with laughter. Max and Lolotte read after that while Ermine and I played chess. Ermine was wearing a low-cut full-skirted evening dress of dark red that flattered the skin of her very

114

bare shoulders. I found myself looking into the front of her dress more and more often as she leant over the low chess table to make her moves, and at last she looked up from the board and caught me. I bent towards her.

"You have an adorable bosom," I whispered.

"Bravo," she cried, "you're learning fast. I shall have to watch out in a day or two."

We looked up from a fit of giggles and caught an alert sidelong glance from Max that made us finish our game in silence.

Ermine got up and stretched.

"Two wins for you and a draw for me—you'll have to give me my revenge tomorrow, Richard. I'm too sleepy to play any more tonight. I feel stuffy. Let's go for a little walk before we go to bed."

"I shouldn't if I were you," said Max, "the bottom's fallen out of the thermometer. There's quite a sharp frost. You'll catch your death of cold in that dress. And anyway, I'd like a game of chess with Dickie before I turn in. Set up the board, old man." He came over smiling genially and held me down in my seat with a surprisingly firm hand. Ermine walked round us, peering at me.

"What on earth are you doing?"

"I'm looking for the sign that says don't touch."

"Pztt," Lolotte spat at her like an angry cat.

"Good night, everybody," said Ermine, and she vanished with a flounce of her wide skirt.

I lost a game quickly to my father, then another, and went off to bed. While I undressed I heard Lolotte and Max quarreling in the living room along the hallway. Their raised voices got on my nerves, and for the first time their brawling didn't amuse me. I lay down but I couldn't sleep. I decided to read, and searched the bookshelves for some light piece of nonsense that would make me laugh without making me think too hard. There wasn't anything there that was quite what I had in mind, and I was about to go back to bed when I remembered that I'd seen a novel that looked amusing in the drawing room shelves. I thought I'd go and fetch it. Silence had fallen and I supposed that everyone had gone to bed. I opened my bedroom door quietly and slipped out.

"Hallo, Dickie, do you want something?" I looked down the passageway. My father was sitting inside the drawing room playing Patience at a card table which he had placed opposite the open door.

"I was going to fetch a book," I said. I walked into the drawing room and began hunting in the shelves for the novel I'd seen, I remembered that it was a green book with gold lettering on it. My father laid out his cards quietly and watched me with an air of satisfaction, the same air with which he had celebrated his victories at chess. He definitely seemed to feel that he was one up on me about something.

"You shouldn't be reading all night at your age. You still need a lot of sleep. While you're growing you want it the way you want good food. And you've a lot of growing and filling out to do before you become a man."

"I generally sleep pretty well," I said, "I just felt on edge tonight."

"I can imagine. . . ." he said dryly. "Good night, old chap."

"Good night, Max." I took the book and went back to my room. He waved at me, with a faint hint of irony in his gesture, as I went back through my door. I stood inside my room holding the book in my hand. Now I had it I didn't want it. I flung it into a chair and went over to the open window. The moon was setting and the hills were silhouetted in velvety black against the pale ashen sky. A dog barked a mile or two away, and the clock in the tower of Saint-Vicaire struck one.

There was a faint rustling noise along the wall to my right. A black shape was crawling along the roof of the dining arbor on the terrace below in my direction.

"Qui est là? . . ."

"Who do you think, you idiot," whispered Ermine. "This roof's as slippery as glass." She inched up to the window. "Give me a hand." She came in over the sill like a big fish. Her hands were icy cold, and she was shivering under her thin pyjamas. She dived into the bed. "Come and hug me tight before I die of cold." She flung the covers up over her head. I looked at the shape of her body under the bedclothes and suddenly realized, trembling a little, though not with cold, what the game of hide and seek we had been playing all day was about.

"Don't make a sound," I said, bending over her. "I won't be a minute."

Her face as far as her nose appeared over the edge of the pink sheet, and she watched me with enormous eyes.

"Don't be a fool. . . ."

I put a finger to my lips, opened the door quietly and looked out.

Max was still there, playing his Patience, laying card on card. He looked up and saw me.

"Good night, Max. Merry Christmas."

"Merry Christmas, old man, sleep well."

I shut the door and got into the joyous bed beside Ermine. We lay in each other's arms in a warm ecstasy of silent laughter which dissolved into a happy, golden seriousness. I discovered that Ermine's skin smelt faintly of honey. I slept very well indeed.

On Christmas day we were all very cheerful and it was a happy week which followed. By day Ermine and I kept up the pretense that we were trying to escape Max and, with mock dismay, allowed him to frustrate us. His feeling that he was saving my innocence preserved his good humor. Lolotte, though I didn't know it, was being kept fully informed of our progress by Ermine, and the success of her plan kept her in a state of bubbling amusement. On our last night together Ermine told me all about the plan. She was sitting in the bed with her legs drawn up and her arms round her knees looking down into my face as I lay nestling up alongside her.

"It's a pity I've got to go tomorrow. I could have done with another week, couldn't you?"

I took her by the ankle and squeezed it. "I'd like to be with you all the time. I wish we could go on much, much longer."

"Well, we can't, and that's all there is to it. You must promise me you won't forget my lessons, and when you have successes with those proper English girls think a nice thought about me."

"I'll always think nice thoughts about you."

"You'll have to think nice thoughts about Lolotte, too."

"What's Lolotte got to do with it?"

She looked at me and smiled, with the tip of her tongue between her bright teeth.

"You must promise not to be angry if I tell you, but you owe a great deal to Lolotte."

"Do I? What? . . ."

"Me."

She leaned over and scrabbled a cigarette out of the Gaulois packet on the bedside table.

"She's an extraordinary woman. The rest of the family rather despise her. They say she's *déclassé*, because she lives with Max who isn't *hochwohlgeborn*. My father says she's disgraced herself—as if she'd gone off with a garage mechanic. We're all meant to marry soldiers. I'll probably marry a soldier soon, now that the army is getting back on its feet. Lolotte tells me I must save myself before that happens. She keeps telling me to get out of Germany. She's trying to get me a job in England through some friends of hers. We're conspirators against the family. She says they're part of the old Germany that's going to sink like a stone—but I don't know."

She took the cigarette out of her mouth and bent down to nibble my ear.

"I was her Christmas present to you. She rang me up three

days before I came and told me about you. How you fell over your feet and hands when there was a pretty woman in the room, and about the way you blushed, and how adorable and innocent you were. And she asked me to come and teach you how to be a man before you turned wooden like all the other English."

She stroked my shoulders, and then ran a finger up and down my breastbone.

"Why do you suppose Max was so against it? Aren't people mysterious?"

For a moment I was angry and bitter, but not about that. "You did it all just for a joke, not because you liked me. . . ."

"Of course I liked you, I wouldn't have done it if you hadn't been nice. It's been lovely seeing you becoming sure of yourself, and good at making love. What's the use of a man who can't make love? Besides, it feeds my vanity. You won't ever forget me, ever. You never forget your first. And if you have a career and become an important man I shall think there he is, I gave him his beginning in life. And it will be fun for me, remembering that I had pleasure with you and you had pleasure with me, whatever happens to us."

I kissed the palm of her free hand. My brief anger with Lolotte passed by; whatever the terms might be on which I had arrived in bed with Ermine, she was a very wonderful Christmas present to get. We stopped talking, and I didn't think of her question again, until after I had said good-bye to her at Nice airport.

Her question revived itself to trouble me after she had gone and I could see, in tranquillity, how much she had done for me. She had taught me to accept my sex without shame, and in her body she had shown me a world of pleasure without guilt. A great question about myself which had darkened a quarter of my life since I had felt the first stirrings of lust in my blood had been answered sweetly and simply, and a cloud of darkness had been lifted from my mind in such a way that I could be sure that it would not return. And Max had wished to deny me all that. Why? I couldn't make it out. I might have resented his attitude very much had I lost the game of hide and seek, but I had won it, and was ready enough to be magnanimous in victory. He was so enormously relieved when Ermine had gone, and he blossomed out with such happy geniality that neither Lolotte nor I could possibly have borne to tell him how things had in fact come about.

We went for a walk together the day before I left for England, along the abandoned single-line railroad track which wound through the hills from Grasse to Nice. Its permanent way was almost overgrown with shrubs and weeds, but the peasant and farm people, finding it a convenient short cut into town, had kept the plate layers' track beside the rails open as a footpath. We sauntered along its dead level for a mile or two in silence and then sat down on the edge of an embankment that looked across tilled fields to the clustered houses of St. Paul de Vence on its hilltop. A few goats were grazing not far off and we heard the bells on their necks clanging faintly from time to time. Without thinking I pulled a packet of Gaulois out of my pocket and lit a cigarette.

"I didn't know that you smoked," said Max.

"I didn't. I just decided I'd start. Everyone else does."

"I suppose Ermine put you up to it, well, it can't be helped. I hope Naomi won't kick up a fuss. Thank goodness there isn't worse for her to make a fuss about."

I smiled inwardly, hoping that my expression was suitably bland and unrevealing. Max lit one of his own Egyptian cigarettes, taken from his thin gold case.

"I hope you aren't angry with me for the way I butted in on you and Ermine all the time she was here. I didn't want to spoil your fun, but I don't think you've had enough experience of life to know how to handle that kind of thing on your own. Ermine's like Lolotte—they belong to East Prussian families from way over on the Russian border. All that country has been marched through, fought over, and revolutioned, and counter-revolutioned, over three or four times, even in Ermine's lifetime. They've had a disturbing upbringing. They've developed a queer sort of psychology unlike anything you've ever had to deal with. They snatch at things because if they wait for them life may snatch them away. I had an idea that when young Ermine set her pretty eyes on you she took it into her head to take a snatch at you. Well, I just didn't want to see you hurt, that's all. I know you're sensitive—a little too sensitive—and I think you've got to be a lot tougher before you can take on a heartless little animal like that. She'd have made you fond of her, and then as soon as something else came along that took her fancy she'd have been off with a hop, skip, and jump, and you'd have been pretty hard hit."

He looked at me wisely, and fondly.

"Ermine wasn't a bit like that. She . . ."

"You're only convincing me how right I was. I can see how thoroughly she's pulled the wool over your eyes. I know she's pretty, and there's something very appealing about those harum scarum ways of hers, but, believe me, she's no innocent young girl. She's had affairs already, and she'll have a lot more before she's through. Don't you worry. I can tell—I haven't been in the world all this time for nothing."

He nodded at me, with that fond twinkle in his eye, age counselling raw youth with patronizing affection, and then his expression became serious.

"You know, Dickie, I feel more than usually responsible for you. I didn't mean to, but I've given you a rotten bad start in life. Naomi and I didn't hit it off, and we never got married. That's our affair, but people know about it. I've lived a fairly complicated life, and there are a lot of stories about me going around that can be given a twist by people who aren't very friendly. Well, it isn't your fault, but they all come back on you in a queer way. If you were to get in a jam now—sup-

121

pose you'd been able to get off with Ermine and she'd let things get out of hand and started a baby—well it happens in the best of families, but if it happens in the worst ones it makes much more noise. Nobody would have said you'd been got hold of by a designing little hussy. They'd have said like father, like son, and you'd have had two strikes on you before you were even out of school. You've no idea how that sort of thing gets round—the world's much smaller than you think and these things take a lot of living down."

He stubbed out his cigarette, and then cupped his chin in his hands. I sat beside him in silence, recalling the extraordinary cleanness and firmness of Ermine's body, and her absolute frankness and honesty about her body's relation to her heart. How could I tell Max how wrong he was, and how could I be so disloyal as to let her defense go by default.

"You know," he said, "I've always been held back by a feeling that it would be unfair to you and unfair to Naomi to give you my side of the story. Naomi's a queer fish and she took the whole thing very hard after we broke up. She has an idea in her mind about the way things happened that isn't very much like the truth. I don't know just when she decided she was a wronged woman, but somewhere or other along the line of her development she decided it was so and she's felt worse and worse about it over the years. To tell the truth, though it's an ugly thing to say, she chucked herself at my head. There's over twenty years between us, you know. In those days I was at the height of my success, forty-two or three, and a public figure of a kind already. The papers used to run reports on what writers were up to in those days almost the way they cover the lives of film stars now. We had a certain glamor. Naomi was nineteen, turning twenty, and I suppose she fell for it. I photographed well in those days, and the papers used my photographs a lot . . . your height doesn't show in your photograph. . . . She found out where I lived and came for my autograph. I'd given orders to my manservant to turn away autograph hunters, and I never answered their letters. Naomi came two or three times and was turned away. I suppose that hardened her determination. She used to write to me every day, and she hung about in the lobby of the apartment house I lived in, and on the other side of the street. When I came out she used to hurry up to talk to me. I was irritated by it all for a long time. I gave the doormen orders not to let her into the lobby, and I'm afraid they were rude to her. After that I'd often look out and see her standing across the street hoping to catch a sight of me. When I went for a walk she used to follow me. I was parted from my wife at that time— she lived down in Cornwall with my two boys. I felt lonely sometimes. When I was feeling lonely I'd often go to the window and look down and see all that adoration and devotion waiting for me down in the street—mine for the asking. She's a beautiful woman now, and she was a very lovely girl then— I don't know—there was a latent fire in her that was exciting. But as soon as I thought about it the stupidity of it overwhelmed me. I'd been in a sort of scandal a year or two before —with a married woman whose husband belonged to my club. There'd been a lot of talk. That was why my wife had left me. I didn't want to get into another scrape. I was involved in politics at that time too. There was a thing called the New World Society that was going to take England over and make it into a new heaven on earth. They were all political dreamers on the management committee and I was trying to shake them up and get them out of a cloud cuckooland of social and economic theorizing and to bring them down to earth. They were my enemies, they didn't want their cozy little discussion group turned upside down and vulgarized. I wanted them to get into elections as a workers' party, and do all sorts of things like making alliances with the unions and the little radical and socialist parties that were springing up—it would have meant letting in all sorts of rough lower-class elements and they were all refined educated persons. They hated me very bitterly for it, and I knew just what they'd do if they could get their teeth into another scandal about me. They did quite a lot with the old one in their nasty backhanded way, as it was. But in the end Naomi won. I came home from a noisy, nasty, argumentative New World meeting late one night. It was raining cats and dogs. I hadn't been able to get a cab, and I'd had to walk all the way up from the Caxton Hall in Westminster to my place on the north side of the park. I'd only an umbrella and I was sopping wet. I was horribly depressed because the old guard of the New Worlders had wangled a lot of trick voting for new members on the executive committee and all my nominees had been beaten badly. Naomi was in a doorway across the street, half soaked, with nothing but a newspaper over her head to protect her. I was furious with her for making such a spectacle of herself, and for making a fool of me. The doormen used to make jokes about my admirer, and the cabmen on the rank at the corner, and the little street Arab who sold newspapers—they all knew about it and they used to make sniggering, meaning remarks. Now she was standing there in the rain, with her hair plastered down in draggles over her cheeks, and her clothes heavy and shining, looking grotesque. I went up to her to tell her that if she didn't stop making a fool of herself and of me I'd go to the police."

We listened to the goat bells for perhaps a minute, and then Max went on.

"I was still furious when I got up to her. But when I started to speak I couldn't say anything unkind. I stood staring at her from beneath the rim of my umbrella. Eroticism is a queer thing—I've tried to notice what it is about one woman that makes her more exciting than another ever since I started to write—each time it's one silly little thing all by itself—the color of the shadow under her eyes—a particular gesture—the way she pulls a comb through her hair—or puts a hair pin in her teeth while she's combing it—something silly and irrelevant like that suddenly becomes the focus of sex itself."

I nodded, remembering the golden down on Ermine's legs, and Max gave me a sharp clairvoyant look.

"It was the way Naomi was so damned wet," he said. "She was holding her two hands up level with her eyes to prevent that soggy evening paper from collapsing over her ears, and the water was running off her hands, down her forearms and dripping off her elbows. She looked as if she'd been in swimming with all her clothes on. She was half scared and half delighted that I'd come up to her to speak to her, and she waited for what I was going to say, with her lips parted. There were beads of water on her upper lip . . . on her eyelashes, on her eyebrows, at the ends of those draggles of hair. There were droplets of water on her cheeks and on her neck. That did it. I didn't scold her, I said, 'You'd better come in and have a hot bath before you catch your death of cold.' She smiled, a timid smile with a hint of triumph about it, I can remember it exactly. I can remember the way she dropped the paper, and picked up the hem of her skirt so that it wouldn't drag in the mud as we crossed the street. Women wore skirts right down to their ankles then, I can remember exactly how the heavy folds of those yards and yards of sodden material looked draped over her arm as we squelched over to the apartment house. She took a tub in the old children's bathroom while I had one in mine. Then we sat in the kitchen in bathrobes and had scrambled eggs and drank hot tea. She told me how she'd been in drama school, how she'd traveled with a touring company, how she was going to be the greatest actress of them all—Duse, Rachel, Bernhardt—they were going to be nothing to her. I sat there and listened, and I loved her beauty, and her greed for life, for success, and for me. That's how it all started. . . ."

Max pulled up a small weed and shredded the leaves off its wiry stem one by one. A faint thymey smell filled our nostrils.

He sat there for a minute or two thinking with the bare skeleton of the herb in his hands, as if he were going to go on with the story, and then got to his feet abruptly.

"Well, there's no use crying over spilt milk. But if Naomi ever tells you that she was wickedly seduced by an older man who took advantage of her youth and inexperience you'll know what to think."

I got to my feet and stood beside him wondering what to say. It seemed so easy for them to say we loved each other, and we had a child, but then things didn't work out and we had to part. It seemed so pointless to go on raking over the business of loving and not loving again and again, year after year, and distilling a lifetime of bitterness and conflict out of the moments of pleasure long gone by. Well, I thought, I am a man now, thanks to my Ermine. I can go ahead with my own life, I can leave behind all this warfare in the heart in which I have no part. My life is my life, I have escaped from Mother's life, and from my father's. I put my hand on his shoulder with deep affection and with pity, it was a gesture at once of consolation and of farewell. He sighed. "You've got so much to learn about life, Dickie," he said. We walked back to Les Orangers in the soft afternoon light in silent, contemplative affection.

3

When I got back to London I was surprised to find how little it had changed. I had expected to find that it had been transformed, or at least that I would see it through new eyes. But though I looked at the women and girls on the streets with a greater interest, the tangle of gray streets, the squares, and the parks still remained the familiar landscape of my childhood. As I looked out of the windows of the taxi between the station and Castlereagh Gardens it dawned on me that despite Ermine I had still a long way to go. But all the same I looked forward to meeting my mother again on something more like equal terms.

She was not at the apartment. It was a matinee day and she was down at the theatre. When I had unpacked my bags I mooned round the quiet rooms looking at myself in my French sports clothes in the familiar mirrors, clinging to the fact that I had changed if nothing else had. I wondered what Mackie would think if she could see me, grown taller than she had been, and beginning to fill out to a reasonable weight for my height. I decided that when the time came for me to write my twice yearly letter to her in New Zealand I would send her a photograph of myself in Lolotte's French rig-out. She had surprised me by going to New Zealand to marry a farmer to whom she had gotten engaged by correspondence, and she had surprised me every year since with a photograph that came regularly every Christmas showing that she had produced another baby; the last had shown her with three children standing on their own feet, and a little swaddled bundle in her arms. Each photograph had shown her looking plumper, softer, and happier, and I had been fascinated by the change that had come over her; now it would be my turn to show her that I had changed, and that "poor wee Dickie" had gone into limbo along with the tight-mouthed woman butler MacEwan.

And then it struck me that kicking my heels and waiting about to see if my mother would come home between the matinee and the evening performance was a poor-wee-Dickieish thing to do, and that it would be more in line with my newly discovered manhood if I went down to the theatre to take her unawares. It would be a good thing to show her that I had some initiative, and that there would be no more shunting me off as I had been for Christmas. On my way up Knightsbridge, and along Piccadilly, towards the Palinode I wondered if I would tease her about her tarradiddles to me and Max, or if I would keep my knowledge of her maneuvers as a private score. In certain circumstances it was a good thing to be thought a fool or a dupe when one was not, and it would be interesting to see what she would try to get away with next if she thought she could get away with that.

She was on stage in her big scene at the end of the last act of Larry Brook's *Frost in May* when I came onto the wings. She was well forward at center stage under a pale blue spot, standing with her face turned up towards the back row of the dress circle, giving an unbearably poignant expression of the grief of a young woman who had given up all hope of her own happiness for the sake of that of the man she loved. Perhaps because she knew that the thing was a rather shabby piece of theatrical trickery she was taking special care that the trick should not fail, and was pushing her emotion right up against the dress circle exit doors, so that there should not be one empty cranny in the auditorium in which any scepticism or reservation could lurk. I watched her with a crawling sensation on the back of my neck, feeling the concentrated attention of the full house in front of her focused on her as sharply as the blue spot, feeling the immense will power with which she was creating the illusion of grief and conveying it to over a thousand people, and feeling, too, the irresistible pull of her animal vitality and beauty. The posture of her body, and the backward tilt of her head, gave her neck and shoulders an antique purity of line as they rose out of the white dazzle of her evening dress. I would have given anything in the world to have her turn towards me, see me, and smile, when the curtain dropped, but I knew that would not happen. When the curtain came down, and she had taken her last calls, she would turn towards her dressing room, diminishing in size, holding herself carelessly, with the light going out of her face as the light dies out of a powerful bulb when the current is cut off. They, the ranks of anonymous people out front, were the ones she lived for, and she kept all this for them.

Perhaps it was because I was already sick with jealousy that I took an instinctive dislike to the man who was standing close to me in the wings watching my mother. I could see at once that he did not belong in the theatre, he was one of them, the others, and he had no business to be standing there, easy and relaxed, in the shadow of a flat with his beautifully polished shoes gleaming among some coils of black insulated cable on the boards. He was staring at her with an appreciative smile which irritated me, and I found that I kept glancing at him. He looked round and caught me with my eyes on him, and after a second of interrogation, flashed his teeth at me as if he recognized me. It was the kind of smile I hated, a little too

129

open, a little too pearly, a little too boyish. Some of Larry Brook's older friends had that kind of smile and I distrusted it; it was the kind of smile that wanted to be friends too soon. I looked away at my mother, and I turned my head when I sensed him moving closer to me on tiptoe. I felt the faint smell of an expensive cologne and wanted to move away, but I was penned in between a flat and a flood on a dolly. He leaned towards me and whispered.

"You're Richard, aren't you—you couldn't be anyone else with those eyes," he said.

I looked at him angrily with an adolescent sense of outrage at such a personal remark.

"It's all right," he said, amused by my reaction, which he had immediately understood, "I'm Colonel Arthur." He gave me his hand. "I'm glad to know you at last. I've heard a lot about you."

We shook hands and were both startled because the action was saluted by a roar of applause from the front of the house, and turning we saw the curtain falling. As soon as its heavy tasseled foot was below the level of her face my mother smiled into the wings at the Colonel. She did not see me for a moment, and while it lasted I had time to remember why his name was familiar to me. I had unexpectedly had a letter from her in the middle of the previous school term which had said, among other irrelevancies to which I could attach no importance, "I've just met Colonel Arthur—he's been a sort of Lawrence of Arabia among the tribesmen in the Himalayas for the last few years. He's a wonderful man, and I think we're going to be great friends." Now, as they glowed at each other, I understood the significance of the phrase, and saw the way the wind was blowing. I had been pushed off to Les Orangers to leave the coast clear for courtship.

My suspicion became a certainty when she came off stage all softness and tenderness and kissed me with her hands on my shoulders in a way which suggested a womanly pride and devotion to her great big boy. As she did it her eyes traveled swiftly over me, from the square padded shoulders of the atrocious jacket down to the thick-soled brogues, and I could feel the effort she made not to say anything about them, clearly it was important that nothing should mar this scene of affection.

"Mother, darling," I said.

"Dickie lamb, it's lovely to have you back." She blushed faintly, "I want you to meet Colonel Arthur."

"Oh, Dick and I are old friends, Naomi," said the Colonel. "We introduced ourselves while you were still 'on.' We've been getting along famously."

"I'm so glad. . . ."

It was dark when we got back to the apartment. As the Colonel was paying off the taxi and we stood waiting to go into the house, the muffin man, with his cloth-covered tray balanced on his head, turned in from Exhibition Road at the top of the Gardens and came down towards us with his bell jangling in his hand. A pang of nostalgia overcame me as I watched him striding from one pool of lamplight to the next, and remembered how when I was very small, and it was still an excitement to buy things with real money, my mother would sometimes give me a shilling on dark winter afternoons and send me down to get muffins for tea. On an impulse I stopped the man as he came level with us and asked him for a dozen. While they were being put in a bag the Colonel came up, saying, "Ha, muffins, a capital idea," and he insisted on paying. "No, no, my boy, it's a pleasure."

Indoors while we waited for Stoneham to bring tea the Colonel began talking about India, and I had my first really good look at him. He was a very handsome man, tall and fair with the rather German appearance of the British upper class, and the characteristic tight upper lip. He was beautifully dressed with the deliberate subdued elegance of a monied Guardsman or Foreign Office career man. Everything about him spoke of money, from his well bathed, well trimmed, well manicured person down to the last detail of his dress. I found him better to look at than to listen to.

"Well the Rajah up there was a very nice fellow—he was at Harrow for a couple of years, and then at Caius Cambridge. A nice chap, one of the best, you couldn't ask for better, although he was a fat little fellow. He looked just like a teddy bear in the British Warm I got for him, if you can imagine a teddy bear in a turban with a great diamond the size of a walnut on the front of it. Well the last time I saw him I was trying to put the kibosh on a mullah who was using a corner of his little kingdom as a base for raids into our part of the world. Whenever we sent a brigade out to round him up he'd nip back over the border into my friend's kingdom and lie up until our chaps went home. Then when the coast was clear he'd sally out and make more trouble. He was getting ammo and rifles from the Russkies, across the mountains from Tazhik beyond the Hindu Kush. Oh it was a rotten show altogether. So the Rajah and I had a confab. 'Now look here,' I told the Rajah, 'we've always played fair with you, and we've a right to ask you to play fair with us. You've got to shut down on this mullah fellow. . . .'"

I stole a look at my mother, and her eye met mine with a steely glint in it.

"So when the mullah slipped over the border next time it was no surprise to us. We had a party laid on, and he walked slap into it. I was identifying the old rascal's body among the dead in the Wadi where we'd caught his fellows when the Rajah rode up on his white Arab horse looking as pleased as punch. 'You see I'm a man of my word,' he said, 'you ought to give me a chit for giving you such prompt delivery, something I can show to your people down at New Delhi next time they say I'm being a naughty boy.' I wrote him a receipt then and there for 'One mullah, damaged in transit,' and we both had a good laugh. . . ."

The Colonel slapped his thigh, and laughed with his head thrown back.

"Oh a capital fellow, the Rajah, capital, we had some good times together one way and another. . . ."

We chatted for a time and my mother asked me how it had been at Max's. She hoped I hadn't been bored. I said that I'd had a very good time.

"I've never understood the appeal of that part of the world," said the Colonel, "the climbing's no good, there's no game to speak of, and the riding's impossible. What's there for a boy like you to do with himself all day? Just you wait till you get down onto my place in Wil'shire. Partridge, pheasant, wild duck in the water meadows—a nice bit of sporting water with some very game trout in it, and miles of open downland without a strand of barbed wire. You'll love it."

I said I didn't know much about guns, and I'd never ridden a horse.

"Well, let me tell you, learning to do that sort of thing is half the fun." He rose to his feet twinkling kindly. "I'd better be running along. I'm sure you two will have a lot to talk over after spending Christmas apart."

My mother saw him out. They whispered together in the hall for a long time, and I moved my position on the sofa so that I could watch them through the partly open door in a looking glass. My mother turned up her face and he kissed her with a certain solemnity. Lord above, I thought, what a stepfather. The front door shut, and my mother came back into the room a little defiantly.

"Who on earth is that? . . ." I said.

"A wonderful man you should be proud to know," she snapped, "and if we're going to ask questions I'd like to know how you got hold of those appalling clothes. That jacket's the most frightful thing I've ever seen, and the shoes are a disgrace. Max must have been out of his mind to let you wear them, he can't have wanted to make you a laughing stock."

"I like them, they're *tellement* frog."

"I don't care what you think about them—I'm not going to have you looking like a French waiter on his day off. You're to go to Poole's tomorrow morning to be fitted for a respectable tweed jacket, and a good dark suit."

"Now steady on, Mother, you know what you give me for a clothes allowance, and you ought to know if anyone does that it only just covers the regulation school stuff. I can't go barging into Poole's . . ."

"Don't be absurd—Jack—Colonel Arthur—has an account there and he's going to tell them to look after you. And you're to go to Maxwell's to get yourself some presentable shoes. . . ."

"Shoes, too . . . from him?" I thought of him measuring up my clothes, and my shoes, from behind his pearly smile, and deciding that I was not fit to be seen with him in public, and I suppose the thought put something sourer than I intended into the remark. My mother flared up.

"Don't be an ungrateful little monster—I thought it was very sweet of him to think of it. He's an angel."

"I'm sorry, Mother, it just rubbed me up the wrong way, the idea of you two whispering about my clothes and making plans for me as if I was a baby or an idiot."

"If you don't want to be treated like a baby don't behave like one. You're too old to sulk."

"I'll try not to. . . ." I felt a swift return of confidence. She was using the old way of making me feel small and it wouldn't do any longer. I was, after all, a man who had a mistress in France, and she just didn't know the first thing about the new being she had to deal with. It was fun holding out on her, and it made me feel pleasantly superior. I thought I'd show her how far from sulking I was. "When are you and the angel getting married?"

She surveyed me with surprise.

"I didn't think you'd take it like this—I was going to lead up to it, and break it to you gently when you'd seen a little more of Jack. He really is an angel. He's kindness itself. I'm sure you'll like him when you know him."

"I'm sure I will, and I hope you're very happy together."

"You really don't mind, Dickie lamb? Because I do love him most terribly, and I just can't do anything else." She said it in her bright party voice, the one belonging to the nice girl having a wonderful time and ready to be grateful to all the world for it. The word love made me look into her eyes, and I saw that Naomi was sizing me up from within the loving ingenue. It was a moment of recognition, and when she turned away to stare into the bright coal fire in the grate she spoke to me without pretense of any kind. "My contract with Kenning and Archer runs out at the end of the month, and I'm not going to renew it. I'm not going to act any more. We're going to live down on Jack's place in Wil'shire."

A coal slid in the fire, which flared up in a wavering red flame. She stared through it, wrapt in a new dream, and the firelight danced on her remote, entranced, face. I was stunned. Castlereagh Gardens was the one fixed point in my life, and I suddenly saw it vanishing. And the stage was the one place where Naomi seemed to have an solid existence. Now even that was about to disappear. Everything was breaking up and dissolving under my feet, soon there would be nothing left but some fancy in her head. To cover my desperation I fixed on the one unimportant point in it all, the cadence of the word Wil'shire.

"You always used to say Wiltshire," I said, hardly thinking what I was saying.

"I'm sure I never did, everyone says Wil'shire," she said.

"Wil'shire," I said, "Wil'shire. I'll try to remember. I'm sure it will please Jack."

She looked at me with undisguised anger, and I suddenly

135

realized both what the implication of the remark was, and that for the first time I had been cruel to an adult in the way that adults are cruel to each other.

"Oh, you're impossible," she said, and left the room.

I felt partly triumphant at having won one of our scenes for a change, and partly ashamed of myself. And because I was more ashamed than triumphant I became angry to cover it. How could she want to marry such a dull man, a man with a sort of Midas touch of boredom who could kill anything he touched? How could she, after having loved Max? I recalled the exact way he had butted in to spoil the pleasure of buying the muffins. My eye fell on the tea tray, there they were under a rounded porcelain cover with a little green and gold handle resembling an acorn on the top. None of us had touched them. I lifted the cover and found that they were still passably warm. I ate one, and then another. They were greasy and leathery, as usual, but somehow delicious. It is difficult to go on being elaborately unhappy or very angry when you are sitting by an open fire eating well buttered muffins in a curtained room, and I soon managed to come to terms with the new situation.

If the Colonel wanted to buy me muffins, and expensive shoes, and expensive suits, let him. And if he wanted to take off to Wil'shire to hunt and shoot and fish expensively, let him. He could put down as much money as he wanted, and all he would do was to find out that some people, at any rate, weren't for sale. This formula, which put taking what was going on a high moral plane, comforted me, and presently I was licking butter off my fingers and thinking about Ermine, and the kind of jokes she would make about someone like the Colonel. I tried to imagine the Grafin married to such a man, but it was impossible even to think of it. And then I thought of the quizzical expression with which Max looked at nice dull people who were boring him, with his head tilted forward, and his thick eyebrows slightly arched, as if he was thinking of some way to startle them out of their dullness. He would know some way to get fun out of the Colonel, he knew how to get fun out of anything. I began to miss him very much, and to feel unhappy and angry all over again. I ate another muffin, but the spell didn't work a second time. In a few days I was back at school in the world of iron bedsteads, carpetless floors, echoing stone-flagged passages, dull food, and compulsory games. I was for once glad to be there, and I went out for track and the school boxing team with a concentrated energy which surprised my house master. He gave me a little talk after a few weeks congratulating me on my new spirit and my obvious desire to "give something to the school." "You'll get on much better in life if you make an effort to fit in, Savage, you'll find it's well worth it in the long run." I couldn't tell him that I was beating people in the track trials for the simple sake of beating them, or that I was boxing simply because I had found that I liked knocking the tar out of my opponents. "Well, keep up the good work, Savage, if you go on as you're shaping I'll be considering making you a Prefect next term. I hadn't thought of it as a possibility before." That would mean having the privilege of beating junior boys who had gone upstairs in the wrong shoes, or talked in preparation, on the bottom with a cane. It was called responsibility. I thanked him very much, and the interview was over.

The marriage took place in the middle of the school term, soon after *Frost in May* closed, and I didn't go to it. I saw some photographs of my mother arriving at the church in a cloud of white lace, and leaving it on the Colonel's arm, smiling through a shower of rice and confetti, but even though they sent me a slice of wedding cake in a neat little cardboard box, I didn't really believe it had happened. I was only convinced that it had when I found myself at Marshwood when the holidays came round.

The taxi from Salisbury turned off the public road just outside Chilmark down a long avenue of beech trees like a green tunnel. At the end of a half mile a white signboard said

MOTORS, TEN MILES AN HOUR, PLEASE! and the tarmac gave way to weedless gravel. We crunched round a sharp curve between banks of Portugal laurel and came in sight of the house. It looked enormous, and the front door was a good ten feet high under the Greek revival portico. When I had paid off the taximan with a pound note I stood on the steps in front of the huge door and looked round, at the chapel in the same Greek style as the house standing not far off in the middle of a group of Lebanon cedars, at a stable behind a shrubbery, crowned with a white belfry, and at the hint of a walled garden and greenhouses behind a bank of beeches. I turned from all this magnificence and rang an old-fashioned bell which pulled in a well oiled socket. It jangled faintly a long way off, and I stood listening to the faint cawing of faraway rooks for a long time before anyone came. When I knew the place better I realized what had been happening while I waited. Manson the butler, who had been sitting in his pantry in a cane chair with his coat off reading the newspaper, folded up *The Times*, put on his coat, left his pantry, walked down the service corridor, passed through the downstairs hall, climbed a short flight of stairs leading to the green baize door cutting off the servants' quarters from the house, crossed a lobby, and opened the door opening into the main hall. Then he reached the front door and let me in. It was a slow business, but then there was no reason for anyone to be in a hurry at Marshwood.

The hall was as large as the lobby of the Palinode Theatre and it was filled with a luxurious hush. All I could hear was the faint conversation of two or three clocks. The butler moved about quietly bringing in my cases and disposing of my coat with a great air of discretion. I listened to the regular ticking and took in the colors of oval space, pale green, pale gray, lavender, silver and white. It was all in exquisite late eighteenth-century taste. The voices of the clocks seemed to tell me that even time was in good taste here, that it did not hurry by as it did outside, and that minutes and seconds were a little longer in Marshwood than they were elsewhere. Manson came back without my coat, he was a small, round-headed man, who did not quite meet your eye when he smiled.

"You'll find your coat in the little cloakroom under the staircase to the left when you want it again, sir," he said. "I trust you had a pleasant journey."

"Oh yes, thank you, very comfortable."

"The Great Western is not what it was, sir, and one hears complaints." I looked at him quickly to see if he was trying to make a fool of me, but he was not. "I'll show you to your room, sir."

We walked up the wide stone stairs, so beautifully balanced between riser and tread that one hardly knew that one was climbing.

"Your mother wished me to say, sir, that she and the Colonel were lunching over at Wilton, and that they would return in time for tea."

"Oh, I see," I said.

We passed across a landing and down a corridor lined with the heads of horned beasts and snarling cats mounted on shields with little gold labels saying where they had been shot, hot-sounding Indian, Malaysian and African names. I was shown into a room rather larger than our old drawing room at Castlereagh Gardens flooded with warm afternoon sunshine which poured in through two tall windows. Everything in it looked very solid and very comfortable. Two huge leather armchairs flanked the fireplace, a kneehole desk under one of the windows had a practical Victorian swivel chair in front of it, and the dark red walls were covered with thirty or forty mezzotints of wigged and curled seventeenth- and eighteenth-century personages.

"I see you're looking at the pictures, sir," said Manson. "They're the Colonel's Admirals. When he was a young man, sir, he made a collection of all the Admirals of the Blue." He smiled as if he were having a private joke with somebody an inch to the left of my breast pocket. "It was the red paper on the wall that gave him the idea."

"I see."

"On account of the Admirals we call it the Blue Room now, sir. It's one of the Colonel's little jokes."

I thought of the simple joke occurring to the Colonel, being kept in mind for three or four years while the mezzotints were accumulated, at last made, and then kept up, year after year. The Colonel was certainly a force in his own way, I had to admit. Manson was unpacking for me, moving about rapidly, and silently, hanging the suits and jackets in a closet, putting the shirts and linen in drawers that ran without a sound or an effort. He put a pair of trousers aside to be pressed, and arranged my personal objects in a neat row on top of the bureau.

"There, sir, I think that should be everything." He looked all round the room, and then once more smiled at the neighborhood of my breast pocket. "You should be very comfortable here, sir. It was the Colonel's room when he was a boy, and it was kept for him when he went into the army. He was very attached to it, and he went on using it for several years after he came into the place. He was very concerned to have everything just so when we opened it up for you last week. He came up here several times himself and looked round while we were setting it to rights. 'Manson,' he said to me, 'Manson, I want Master Richard to feel thoroughly at home here. Do you think the boy will have everything he wants?' I pointed out to him that the hearth rug was a little worn, and he said, 'I know what, Manson, we'll give him one of my bears.' It's a Kodiak bear, sir. The Colonel shot it himself in his younger days. He's very proud of the bear, sir, and I know he wouldn't have had it brought out if he didn't think a lot of you. He's a very warm-hearted man, the Colonel."

I looked at the huge pelt. I felt that it was a rather overpowering token of esteem and regard.

"That was very nice of him," I said.

"Well, sir," said Manson, "I'll leave you to settle yourself. I expect you'll be able to find your way about downstairs."

When I had spent some time at the windows taking in the vastness of the smooth green lawn which spread out in front of the house, and the quiet of the gentle park which stretched away for half a mile or so to the south, I went down to explore. There was a great deal to look at in room after room filled with precious things, but everything seemed stiff and uneasy as if the chairs and sideboards and the elaborately framed looking glasses were all conscious of their quality and afraid of being scratched or fingermarked or sat on by an interloper like myself. The family portraits in which I saw the Arthur face again and again, now on a woman, now on a man, now old and now young, with never a trace of lightness or humor in the eyes or at the mouth, daunted me. I could laugh at the modern portraits, by Millais and Sargent, and Boldini, but the eighteenth- and seventeenth-century Arthurs and the Elizabethan Arthurs were another matter. They had the air of knowing who they were, and where they belonged. Their clothes changed as they receded in history, and the pictures of Marshwood in the backgrounds showed that it had been torn down and rebuilt two or three times, but they were all of them Arthurs. All I knew about the Savages was that there was a Naomi Savage, and all I knew about Max Town was the one glimpse into his father's cottage that he had given me. I had never met another Savage or another Town, I didn't know where they lived or where they had lived, or who they were or what they had been, and until I encountered this silent regiment of the Arthurs of Marshwood I had never even thought about my ignorance. I tried to find a room with no portraits in it and found a library with a gallery, lined from floor to ceiling with books. But all that I could see were brown leatherbound eighteenth-century books or older, with long F's for S's, and the air smelt dead as if no one had sat there for a long time, so I moved on. In the end I settled in the pink and white drawing room and sat there reading the magazines that were spread out on a low lacquered table, *The Sphere, Country Life,* the *Illustrated London News* and the *Countryman.* When I looked round me everything was pink and white, the enormous, swollen armchairs and sofas in their pink and white loose covers made me think of barmaids in summer dresses. Half a dozen white and gold occasional tables were scattered among them covered with pink and white porcelain knickknacks, and flower stands loaded with pink-and-white-blossomed pot plants stood in the window bays. When I stopped reading I heard the gold clock above the fireplace ticking quietly, saying another second, and another, gone, another minute gone, and another second. Through the open French window leading out into a formal rose garden I could hear the rooks talking as they settled into the trees behind the church. Caw, they said, caw, caw, caw. I went and stood in the window listening to the monotonous sound, and watching the clear afternoon light ripening insensibly into the gold of evening. It was a Wednesday: the matinee crowds would soon be coming out in London, and the hum of the city would be deepening into a roar as the rush hour began. The pavements would be crowded with people hurrying home, and in an hour or so that throng would give way to another making its way to restaurants and theatres, concert halls and cinemas. How could Naomi give up all that, for this? The room behind me suddenly became filled with a friendly roar.

"Hallo there, Richard my boy! Here he is, Emily . . . my dear fellow." He pumped my hand and patted my shoulder. "It's good to welcome you home, Richard." He was immensely genial, the room was filled with the warmth of his smile, and his loud hearty voice. "I wish we'd been here to meet you, old chap, but the Davincourts asked us to lunch, and Emily accepted without remembering what an important day it was. When we remembered it was too late to put him off. I could have kicked myself when I realized what had happened, but there, these things happen—and as I said to Emily, 'Richard's not a baby any more, he'll have as much fun explorin' the house by himself as he would if we were showin' him round, I know he won't mind. . . .' "

He stood there smiling at me in his big tweed overcoat, but I could see that he really was concerned. He'd come straight from the car without stopping to take his coat off, so that he wouldn't lose a minute before delivering his explanation of what had happened. When I had made it clear that I didn't mind a bit he patted my shoulder again, and this time it was with a real friendliness that surprised me. When my mother came into the room he looked down at himself in mock astonishment.

"Good Lord, here I am in the drawin' room in my topcoat —I'll just hang it up and wash my hands before tea." I knew from the way he said it that he'd be gone some time, and now I wondered if he'd kept his coat on in the first place in order to contrive a way of leaving us alone together.

We faced each other. I decided not to ask why the Colonel had taken to calling her by the name she had dropped when she first went on the stage. I saw at a glance that she had assumed a new personality for which Emily was the best possible name. She was wearing a tweed coat and skirt, a pale pearl-gray blouse, and flat-heeled brogues. There was a trace of lipstick on her mouth, but hardly any make-up on her face. She waited for me to speak with a curious expression that I found hard to interpret, it was that of a child expecting uncomprehending criticism of an imaginative drawing—"but, dear, horses don't have wings. . . ." We evaded everything there was between us with a silent kiss, and then went and sat side by side on the sofa.

"You're looking very well, dear, did you have a good term?"

"Oh, pretty good."

"I hope the wedding cake we sent you was a success?"

"Yes, it was a great success."

"You might have written to say thank you. It was Jack's idea, and I think he was hurt that you didn't write."

"I'm sorry, but you were off on your honeymoon, and I didn't know where you were."

"You could have written here."

"I suppose so. I should have thought. I'm sorry."

"I wish you'd think. Things like that are so easy to do, and they're so noticeable if you don't do them."

It was like so many of our dull conversations, my mistakes being niggled over; the tension between us being boringly converted into boredom.

"You needn't look so upset—I'm not really angry—it's just that I do love it when you do the graceful nice thing without being prompted. . . . I don't like nagging at you. I just can't bear it when you aren't absolutely perfect. . . . Manson will bring tea in a minute. I expect you're hungry after your journey."

She was nervous and ill at ease, and she kept looking at me, and then round the room, at the banks of flowers, the pinkness and the whiteness, as if she was trying to see it through my eyes.

"This is a lovely room, isn't it . . . and oh, Dickie lamb, even if you do hate it all pretend not to for my sake. Say you like it, Jack loves it more than anything in the world, and he does so want you to like it. . . ."

"It's the most wonderful place I've ever been in," I said.

"That's true enough," she said, and the old Naomi looked at me piercingly out of the new plain country face for an instant, until the Colonel came beaming into the room.

"No tea yet, dear? If Richard's got half my appetite he could eat a horse. I hope Manson's got some cinnamon toast for us. . . . I'll tell you a funny thing about Marshwood, my boy, there's something in the air that makes you eat. Now when I'm abroad, or in town, I eat like a bird—I just don't seem to want big meals. But here, why, I'm always eating. At Marshwood I eat a good breakfast, I'm ready for lunch, and no matter what I've had for tea I'm ready for dinner. I don't know how to explain it, but there it is. . . ." Manson came in and set up the tea things in front of my mother. "Ah, there you are, Manson, there you are, capital, capital. I hope you've got some of our cinnamon toast under that cover. I'm very eager to see what young Richard here thinks of our cinnamon toast. . . ." He twinkled at me. "We're proud of our cinnamon toast at Marshwood, it's one of our things. I remember when I was at school, and, to tell the truth, even after I'd joined the army, one of the things that I used to look forward to was having tea and cinnamon toast back at Marshwood. It's a silly thing for a grown man to admit, I know, but I still look forward to it whenever I'm away. . . ."

I couldn't quite believe in him as I listened to the steady flow of his cheerfulness pouring out relentlessly. Larry Brook and Naomi might have invented him jointly in the old days, less than a year before, and have kept him going as a running joke while they were at Bournemouth or Manchester for a week giving a play a tryout before its London opening. It was incredible that she should have put the rest of her life into the hands of a joke come true.

Tea came to an end, and at half past six we all went upstairs, took baths, dressed for dinner, came downstairs again at half past seven, sipped sherry and ate little cheese biscuits for half an hour, and then went in to dinner at eight. The three of us sat at one end of a table that would have seated ten, and ate and ate, while the Colonel talked and talked. He described the way that farming had changed in the neighborhood since he was a boy while we ate leek soup, sole Mornay, roast guinea fowl with Brussels sprouts, baby carrots and roast potatoes, followed by an apple tart with Devonshire cream. Occasionally my mother would break into the Colonel's stream.

145

"Are these our carrots, Manson?"

"Yes, madam, McGregor sent them up this morning."

"They're delicious."

"Thank you, madam."

Manson was pouring wine from a decanter into my glass.

"That's a Corton twenty-one, my boy, one of the great years. I don't suppose you'd remember it. It was the dryest summer I ever struck. They had the corn cut and stacked hereabouts before the first Sunday in August—I don't suppose I'll see that again in my lifetime. I don't think we had a drop of rain after May the first until we were into October. They say it was all that sunshine and dry weather that made it such a good year for wines. . . . Ah, well, Richard, if there's ever another summer like that we'll have to keep our wits about us and lay down a pipe or two of good Burgundy in the autumn, right away before the merchants collar it all and wait for the price to go up. My father, bless his heart, put down forty dozen of this Corton in the spring of twenty-two. That sounds like a tremendous lot of wine—but we could have done with double the quantity. Why, come to think of it, Manson, how much of the Corton twenty-one do we have left? I don't suppose we could raise a dozen if we wanted to, could we?"

"No sir, I'm afraid not, sir." Manson smiled discreetly at my left armpit from his place beside the sideboard. "There are only seven bottles left, sir."

The Corton joined the Kodiak bear as a component of the overpowering demonstration of good will. I felt squeamish, remembering that the dinner jacket I was wearing, and the suit I had changed out of, both came from Poole's and had been on the Colonel's account. I looked at him hard to see if he was by any chance trying to make me squirm, but once again I was surprised by the transparency of his good intentions; he was really welcoming me. I felt ashamed of my suspicion, and lifted my glass to drink in confusion. I was all

146

wrong to despise him for being such a bore, he was a really good and kind man.

The evening stretched out, and by half past ten we had all yawned covertly two or three times.

"Well, who's for Bedfordshire," said the Colonel, slapping his knees and getting to his feet. It seemed ridiculous to be going to bed so early, but what else was there to do? I thought of reading when I found myself alone in my room, and searched the bookshelf beside my bed. But the Colonel's tastes were not mine. I glanced at the covers of *Jorrock's Jaunts and Jollities, The Tactical Use of the Heavy Machine Gun,* and *The Heavy Mortar Company, Help or Hindrance to the Infantry Battalion,* and I glanced away. I did not feel like reading after all. I found myself yawning and yawning, and within a few minutes I was in bed and asleep.

The next morning we went rook shooting.

"Talbert down at the home farm says the rookeries are overcrowded," said the Colonel. "There are about two thousand too many of the black villains on the place. We've got to thin them out. Now they're nesting it's the time to do it. They can't stay away from their eggs or their fledglings for long, so we can get plenty of chances at them as they go in and go out. It's not exciting shooting, but you'll get a good chance to get the feel of a twelve bore, and you'll learn how to take high wing shots. There's nothing like vermin for learning on."

We went off to the rookery followed by two keepers soon after breakfast. Low gray clouds were breaking up, and islands of vivid blue sky were beginning to appear in the rifts. The air had the wonderful freshness of a spring morning after a night of rain, and the green of the new leaves on the trees was as bright as blossom.

"Rain before seven, fine by eleven," said the Colonel, snuffing the soft breeze with his head thrown back. "We're going to have a good day."

As we came in sight of the clumps of beeches where the rooks nested, the thousands of black birds rose clamoring in protest at the sight of the glint on our gun barrels. They circled cawing for twenty minutes out of range while we took our positions under their trees. We waited, tweedy and relaxed, while the eggs cooled and the nestlings piped shrilly for food in the big shapeless nests. Then they began flighting in desperately.

"Take them as they drop onto the nests," said the Colonel, "when they spread their wings wide to slow themselves up— you've got the best target then."

I remembered what I had been told: Don't think about aiming, swing on the bird, and when you feel it at the end of the gun, fire. Don't think, follow your instinct.

"Lead them by about a foot, sir," said the keeper behind me.

The birds began to drop, loose bundles of feathers that bounced as they hit the ground, and made an *ankh* as the last gustful of wind was knocked out of them. The lamenting survivors circled out of range, but time and time again came back to their young and their cooling eggs. I hit twenty-seven birds in thirty-five shots, ending with a left and right that brought two rooks plummeting down out of the sky. I saw them fold and drop, and then watched them flexing their blue-gray talons and slowly moving their wings, as if they were trying to push the crushing weight of death aside.

"Good shooting, Master Savage," said the keeper who was loading for me. I looked across the carpet of red-gold leaves from the last autumn, littered with scarlet and brass shells, and dotted with dead rooks, to see if the Colonel had observed my triumph. He gave me the thumbs-up sign without taking the finger out of the trigger guard of his gun, swung up onto a bird making a pass at its nest, and brought it down through the twigs and boughs to fall, stone dead, between us.

"He kills very clean, does the Colonel," said the keeper,

148

handing me a loaded gun and taking my empty one. "Not that you aren't doing all right."

I missed my next four shots in my eagerness to show that I too could kill clean.

We ate a picnic lunch in the shelter of a group of round wheatstacks on the edge of the wood: blue vinney cheese, sweet whole wheat bread, a half pint of Whitbread's, and an apple, pale gold and sweet. While we ate the keepers replied to the Colonel's questions about where the partridges were nesting that year, and in what strength, in soft burred Wiltshire voices that gave me a strangely comfortable feeling, as if they were speaking a language that I had always been familiar with.

We shot on through the afternoon, and by the time the light began to go we had killed nearly three hundred rooks. When we got back to the house I was ready for an enormous tea, a bath, an enormous dinner, and bed. I was in the Marshwood swing.

When we were not shooting we were riding, and the Colonel and I spent many hours hacking along the grass tracks that crisscrossed the bare, empty expanses of downland. These untraveled, solitary ways ran for mile after mile across the grain of the valley life, and road network, and it was easy to get the impression that England was still an unpeopled farm country with more sheep than men in it. We would ride for miles, hour after hour, without meeting more than three or four people, and only seeing cars when we came down from the crests into the broader valleys to cross over from one ridge to another. The Colonel loved these forgotten sheep walks and cattle droves, and the wide emptiness they passed through, with its old prehistoric hill forts melting into the grassland, its fading traces of Roman roads and camps, and its dry valleys, like great amphitheatres, with the hawks circling above them. We used to ride off in the early morning and get back late in the evening, often too late for tea, take baths, eat dinner half asleep, and go straight to bed. I scarcely read a book all the holidays, and I forgot that I was missing a dozen new plays and films.

I was enjoying myself, but there was more to it than that. Every time we rode off to the south of Marshwood, and crossed the Nadder Valley to get under the vast open sky which stretched over the whalebacked ridges running west and southwest of Salisbury towards Shaftesbury and Bland-ford, I had a strange feeling that I was in my own country. Once or twice we passed along an old sheep walk that ran along the crest of the downs above Plummer's Dene, and as I looked down at its two or three farms, and its cluster of cottages nestling round the square-towered church, I felt a movement of the heart. I wanted to go down there, as if I expected to find someone I knew waiting there for me.

We came on it on our way home one day towards the end of the holidays. The horses were walking, tired by the long climb up the side of the down, and the sense of familiarity was so strong that I reined in my animal and stopped. The Colonel stopped beside me, and we looked down at the gray church and the thatched houses together. The horses dropped their heads and pulled at the close, violet-strewn turf. A great flock of fifty or sixty golden plover swept over us. Their black wings and gleaming white bellies flashed in the sunlight, and as they swept over us we heard the magical whisper of their wingbeats. Delight released my emotion.

"It's queer, I've never been here before, I'm sure of that, but ever since I've been in this part of the world I've had the oddest feeling—as if I'd come back—as if it was home."

"I'm glad you feel that, Richard. I've been wanting to say this to you for some time. It is your home. I want you to think of it that way, always." The Colonel turned in his saddle and smiled into my eyes. "I want you to think of me . . . well, as if Emily and I had met each other when we should have if this had been the best of all possible worlds—a long way back—as if we'd all three been together from the first. I want you to feel about Marshwood just as I did, when I was a boy. It was where my father and mother lived. It was home. It was where I belonged."

I was taken aback. It was Plummer Dene spread out a couple of hundred feet below us, and the soft spread of the Nadder Valley that had stirred me. Nothing had been further from my thoughts than my dubious relationship with the Colonel. If as he put it "we'd all three been together from the first" he would have been my father. Every bone in my body, every muscle, every corpuscle in my blood, recoiled from the idea. Max was my father. I looked in the Colonel's eyes and saw nothing but kindness there, and the instinctive revulsion died. I remembered how little of a home Castlereagh Gardens really had been, and I remembered sitting looking across the harbor at the old town of Cannes, thinking that all places were alike to me, the dwelling places of strangers. He knew that and he wanted to change it. It was not a moment for words, and we leant out of our saddles and clasped hands in silence.

It was a long way back to Marshwood, and it was quite dark when we arrived. Bars of light from the lighted windows stretched out across the lawns, and the cedars hanging over the chapel seemed to be made of black velvet. A new moon, sharp as a knife blade, hung low in the sea-green sky over Chilmark. A roosting pheasant, alarmed by a passing fox or by the trampling of our horses, called out from the shadowy bottom of the nearest covert, and the gun dogs in the stable yard began to bark. The Colonel put his arm over my shoulders as we went indoors, and I felt that perhaps I had found a home after all.

The last few days of the holidays went by very quickly, and I was sorry when they were gone. While they lasted we were all very close together. The Colonel felt easier in his mind about our situation, and his flow of talk became funnier and less boring. My mother saw that we were getting on well, and the tension and strain of our first encounter in the pink and white room vanished. When I got into the car to go to Salisbury on the first leg of the journey back to school they stood together arm in arm at the top of the steps smiling at me as if they really were my parents, and Manson stood behind them smiling at the back of the chauffeur's neck just as if he were seeing off the son of the house.

But it was never to be as easy as that again. The English summer term lasts for thirteen weeks, a long time in which a lot can happen. In it my mother found her feet at Marshwood, and got the feel of her new role. When I came back I found that she had got to know the neighbors. By that I don't mean the pleasant clergyman who was the Vicar of Chilmark, or Doctor Stebbings, or any of the other friendly people who lived close at hand, though she spoke to them quite affably. In our new language the neighbors were people who lived five, fifteen, or twenty miles away, in houses as large or as expensive to keep up as Marshwood. The numberless flock who, counting their pennies, lived in smaller houses, among less precious things, did not qualify as neighbors. They did not count.

I soon found out about this. During the summer I had struck up a new friendship with a boy at school called Gresham. We met at the school poetry society meetings and discovered we liked the same new poets, and were trying to do similar things in the poetry we were writing. We had endless talks and arguments in which we threshed out the ways in which our work would have to be done if it was to bring about the complete reform of life, literature, and the arts. Gresham lived at Teffont a mile or two downstream from Chilmark and Marshwood, and we planned to see a great deal of each other during the holidays. I told my mother and the Colonel all about Gresham at dinner the first night I was back at Marshwood.

"Gresham?" said my mother, "I didn't know that anybody called Gresham lived in Teffont. Who can they be, Jack?"

"I don't know, my dear, I've never heard of them. I daresay they haven't been there very long."

"Gresham says they've been there for several years," I said.

"Well, there's a funny thing," said the Colonel. "And I thought I knew everybody in Teffont."

Gresham's father was a retired naval officer living quietly on his pension and not much else. His wife, the daughter of the headmaster of a small grammar school in the midlands, had bought the cottage in Teffont a year or two before he retired with a little windfall that had come her way when a bachelor uncle died. They both loved the village, with its row of gray stone cottages in neat gardens, and the clear fast-running brook that chattered through a conduit alongside the main street. Their only concern was that it was a rather lonely place for their clever son, who had to go a long way to find anyone who shared his interests in painting, poetry, and music. They were glad to hear that he had discovered a friend as close to home as Chilmark, and a day or two after the holidays began Mrs. Gresham telephoned to ask me over. I was out when she called so my mother took the call. I don't know in what spirit she accepted the invitation, but when Mrs. Gresham asked her, as one mother to another, to come along, she said she would adore that.

"What an amusing little house," said my mother smiling graciously as we stepped through the front door, straight into the tiny living room of the Greshams' cottage. She was wearing a white woollen dress, and some very plain, very heavy gold bracelets on her right wrist. She sat looking very expensive and cool while Mrs. Gresham made tea.

"It must be such fun doing everything for yourself, without any bother about servants," my mother said. She went on to tell quite a funny story about one of the Irish maids who had fallen passionately in love with Manson and had had to be sent back to her family in Ireland. Commander Gresham came in, naval and blocky, and my mother shook hands with him. I noticed that she had a new way of doing it, she held her arm up, and the Commander took a bunch of inert fingers which lay dead in his hand.

"I'm sorry I'm late, Mrs. Arthur," he said, "our wretched bees took it into their heads to swarm this afternoon, and I've been settling them into a new abode. I had to climb an apple tree to collar the swarm. . . ."

My mother was interested. McGregor, the head gardener at Marshwood, was so good with bees. He had a new Italian strain that was said to be very wonderful. She was sure that if Mr. Gresham was having any trouble with his bees McGregor would be delighted to help.

There was cherry cake for tea, yellow sand cake with big pieces of scarlet crystallized cherry in it.

"What a delicious cake!" said my mother. "I'm always trying to get Mrs. Lockett to make me a real old-fashioned cherry cake like this. I'd love to copy your receipt, if it isn't a secret."

"We get it from the International Stores," said the Commander, looking puzzled, "they cut it off a whacking great slab. I thought everyone knew the jokes about the cherries in slab cake being made out of red mangolds. . . ."

"Oh, dear." My mother put her hand to her mouth. "I do hope Mrs. Lockett never hears that I tried to get the receipt of a shop cake for her . . . but it's so good I'd never have guessed."

After tea we went out and looked at the garden. The delphiniums were good strong plants, but they were all old-fashioned colors. My mother talked about the new pinks, clear blues, and strong purples. McGregor must send them down some roots when the borders were broken up in the autumn.

As we walked round the tiny enclosure, neat as a pin, we could see the back of Teffont House rising above the roofs of a few intervening cottages, and the walls of its gardens. Did the Greshams know the Bennets, asked my mother, they were such nice people. She must bring the Bennets and Greshams together, she was sure they would get on. Betty Bennet was an Archbold before she married, she was a great dear.

The Commander's face, which had become expressionless during tea, performed the remarkable feat of becoming more expressionless, it was a secret he had learned in the service, I suppose. He took his short bulldog pipe out of his mouth, and observed that he had known an Archbold once. My mother was interested: was it the Admiral, or his wild younger brother who had *H.M.S. Vincent* now, and was doing so well? The Commander smiled, his bright blue eyes as innocent as a child's in his mahogany face.

"No, I shouldn't think it was one of them. This was an awfully nice fellow. Tubby Archbold, Chief Petty Officer on the *Artemis*—left the service a year or two ago—keeps a pub now, the Admiral Benbow over at Clenchford—pretty little place—they give you a very good tea there, and Tubby always makes you feel welcome."

My mother reddened slightly.

"I'm sure Mrs. Bennet is very nice, she always looks so pretty," said Mrs. Gresham, desperately trying to make peace.

"Yes, we've seen her walking by the garden gate quite often in the past seven years," said the Commander unmaking it again firmly.

"What impossible people," said my mother on the way home. "You do choose the oddest friends—though I suppose it's very hard to tell about a boy's background when you're at school with him. He didn't seem to come up to your description this afternoon—he just sat there staring at me like a booby all through tea, and yet I suppose he must be quite brilliant to have a scholarship."

"I suppose you say that because you want to say that people like that couldn't possibly afford the school fees—" I was hot with anger. "I think he's there on the same footing as anyone else. I suppose his people pinch and scrape for things the way we did a year or two ago. I think they're very nice, even if they aren't rolling."

"I wish you'd check your taste for what's low and ordinary," said my mother sharply. "I don't want to choose your friends for you. But little people like that are so narrow and dull. I can't see why you want to waste your time on them, that's all."

We rode home in silence. I knew that the only thing wrong with the Greshams was that they were as poor as we had been before Colonel Arthur had come along. A sort of nausea came over me as I thought of the Colonel saying, "Well, that's a funny thing, and I thought I knew everybody in Teffont." I caught a faint first glimpse of the price of the Colonel's gifts.

Gresham was asked up to tea at Marshwood a day or two later. We had it on the lawn in front of the house, in the shadow of a huge tulip tree. The gardeners had set out Bermuda chairs and an iron table with a glass top. While we played a game of croquet Manson and two maids brought out the tea. It was a hot day and dead still, but it seemed cool in the shade listening to the birds fighting for the ripening berries in a big mulberry close by.

The Colonel and my mother tried to draw Gresham out. He did not ride, and did not shoot, he was not very good at tennis. He did not think as much of Kipling as the Colonel did. I knew how lively and quick his mind was when he was talking about what interested him and I sat watching miserably while the stream of questions turned him into an awkward clod. He dropped a cucumber sandwich into his lap and everybody pretended not to notice while he dealt with it.

Reaching out for a third cup of tea he tripped over his own feet and dropped the cup into the tray.

"Really it doesn't matter," said my mother, looking agonized as she rescued the browned traycloth and a plate of soggy macaroons from the swimming tray. "I'm sure it won't stain."

"I'll just pop in and tell Manson we've had a little disaster . . . don't you worry." The Colonel patted Gresham forgivingly on the shoulder and reduced him to a jelly of misery as he went indoors to get help. Gresham sat silently by while Manson and a maid replaced the devastated tray with a fresh one and the Colonel said how much good, simple, poetry "with the breath of England in it" had meant to him when he was in India. I was sorry I had said anything about Gresham's interests in that line, it seemed like a kind of betrayal.

A breeze sprang up, and there was a sudden surf-like whisper from the trees.

"Ah, that's a sound I love," cried the Colonel, "that's the sort of thing a poet ought to write about—instead of carrying on about love and suffering—that's the sort of thing you really feel. . . ."

"They have written about it," said Gresham, looking as if he was startled to hear his own voice. "Tennyson did—don't you remember—'summer woods, about them blowing, made a murmur in the land. . . .' It was in a place like this too. . . ." He shut his eyes and gathered in the full quotation.

" 'They by parks and lodges going
See the lordly castles stand,
Summer woods about them blowing
Made a murmur in the land.
From deep thought himself he rouses,
Says to her that loves him well,
Let us see these handsome houses
Where the wealthy nobles dwell. . . .'

"Don't you remember?" he went on, fatally, "it's the only decent line in that gloriously snobbish poem about the Lord of Burleigh. You must know it, about the cottage girl who dies of her husband's immense grandeur." Lost in his pleasure with the gross idiocy of the poem, he threw back his head and quoted again. "You must remember . . .

> " 'And while now she wonders blindly,
>   Nor the meaning can divine,
>   Proudly turns he round and kindly,
>   "All of this is mine and thine"
>   Here he lives in State and Bounty,
>   Lord of Burleigh, fair and free,
>   Not a Lord in all the county
>   Is so great a Lord as He. . . .'

"Dear old Tennyson," said Gresham and laughed, and I laughed with him. But no one else did, and I found it hard enough. My friend felt the sudden coldness, and then, blushing, fell silent.

"Well, dear, we'd better be thinking about dressing, I suppose," said the Colonel. "The Denshams dine at eight, and we've nearly twenty miles to go. I hope you'll excuse us, Mr. Gresham." We all got up. "We've got to be off before seven, so give yourself time to get changed, Richard, we won't want to hang about."

We were left on the lawn, and presently I was watching Gresham pedaling away down the drive on his battered old bicycle. His tweed jacket was too short in the sleeves, and the volume of poetry in his pocket gave it a shocking hang. I knew he wouldn't come back, and I knew I wouldn't ask him to. We met once or twice afterwards on neutral ground, but there was a wall between us. I was ashamed when I met him because I wasn't fully loyal to our friendship, and he was ashamed of himself for being overwhelmed by Marshwood, and, deep inside himself, of the lack of money in his home. I couldn't make up my mind which side I was on, that of money or friendship, and while I hesitated we drifted apart and I found that I had taken the side of money without knowing it. I had dropped my friend, because he was, by Marshwood standards, "impossible."

Step by step I was being taken over by Marshwood. Although it was high summer the Colonel was already looking ahead. He planted several mentions of the Christmas rituals of the place in his talk, and though he described the annual ball, the party for the tenants' children, and the trip to Salisbury for the choir school carols in the past tense, he managed to suggest that I would be enjoying these things next Christmas, and that I would not be with Max in France. Each time the hint was so slight that it was not possible to make an issue of it, but each one settled into place like a feather adding its unnoticeable presence to a sum that amounted to something considerable. Sooner or later the day was going to come when the Colonel would say, "But it's been understood, my dear boy, from the very beginning. You're spending the holiday with us. . . ."

My mother didn't concern herself with hints and intimations. But our common experience was going into the discard implacably. I could refer to things we had done together or seen together without producing anything more than a vague, "Did we? Do you know, I've quite forgotten. . . ." or, "Did we, Dickie lamb? I'm sure I'd remember a thing like that— perhaps you dreamed it. . . ." As for the stage and anything to do with it, a curtain had fallen on all that. I spoke of Larry Brook once or twice, and she pretended that she had put up with him because she'd been forced to by professional necessity. "You can't do anything in the theatre unless you keep in with that dreadful homosexual crowd. I suppose he was an amusing little beast in his way, but he made my flesh creep, and I hated to see him being friendly to you . . . you're still too young to understand what Larry Brook really is—I can't tell you how glad I am that we've escaped from all that." I only realized the strength of the determination behind this apparent forgetfulness when I took it into my head to try to recover the books which I had treasured at Castlereagh Gardens, and which had vanished in the move.

"I really don't remember where all those things went—I believe Manson had them stored in the attic, I'll ask, if you like. . . ." My mother turned the subject, days passed.

"Oh, I meant to tell you. Manson says everything from Castlereagh Gardens is in cases in the store room—they aren't numbered or labeled and it'll be frightfully difficult to find your books—do you really want them terribly? It will mean getting a man to open the cases. . . . It's rather a bore, just now."

She was in the flower room arranging a great bunch of late summer flowers and early autumn ones in a large glass jar. She kept her eyes on their dusky browns, reds and purples, and not on me. Sunlight flooded into the little white room and her face glowed with the newer, calmer, beauty of her country personality. Half my mind said, let her alone, don't bother her; what after all does that old stuff matter . . . and the other half was remembering the old stuff. Since he had begun to recognize my existence my father had sent me each of his books as it came out, inscribed from father to son, and realizing at some time or another that I had missed his early novels, he had sent me the first collected edition of his works as a glorious birthday present. Those inscriptions were precious to me, and I wanted to see them again. So were the volumes of poetry which seemed to have in them the secrets of why life really was worth living. I looked at my mother's long-fingered hands, touching the flower stems as she perfected her arrangements, and wondered how to say that I did very much want the old things. My eye followed the flower stems down into the water and their greenness, starred with tiny silver bubbles, brought the Korean bowls that I had given her into my mind. They were boxed up in the storeroom in the dark. I felt a passionate desire to see their green by sunlight again, to liberate that small token of the past if nothing else. My mother broke in on my thought.

"You don't really mind, do you . . . if there's any book you really feel you must have you can get it at Eastman's in Salisbury next time you go in—we have an account—I'll tell them you can charge things," she said.

I didn't go to Eastman's. Some instinct took me to Manson's pantry a day or two later. I watched him rubbing the silver to a velvety whiteness with his thumbs and pale pink rouge for a minute or two, and then asked him if he knew where the cases from Castlereagh Gardens were stored.

"Cases, Master Richard," he said. "I don't think anything's left unpacked. Not that I know of. Everything's either in the china cupboards in the old still room, or in the north attic. Was there anything special you had in mind? I could very easily get you anything you had a fancy to have out."

I thought for a moment about the books, but if I could have them whenever I really wanted them they were all right where they were.

"There were two bowls, a pale sea-green, they looked Chinese—I'd like to have them in my room if it isn't a bother to get them out."

"No trouble at all, Master Richard." Manson wiped his hands on his striped apron. "We could go and get them now if you like."

It was strange to find all the familiar little gewgaws from Castlereagh Gardens on the still room shelves, neatly arranged behind glass-fronted doors among the secondary treasures of Marshwood. There were pretty Sunderland jugs that hadn't yet become fashionable, a Kuan Yin striped in soft colors who would have been valuable if her lily hadn't, at some time or other, been broken, and next to a pair of Dresden china candlesticks smothered in forget-me-nots that I'd quite forgotten, the green bowls.

"They're very unusual," said Manson.

"They're over six hundred years old," I said.

Manson looked at them with greater respect: "Come to think of it I've seen a green like that. The Colonel has a piece or two, Celadon ware I think he told me it was. But they've got a smoother finish. It's another class of article if you don't mind my saying so."

"I'm very fond of these particular bowls, of this particular green, I don't know why."

"It's funny what you can take a fancy to," said Manson shutting the glass doors.

"Oh, one other thing," I said cradling one of the bowls, "just where are the old books? I'd like to be able to get at them without bothering you, another time."

"Ah, the books now," said Manson, "that's another story. The Colonel was for having some shelves made in the old schoolroom to take them, but Madam didn't think it was worth the expense, and the bother. They were all sold. Mr. Buttress who keeps the bookshop by the gateway to the Cathedral Close came and fetched them away."

"Oh, I see. . . ."

I heard the stable clock chime the first quarter of an hour, and I noticed that Manson was looking me in the eye for the first time.

"That wasn't very far back, sir," he said in a whisper, "you might find that Mr. Buttress still had some of the books left. . . ."

"Thank you, Manson." I did my best. "They weren't of any importance."

But I bicycled into Salisbury that afternoon.

Mr. Buttress's low-ceilinged shop was very dark after the glare of the sunshine outside and it took me some time to find the shelf where fifteen or sixteen of Max Town's books clustered together. I looked through them, searching for inscribed flyleaves, but there weren't any. Mr. Buttress, thin, lean, and

162

with slightly trembling hands came out of the rare book room, where he sat watching all his customers by means of a complicated arrangement of looking glasses, thinking that I was hunting for first editions.

"Was there anything special, young man, I could help you to find?"

I looked into his enormous pale blue eyes behind their thick pince-nez.

"I believe you bought some books up at Marshwood, a little while ago. I'm looking for some inscribed copies that were sold by mistake."

"I don't think there was any mistake and I don't think you'll find any inscriptions."

"But they were my books, or some of them were, and I know they were inscribed, Mr. Buttress."

He took the book I was holding and looked quickly into it. He blinked once or twice, and then took off his glasses.

"Come into my office, and I'll show you something. The light's better in there."

He sat me down at a table and put the book under a flexible-stemmed desk lamp.

"Have a good look. These editions all have a fly leaf, and then a page blank one side, with the dedication on the other, facing the title page. The fly leaf has been cut out on this one, with a razor blade I would say. There's the rib of paper that's all that's left of it, and you can see the score on the end paper where the razor blade cut into it. It's disgusting what people will do to a book. I could have given a fair price for a Max Town first with his name in it; they're not much sought after, but they still have a price. But these are just junk now. . . ." He put his glasses back onto his nose and peered at me curiously. "I generally have a cup of tea about this time, if you'd care for one. They send me a tray over from the Cathedral tea rooms. . . . Don't take it to heart, boy."

I fled from his sympathy out into the sunshine, and bicycled back to Marshwood. I felt as if I'd had a bad beating, and all I could think, over and over again, was that I had to hurry or I wouldn't have time to change for dinner, and we were expecting guests. When I got back I found that there was plenty of time, and the quiet stillness of the house gathered healingly round me. I went upstairs to my room and found that Manson had put the two bowls on my bureau. I sat in my leather chair looking at them, and collected myself. After all, what did words written on a piece of paper matter. I knew that they had been there, and what they said, and there was no way the knowledge could be taken away from me. I had been emotional and stupid about the whole thing. In a way I had gone to Mr. Buttress's shop to hurt myself. It was no way to live. In a few years I would be through school and the University and I would be free, and until then I would just have to take things as they were, and be a bit tougher. Ermine's brave carelessness came into my mind, that was the way to take whatever life slung at one. I thought that I hadn't written to her for more than a week, it was high time that I let her know how much I loved her again. After I'd taken a bath and begun to dress I stood in front of my looking glass practicing a new smile; the slightly ironic smile of a cynic, tough as nails, for whom life was amusing, however serious it might seem to those who didn't fully understand it.

My mother came into the room before we went down to tell me who the dinner guests were going to be: Walter Dayrell of Hamborn and his wife, and Sir George and Elizabeth Carrow of Long Easton. She hadn't got very far before the bowls caught her eye.

"How odd of you to get those Chinese things out, they look all wrong in here—with this red wallpaper. You ought to have better taste, you must see how they fight the room. I'll see Manson gives you something more suitable if you need ash trays."

"I like them, and besides—" it seemed an occasion for the new smile, "they remind me of Castlereagh Gardens."

She gave me a quick look. "I hope you didn't get them out to annoy me—you've been so oddly sullen lately—you aren't still sulking about those deadly Gresham people, are you?"

"Of course not, it's just that I think they're beautiful, that's all." I should have stopped there, but an unlucky impulse made me go on. "Why did you tell me that all the old things were in cases . . . you must have known that Manson had unpacked them all and stored them in the house?"

"I? I never said such a thing!" She looked at me round-eyed in astonishment that would have convinced the gallery in the Palinode. "I don't know what you're talking about."

"But you must remember. You were arranging flowers—I asked about my books, and you said that if I wanted any particular book I was to go to Eastman's and charge it to your account. Surely you haven't forgotten that. . . ."

Her eyes narrowed. "My pet, you must have dreamed this whole thing. You must have meant to ask me—and then forgotten. I've really no idea what they did with the things from Castlereagh Gardens. Manson would know. I hadn't thought of letting you use our charge account at Eastman's—your allowance is really more than enough for that sort of thing—but of course you can if you want to."

"I should think I'd have more chance of finding what I wanted at Buttress's place, don't you?" As soon as the new cynic had delivered himself of these words he deserted me, and left an angry child to go on blurting out its fury. "I've seen the books Max gave me, in Buttress's. That's why you told me all that about the things being so hard to get, wasn't it?" The fat was in the fire.

For a few seconds we faced each other with candid hatred, and then her eyes filled with tears.

"You don't understand. . . ." She turned away from me

with a helpless, appealing gesture. She lent on the chimney-piece with her head bowed for a minute, gathering herself. Her hand was to her mouth, and she nibbled at a knuckle. I realized how stupid I had been, and waited knowing just what was happening. A new role was taking shape in her mind, so many seconds were being given to working it out, so many seconds to making me feel cruel and guilty. I thought of the razor shearing through the pages of the books, her long strong fingers crumpling them as they came free, and throwing the wads aside into a trash basket. She could do her worst, it wouldn't affect me this time.

"You don't understand anything about Max and me. How could you? You were only a baby when it all happened—and you weren't even born when it all began. You've no idea what it was like for me. You've no idea what went on. No one who wasn't with us night and day could possibly understand." She walked over to the window, and stood facing me with her back to the light.

I held on, and admired the tactical device as she became a dark silhouette. She clasped her hands.

"You think you know Max because he's played with you and amused you since you grew old enough to be company for him. You've forgotten all the years when you needed him and he didn't care if you were alive or dead. When you were small he wouldn't have bothered to cross the street to see you. You don't remember all that. . . . And now you've come to believe that some wickedness of mine has deprived you of a father—that I've tried to come between you in some way."

She came slowly down the room and put her hand on my shoulder gently and sweetly.

"Poor lamb; you're so big now, and so much of a man that it's always a surprise to me to find out how much you still have to learn about life. I can't tell you how unlike anything you've ever known the world was when you were born, how unimaginably different everything was. . . ."

She took her hand from my shoulder and began to walk up and down beside the great bearskin with her eyes fixed on far off things.

"Writers were so much more important in those days than they are now. They were public idols the way that film stars and band leaders are now. The papers told you all about them all the time. You knew where they went and what they did. They were glamorous and exciting. I was a very silly little girl, I'd come to London with all sorts of foolish dreams about being a great actress, and I was full of wild ideas I'd picked up through taking Ibsen too seriously. Your generation can't imagine what an issue personal freedom was to women and girls in those days—it was thrilling to go for a walk alone in the city, and to get your own latchkey. I was a suffragette, and I belonged to the New World Society that was going to reform everybody and everything. Lots of us used to go there, wearing special progressive pure wool clothes from Jaeger's, to worship the leaders—Shaw and Wells, Graham Wallas, Stephen Merlin and his wife, and your father. We used to go to tea shops afterwards and go over every word that had been said; it was all tremendously exciting and important to us. I went up to Max after one of his speeches to the New Worlders and congratulated him for saying exactly what I thought about something or other. He was nice, and he smiled that wonderful smile that would draw a bird out of a bush, and asked me questions about what I was doing and what I wanted to do. And then he looked round and said, 'Look here, we can't talk properly here. I tell you what, why don't you come and have lunch with me one day to tell me all about this business of coming to London to take the whole world on single-handed. I've got a girl in a book I'm writing who does that and I don't believe I've got her right. I wish you'd help me with her. I want her to come alive. . . .' Of course I said I would. And then it was, 'Let's have lunch again, this has been fun.' You can't imagine what it was like for me—a girl of seventeen—to have one of the big men of the day hanging on my words by the hour, canceling engagements to make time for meetings, taking me to all the places that were symbols of success. It was all such a glorious short cut to the top of the tree, and there was no one to tell me what a fool I was being. . . ." She was silent for a few seconds.

"If you ever make a thorough fool of yourself you'll find out how I felt. I don't really blame Max for what happened. I can't think of any man who wouldn't have done the same thing. I was infatuated . . . I didn't care what happened. I didn't know what I was letting myself in for. Before I knew what I'd done people were talking about me . . . oh, everywhere . . . you'll have to forgive me for not wanting to be reminded of it too often, that's all. I can remember it, the hateful gossip, and the sneering, without any reminders. I've been living it down ever since . . . I suppose I am a little bitter, but I had a horrid time."

She stopped and faced me, a desolate little girl.

"I don't want to be beastly about your dreams of what your father is. I know he's a wonderful man to you, and I want him to be. I want you to love him as much as I loved him. But I don't want you to be hurt by him the way I was. You've never had to rely on him when you were in trouble. You've never had to deal with his twistings, turnings, and evasions when it comes to squaring up to something he doesn't want to face. I don't want you to have to find out what that's like. Admire his public reputation if you like, and get what fun you can out of him. But never trust him. And don't ask me to share your pride, or your amusement. You'll understand what I've been through some day, as Jack understands."

I stood looking at her in confused silence, with my father's version of this story echoing in my head. This, too, had the unmistakable ring of truth. There was nothing to say. She came close to me, and gently kissed me on the cheek.

"My poor love, I've told you a horrid story. Sit here and

collect yourself for a little while before you come down. I don't think anyone has arrived yet. I've got to run, there are one or two things I've got to tell Manson. . . . I'm sorry if I've upset you. It's the last thing I wanted to do, but the time had come to tell you the truth. There . . . come down when you're ready."

She smiled bravely, and was gone. She took her magic with her, and as soon as I was alone I didn't believe a word of her story. From her first move over to the window every step she had taken, every gesture, had been calculated. She had been doing her best to disgust me. I wanted to pack my things and leave the house at once. If I was gone she would have a free hand to rewrite her life altogether. If I wasn't perpetually there to be explained no explanations would be necessary, she might even find it possible to tell the truth all the time : she could make an absolutely fresh start with the Colonel. But as soon as the idea came into my head I could see that it was impossible. If I vanished now my disappearance would have to be explained, there was no short cut out of the maze in which we were involved. I would just have to sit out the next year or two. When I left school and went to the University I would be able to travel and go abroad in the long vacations at least, and when I graduated I would be free of it all. There was a good time coming.

But I was reckoning without the Colonel, his overwhelming goodness, and his obtuseness. On the morning of my birthday, a week or so after the dinner party, the Colonel and I went for a walk after breakfast. We climbed up the rounded side of Chilmark Down, and strolled through the yew wood which sheltered in a dell high up under its shoulder. When we came out onto the crest we could see the whole of Marshwood's park and the smiling valley which spread away from it to the south, a patchwork of well kept farms beautifully supervised by the estate office. The Colonel lifted his stick and showed me where the boundaries ran.

"It's better than looking at it on a map," he said.

Small clouds were sailing slowly in from the Atlantic on the southwest wind, and their shadows ran across the landscape. Fifteen miles or so to the north, perhaps further, we could see the blue line of the Marlborough Downs, and closer at hand to the southeast the thin pencil of Salisbury spire stood up out of the greenness of the Avon Valley.

"Your ancestors picked one of the loveliest places in England when they settled at Marshwood," I said.

"What I like to think of," said the Colonel, "is the way that Marshwood goes on—there are hundreds of years behind it. We've loved it and cared for it for generations. And it makes me happy to know it'll be loved and cared for after I'm gone."

I didn't say anything. Both the Colonel's brothers had been killed in World War I. His only uncle had died, childless, in Florence in the early twenties. There were no male Arthurs left. Some curious fatality had brought the family to the point of extinction.

"Responsibility is a funny thing," said the Colonel. "Sometimes it takes you unawares, and you get knocked off balance by it. If it comes as a shock it's liable to come as a burden. Marshwood isn't just a place to live in comfortably, it's a going concern. It's the livelihood of a good many people, and the farms are the lives of eleven decent families. I've done my best to look after it, and I've given looking after it a lot of thought. You'd be surprised to know how much there is to learn about land, and timber, and buildings, before you know how to handle an estate. When I came into the place I was ready to take it on—I was used to the idea. I want you to be used to the idea. You see, I want you to carry on here after I'm gone. I don't want you to think you're just spending a little time here while you grow up because your mother happens to be my wife. What I said the other day wasn't a manner of speaking. When I said I wanted you to think of the place as home I meant it. I didn't mean it was a place you'd always be welcome when you were hard up, or anything like that. It's all been arranged with the lawyers now, you're my son and heir, and when I die you'll have Marshwood. I hope you'll think about that when you make decisions in the next few years. It means a lot to me, and I hope it will mean as much to you."

"But, sir . . ." only one thought came into my head, "have you told Mother about this? . . ."

"Not yet, I wanted it to be a surprise for your birthday. I wanted to make it a big day for you both. I know it'll make her happy. She worries about you a lot."

I looked at the Colonel, recognized a man, and pitied him as I had never pitied anyone in my life before. I had often tried to put myself in his place. If I had married a woman for all the reasons that make one particular woman attractive beyond all the others I would have found it very easy to dislike her son, if he had been jealous, attached to a brilliant father, and to a literary world with which I had no sympathy, and above all to the world of the theatre from which I had detached his mother. In his place I would have been eager to hurry the son along so that he could get out into the world of his choice and away. But the Colonel was larger than that. As time had run on I had come to despise some things about him more and more: his dead insensitivity to poetry, painting, and the arts, to the things that counted more than anything else to me. And at times I almost hated him for his lack of quickness, and wit. But all these shortcomings were trivial irritations when they were set off against his ability to love. He worshipped my mother and his whole life was given up to making her happy. I had done my best to mock this devotion. In my letters to Ermine I always called the Colonel Gelert, after the hound faithful unto death in the Welsh story, comparing his devotion to a dog's. But the integrity of his love bore me down, and I was forced to realize that I was being worse than petty about it. It did not matter that my mother was playing a part for him, and making a fool of him by pretending to be something she was not for twenty-four hours in the day. By some instinct he had seen through her pretenses and seen that her dream world needed a guardian. It was nothing to him that he might look like a fool as long as she was happy.

And now I saw that he had been completely, and terribly fooled, not by her, but by the simplicity and purity of his own mind. He was including me in the warmth and generosity of his devotion so that she could discard her last anxiety and feel without regret that she had made no mistake in her life, and that she had nothing in her past to abandon. "It's been a great happiness to me to see how you've taken to Marshwood," he said, "you don't know what a comfort it is to know that I've got someone to hand it on to after all." That was the heart of it, my mother's error was not to be an error at all. It was to become providential as a contribution to the flowing stream of comfortable family life at Marshwood, and to provide the one missing element in the Colonel's life. Through the woman he loved he would be able to go on loving Marshwood after his death. The chain of continuity would be preserved, there would be cinnamon toast at teatime in winter, the clock in the stable turret would be kept going, hunters would stamp in the stables below, the gun room would smell of clean oil, and all would be well. My mother would have fulfilled his dearest wish.

As I fumbled for the right words with which to thank him for his splendid gesture, finding that all the usual forms were inadequate, he rose to the occasion in his own way.

"You don't have to thank me, Richard. There's nothing to say. We're only recognizing the facts of the situation. All you can do for me is to be ready when my time comes, and see there's someone ready when your time comes."

"I'll do my level best. I only hope I'm good enough." My eyes were misty with tears. I wanted to warn him against what might happen but I didn't know how. As we walked down towards the house I couldn't think of anything but what my mother might do to him, and to me, when she found out that she hadn't got Marshwood for herself, but for me. As he walked beside me he sang a song from *The Bohemian Girl*, and twirled his stick; he was full of happiness at the way things were turning out.

4

I expected Naomi's reaction to be violent and immediate, but she seemed to be delighted and said so. "It'll give you a fixed point in your life, Dickie lamb," she said, "and, God knows, I've always wanted that for you." The fears that had overcome me when the Colonel had told me about his will melted away, I found a new pleasure in walking in the park and across the Marshwood farms. It was solid ground under my feet, or so at any rate I supposed.

A couple of days before I went back to school I went for a walk alone with her. She was, tremendously, Emily, in a coat and skirt of Galway tweed, woollen stockings, and brogues. On her head she had one of those shapeless tweed hats that the county of either sex wear when they are beagling or fly-fishing or pottering in the open air, and she carried a cane as one always does when going for a walk from a properly organized country house. We reached the crest of the downs and stood for a few minutes looking out over Chilmark and the wide expanse of Jack's estate, cloud shadows moved quietly across the undulating landscape; it had the cozy domesticated look of the English countryside and it was immensely reassuring.

"I'm so glad you and Jack have hit it off," she said. "I was afraid you were goin' to be adolescent and difficult."

I noticed that she had begun to drop her final on certain words as Betty Bennet did.

"It would be very hard to dislike Jack," I said. "He's all goodness and decency."

"Will you think about him when you're deciding what to do with yourself in the next few years—you're getting to an age when you'll have to decide on a career, you know." She gestured along the crest with her stick. "Let's go along that way, on a day like this we ought to be able to see across Stonehenge to the Marlborough downs." We stepped out briskly. "He won't try to influence you one way or the other, I know, but I know what he'd like."

"Don't you think he'd like me to write eight or nine really good plays?"

"Well, perhaps. But you know I think he doesn't really understand that kind of thing." She linked her arm with mine. "Perhaps artists are the one thing he doesn't understand at all. He thinks that kind of thing is living for oneself, it seems to him rather self-indulgent." She frowned. "It's hard to explain. But you see he has this idea about Marshwood. It's something wonderful life allows him and he has to make repayment for it somehow. I don't think he'd see plays as the right kind of repayment. Being a success in the theatre would be like getting something for yourself, another kind of Marshwood, it wouldn't be giving anything back. Do you see?"

"I'm not sure that I do."

"Well, he didn't have to go into the army. He didn't have to any more than Charley Bennet had to go into the Colonial service—but there has to be an army, just as the Colonies have to be governed, so he went into it as a duty. I don't suppose the army will appeal to you very much, though I think your prejudices about it are probably unreasonable, but I think you might be very happy in the Foreign Office or the Civil Service. I wish you'd think about it really seriously."

I saw myself going to a Government office every day, correctly dressed, and I didn't like the idea at all. The huge landscape spread round us, and the wind smelt fresh and clean. I wanted to be free to enjoy that kind of thing, and to write.

"There are so many places I want to see, Morocco, and Persia."

"You'd go to places like that if you were in the Diplomatic Service. You might see them better that way than if you were idling about on your own."

I looked over my shoulder at Marshwood among its dark cedars and beech trees. This I supposed was the price to be paid for it, I had been very unreasonable to suppose I would get something for nothing.

"Did Jack ask you to say this to me?"

"Don't be stupid. Of course he didn't. I know how he feels, that's all, and I don't want you to disappoint him. I'm not suggesting that you should do anything out of the way. It's just the kind of thing people in our position in life have to do to justify it. That's all."

At that moment I saw in my mind's eye a vision that existed more vividly than the open fields through which we were walking. A curtain went up on a lighted stage, and on it something altogether new began, something that had never been done in the theatre before and which would add to it. Faceless actors mouthed words I could not quite hear, they were my words, but they were already taking on a life of their own, a life given them by the actors, and by the minds of the audience. I glanced at Naomi, saw the profile of Emily outlined for a brief instant against the sky, turning away from me towards the vague blue shadows on the horizon that might have been the Marlborough Downs, and then remembered her as Cleopatra filling the dark theatre with magic. The man who had written those words for that night had been dead for four hundred years, and the Queen whom he had made as alive for me as Naomi herself had been dead for two thousand years.

"I want to write plays," I said. "I'll have to learn the theatre backwards, the way Ibsen did. I thought I'd ask Larry to help me to get a stage manager's job—I suppose I'd have to start off as assistant stage manager—in a repertory theatre somewhere. I've been wondering if it's worth going to a University —I've an idea I'd waste too much time that way. I don't see how I'd be able to do anything about the Civil Service or the Foreign Office. It just doesn't fit in."

"Oh, my God . . ." Emily had vanished, Naomi swept the tweed hat off her head with a gesture of exasperation. "What have I done to deserve such a child? How can you be such a fool as to want to go back to all that? Have you forgotten what it was like . . . Don't all the sacrifices I've made to get you out of it mean anything to you? Jack has all sorts of important friends, he'll do all he can to help you to make a good start in any service you choose. Can't you see what a fool you'd be to throw away all this for the sake of spending your time with spotty pansies in camel's hair coats and stupid stage-struck girls . . . there isn't one person in a hundred in the theatre worth ten minutes' worry. You won't find one friend like Jack there, not if you spend a lifetime in searching. The theatre's a bad place for women, and it's an awful one for men. It's gone all wrong, it's a place for second-raters, for people like Larry—you seem to admire him, but I can't think why. I suppose you were too young to see what he was, and I didn't want to rub your nose in ugliness by telling you. I was terribly afraid he'd get hold of you—I should have spoken out more plainly, I suppose, and warned you that he was a homosexual, a quite dreadful kind of pervert. He probably would have been quite a nice boy if he'd had the chance. But he never did. Some dreadful chorus boy got hold of him when he was working as an assistant stage manager and that was the end of him as a man. I know he's successful, and I can see that a child might envy his life, getting up late, eating after midnight every night, and being best girl friend to all the prettiest women on the stage, but how you can give up the position in the world that Jack would like you to have for that sort of thing I can't begin to understand. . . ." A look of wild suspicion crossed her face. "This isn't one of Max's ideas, is it? He hasn't put you up to choosing this dreadful career, has he?"

"No. You know how Max feels about the theatre, or you ought to. He thinks all actors are exhibitionists who only play for the sake of the applause. . . ."

"So that's the picture of me he's tried to plant in your mind, is it?"

"No. It's just an idea he has about actors in general. . . ."

"He never began to understand what endless hard work there is in acting, or what a drain it is on one's whole being. He . . ." She bit her lip. "Oh, Dickie lamb, how can you do this to me and Jack? How can you? Promise me that at least you'll go to the University."

"That isn't fair, you know it isn't."

"I'm not going to be fair when it comes to standing by and letting you ruin yourself."

A silence fell between us, and a huge flock of starlings, floating through the air like an enormous muslin veil, passed overhead.

"That sounded more quarrelsome than I meant it to," she said. "It's only that I found the sort of success you can have in the theatre, and at the very top, didn't amount to much. With Jack, and all this, behind you can do so very much better. If you went into the army or the Diplomatic Service for a time, and if you married well, you'd find it so easy to make yourself a real career—in Parliament—anything—somewhere where you'd be really respected, where you'd make a real name for yourself."

For a moment I saw myself in evening dress under chandeliers, with the scarlet ribbon of an order across my shirt front, and with other decorations gleaming on my lapel, speaking to an Ambassador, perhaps to the head of a foreign state, but not for myself. "His Majesty's Government wish it to be clearly understood . . ." Sir Richard, or perhaps even Viscount Savage of Marshwood by then.

"I don't want you to waste yourself on dinginess and Bohemianism. . . ."

"It's very nice of you to have such grand dreams for me. . . ."

I took her arm and squeezed it, feeling almost tender about the discrepancy between her dreams and my own.

When I was back at school Max suddenly ended the eight months' silence that he had preserved since I had last seen him with a spate of letters telling me of new departures in his plans for living. The first arrived a day or two before my birthday in October, with a check for fifteen pounds.

"You might buy a typewriter with it—if poets like using such things—but I daresay it will meet some other more pressing need such as Egyptian cigarettes or surrealist magazines. Anyway here it is, and have a good birthday.

"I've been thinking about you a lot lately. I've got plans. It's ridiculous that you should have two half-brothers you've never met—we're a scattered family, and it's time we all got together. Fred and John are two very good fellows, and as they are your brothers you ought to get to know them. They've got lively minds, and I'm proud of them, though I don't tell them so—I think you might find them good value. Fred's wife Amabel has two nice little beasts of children who are fun to play with, and John's Maeve is a great beauty and a great dear. We'll all get together in London over the holidays, and I'm sure we'll have a very good time. John has picked out a very jolly little house for me in St. John's Wood with a big drawing room looking out over a garden, which sounds good for parties, and I'm letting Maeve have her head with decorating it—she has quite a talent for that kind of thing. I know I can trust them to make an amusing place to live, and I'm quite looking forward to having an English home again.

"Lolotte sends you her love. She's threatening to leave for Arabia or the High Atlas rather than face a winter in England, but I think I can persuade her to come. . . ."

There were two or three more letters introducing me to the family with an easy run of gossip, and by the time the holidays came round I had quite a clear picture in my head of the brothers and their wives that I had never seen. I imagined the house as white and light, and full of gay colors, and peopled it with younger editions of Max, quick, amusing and full of ideas that rapidly expanded into jokes and flashed off into new ideas. Amabel and Maeve would be like Naomi and Lolotte, warm and passionate creatures, above, or at least unlike, the common run of womankind.

Presently the letters told me that I was to spend Christmas with Max in London, and threw me into a state of feverish excitement. Perhaps Lolotte would come too, and bring Ermine with her. I couldn't really believe, in spite of all the time that had gone by, that I had lost her. I wrote to her, begging her to try to come.

"You don't need, now, to marry some wretched soldier. I'm heir to seven thousand glorious acres of Wiltshire farmland, with the nicest house you've ever seen in a park in the middle of it all. If you can wait a year or two we can get married. And, oh, Ermine, I do wish you would because there never was and never will be anyone quite like you. . . ."

She answered at last.

"Dear silly, suppose I want a tiny little four-roomed house on a sunbaked rock beside the Mediterranean, and hate parks? Don't you find it terribly boring trying so hard to stay in love with someone you haven't seen for a whole year? If you've been being faithful to me, like an old hunting dog, and forgetting all my lessons I'll be very cross with you. I hope you'll have all sorts of amusing stories about English girls to tell me when I meet you again, whenever that is. Have fun and don't be too serious. Yours, Ermine."

She enclosed a photograph of herself with a number of half-naked and gleamingly handsome young German boys and girls crowded onto the deck of a sailboat on an Austrian lake. I discovered by peering at it carefully that she had one arm round the waist of one young man, and the other draped over the shoulders of another. Looking at it I thought of Dulcie Robertson-Scott, who had taken me to look at the stables over at Chartlands House. When we were alone in the tack room looking at the rosettes she had won in jumping competitions at horse shows, I had breathed in the sweet smell of saddle soap and lucerne hay, and looking at her snug-fitting jodhpurs had murmured that I thought that she had a delicious little behind. "Are you batty or something?" she said, frowning in honest bewilderment first at me and then back at the red, orange and blue rosettes. "I don't believe you're a bit interested in horses. . . ." It seemed to me that I wouldn't have very much to tell Ermine, and it looked as if Ermine was going to have altogether too much to tell me. I wondered if I would be able to laugh when she did.

I went down to Marshwood for a week before I joined Max in the new house in St. John's Wood, and the time passed very quickly. I went out hacking for a couple of days with the Colonel, and I was surprised to find that the winter landscape, with its bare glistening woods, was as lovely as the summer and spring one. When Marshwood was hemmed in by the early darkness, the soft glow of lamplight and firelight in its curtained rooms made it seem more intimate and friendly; and as Manson and the maids put up Christmas decorations of holly, fir, and laurel it began to look more and more like a warm and happy house. I remembered going with

Mackie to get five shillings' worth of holly and a bunch of mistletoe from the shop around the corner in the old days— for the kitchen, it was too bourgeois to have Christmas decorations in the drawing room according to Naomi. Now Emily was despoiling plantations for Marshwood. She was also endlessly busy buying presents for the tenants' children, and for the cottagers, and making arrangements for the Christmas and New Year balls for the tenants, the hunt, and the county. In the middle of all the checking of lists of things, of invitations, of acceptances, and so forth, I felt out of things and sorry that I was going away. The Colonel only spoke about the situation once.

"It's a pity you aren't going to be here for the fun."

"I'm sorry about it too, but this family get-together really seems to mean a lot to the old man."

"I know. I wouldn't want to spoil it for him." The Colonel hesitated. "But I'll miss you, and I know your mother will."

"I wish I could please you all. Perhaps I could tell him I can't get away until after Christmas."

"I shouldn't do that; he's an old man, now, and I think you owe it to him."

"We'll do things properly another year."

"Yes. We'll do things better next time."

On the morning of Christmas Eve I went the round of the cottages with the Colonel in the estate truck delivering the Christmas parcels, boxes put up by a Salisbury grocer containing a bottle of whisky, a bottle of brandy, a turkey, a plum pudding, a dozen oranges, and a big packet of almonds and raisins.

"It's an old Marshwood custom," said the Colonel. "It's getting more ruinous every year, but I'll keep it up as long as I can . . . poor devils they'd have a thin Christmas without it."

The cottage women came smiling to the doors, saying "Merry Christmas Colonel, Merry Christmas Master Savage" in their broad Wiltshire voices, their breath making little white puffs in the sharp air. Through the windows behind them I could catch glimpses of paper chains and bells crisscrossing the low-ceilinged rooms, and in one or two windows small Christmas trees. It was all very cheerful and Dickensian. In the afternoon my mother drove me to the station, and the same atmosphere ruled there. The long curved platform was crowded with groups of soldiers and airmen going home on leave from the camps on Salisbury Plain. Many of them had sprigs of holly in their cap bands, and their faces were red with pleasure and excitement.

"It's a shame that you're going just now," said my mother, snugging her face down between her fur hat and her fur collar and turning her back on the wind.

"I wish I wasn't," I said, and for the moment really meant it.

"I think it's time you told Max how things are . . . you've got a complete life down here—he really oughtn't to break it up whenever he feels like it. Christmas means an awful lot to Jack, and I know he's hurt, though he doesn't say so, by your going. He's really very fond of you."

"He's been wonderful to me—I like him more and more."

"I can see that and it makes me very happy—I was so afraid you might be silly and neurotic about my marrying—I was so afraid you wouldn't get on." Her face looked innocently pretty surrounded by the soft fur. "It means a lot to me that you do. But I don't think you ought to just take what he's ready to give, you must make a return. I think the least you can do is to be here for the big things that count with Jack—his birthday at Easter—and Christmas. I didn't make a fuss this time, but I nearly wrote to Max about it, and told him what I thought. . . ."

"It was nice of you not to."

"It went against the grain really. . . . It's so like Max; this whole business of bringing the family together round a Christmas tree . . . it might have meant something when you were little, but now you're nearly twenty and they must be in their thirties . . . you were such a lonely little boy and he didn't do anything for you then. . . ."

There was a faint murmur in the air, the first intimation of the coming train. There was a great stir along the platform, as people picked up grips and kit bags. Emily took my arm and squeezed it.

"Max has got to see it . . . that Marshwood's something you've got to take seriously. I think it would help if you told him Jack had made you his heir. That would bring it home to him, or it should. . . ."

"You think I should—it seems, oh, I don't know, like putting it up to him to do better; rubbing it in, almost, that he hasn't, well, done anything like that."

"But that's absurd," she laughed. "Nobody could take it like that. You don't want to bring it up of course, for the sake of talking about it. But if he asks you what your plans for jobs and things are—well, then you ought to tell him that Marshwood's there, solidly, behind you, and has to be taken into account. . . ." She raised her voice against the approaching train. "And you musn't be neurotic about talking about money . . . there's nothing sillier."

The engine slid past us, rolling slowly to a stop in a cloud of snowy exhaust steam, and within a few minutes I was on my way towards London. Perhaps the storms of the past were all blown out at last, I thought, as I sat looking out of the steamy carriage windows at the hurrying landscape. Perhaps the mutilation of the books had been the one last violent gust before calm fell—perhaps we were all going to be friends from now on, and gentle with each other.

Max's new house in London was something of a surprise. It was a gothic villa in a row of discreetly varied stucco houses that radiated suburban decency. Although it was the dead of winter it took no imaginaton to see what it would be like on a late summer afternoon, with the men, bulldog pipes in their mouths, doing a little gardening after a day at the office, mowing lawns and spraying roses for greenfly between tea and dinner. In spring there would be a great deal of pink may, and mustard-yellow laburnums would drip over the stucco garden walls. I stood for a moment after I'd paid off the taxi, looking up and down and savoring the particular unsuitability of the street as a place for Max to live. As I looked I saw out the corner of my eye a movement at a second-floor window of the house next door, a curtain was drawn aside and a narrow segment of face peered out. I spun round quickly and caught sight of another curtain dropping back into place at a window in the house opposite. Shades of Castlereagh Gardens and its maiden ladies, I thought; it was a very respectable little street.

I walked up the front steps and rang, hoping I'd find Lolotte inside, in what I had in mind as a Maxish interior, alive with paintings, bright colors, and amusing things. But when the pleasant-faced little cockney maid, in a neat cap and apron, had let me in I felt for a while that I must have made some mistake about the address. It wasn't at all like anything I'd expected.

Everything was in such very good safe taste. The carpets were pale pastel colors, there was a great deal of slender elegant Regency furniture, there was a great deal of rubbed gold leaf and pickled oak. In the drawing room there were bookshelves, not the open reader's bookshelves that I associated with Max, but glass-fronted affairs inside which the books were held prisoners. You had to turn little keys to get at them. And the books were in sets, in genteel library editions. Over the fireplace there was a portrait of an intensely serious young man, looking eager, a little overweight, and entirely humorless. I studied it for a while before I realized that it was supposed to be Max. The painter had missed everything he was, and had made him dully good-looking. I went up to it and tried to find a signature, wondering who was responsible for this grotesque misrepresentation. And just as I discovered the squiggle of the creator my father came into the room behind me. I looked over my shoulder, and there he was, compact and buoyant, watching me with a twinkle in his eye.

He came over, patted my shoulder, gave me a little pecking kiss on the cheek, and then jerked his head up at the canvas.

"You'd never know it was me, would you?" he said and grinned. "As a matter of fact it isn't—it's a portrait of two chaps who died. It's very sad because they were both full of promise, both of them. One was Max Town the serious writer —he would have been a sort of British Dostoevski—he would have written, oh, tremendous novels about people being perfectly miserable in the industrial north. The beginning of one of his novels still sticks around, I stole it, and made it into a pretty good short story. That Max was furious. He had started off with two people having a love affair in a steel town —the woman's husband was manager of a steel works, and the lover pitched him into one of his own blast furnaces. That Max wanted the lovers to go on being horribly guilty and tormented for a hundred thousand words or so, with the blast furnaces in the background symbolizing uninhibited passion, and so forth . . . but I wouldn't let him. He never got over the disappointment, and he died almost immediately after it. He haunted me for a long time. He'd crop up at two or three in the morning when I was overworking and not sleeping. He'd point his long white finger at me and say, 'Why are you always joking, Max, how dare you have so much fun? Don't you know the world is a fearfully gloomy place . . . you aren't depressing enough. You'll never be a great writer.' Then he'd vanish away and I'd get up and make myself a pot of tea. It got to be a habit. There must be very few men outside Russia who've drunk as much tea between three and four in the morning as I have."

"And what about the other one, would he have been a writer too?"

"Oh, no. He was a revolutionary, red-hot stuff, all for barricades, speeches from the town hall steps, and so forth. A sort of wilder Lenin, with a whiff of Lamartine about him. He was at his best talking to cheering mobs . . . he had a dead-white face and fiery eyes . . . there were generally torches or burning buildings somewhere nearby to make interesting lights and shadows on his face when he was talking. He'd really have turned England upside down if he'd lived. . . ."

"He must have been hard to finish off, with all that fervor in him."

"Well, he wasn't. . . . He was about eighteen inches too short, you see, and then he put on weight too quickly. When you got a good look at him in daylight he looked like a jolly little man. And then there was something about his voice. When he tried to reach the people at the back of the hall, and when he got excited, his voice went up two tones—to tell the bitter truth, he squeaked. When he tried to sway the mob the mob said things like "louder" and "speak up" and "carn't 'ear a word, mister," and then the chairman at the meetings would tug at the back of his coat and make him sit down . . . he died without much of a struggle, poor fellow."

"Does he ever do any haunting?"

"He did for a bit—until I saw the countries where people like him had had a free hand—it was all mess and misery, food queues and waste. You don't get anywhere by smashing things up, that old revolutionary game is played out. If he'd succeeded, portraits like that damned thing would have cropped up in public buildings and schoolrooms—to conceal the fact that he was just an impatient fool who smashed up a lot of things and people because he didn't have the sense and the patience to make people see reason. All he promised was a lot of trouble and a big name in the history books—I'm glad he died."

"Then why do you have him hanging up there?"

"To tell the truth, Richard, it's to please Amabel. It's a mistake of hers. She thinks it's an awfully good picture of my serious side. She's a great dear, but she does want me to be respectable. She thinks that chap is much more likely to get given the Order of Merit or a Knighthood than I am, and she hangs him up there as an example to me. She doesn't know it's really a warning."

"What's Amabel like?" I said.

"Oh, don't you worry . . . you'll get on with Amabel all right," he said.

Unfortunately it wasn't so. Amabel was Scotch, and she had the Scots look of good health and a consciousness of superior virtue. When she came into the room a few minutes later she smiled as if she was doing me a favor against her better judgment. I took an instant dislike to her, and I knew, instinctively, that there was no question for her of either liking or disliking me: she knew the facts of my origin, she disapproved of passion, actresses, love outside the marriage bed, and bastards, and she therefore disapproved of me. There was nothing more to be said, whether I was a nice fellow or a nasty one was entirely irrelevant. Part of my instant dislike sprang from the highly principled hostility she emanated, another cause of it was her appearance. I was used to women, like Naomi, and like Lolotte, who were proud of their femininity and their bodies, and who dressed themselves accordingly. Amabel was wearing a biscuit-colored tailormade that was simply a covering, and she carried her body with a round-shouldered stoop that was designed to conceal so far as was possible the fact that she had a bosom. Her hair was cut short in the plainest page boy bob, chosen not because it suited her but to give her the least possible trouble. A sense of outrage radiated from her. One had only to look at her to see that she was constantly angry and ashamed because nature had played her the dirty trick of making her an inferior creature, a woman. We were old enemies by the time my father had finished introducing us.

"I expect you'll want to see your room, Richard," she said,

after a little while, and led me upstairs to another combination of safe furniture and pastel colors. It was like a room in an expensive hotel, a place nobody could object to, and nobody could like very much. Amabel moved round touching the tops of the pieces of furniture to see if the girl had dusted them. She showed me a washbasin in a closet in one corner of the room.

"The bathroom is on the other side of the landing . . . please be careful not to splash too much when you wash, and please don't make more mess than you can help. Rose has a great deal to do. I don't think you should smoke in your room —it makes work, emptying the ashtrays and so forth. . . ."

I said I'd make a special effort to be tidy.

"Oh, about meals. Rose will give you breakfast at nine, lunch is at one-fifteen, and dinner at eight. It would be easier for Rose to do the shopping if you could leave her a note at breakfast time saying if you were going to be out for any meals."

"A note?" I was surprised. "Wouldn't it be much easier just to tell her?"

"I don't think it's advisable to speak to that kind of person more than you can help. . . . They take advantage. I think a note would be best. And don't bother Rose more than you really have to for little things. She has a great deal of work to do, and the less bother you make for her the better."

She left me after a minute or two in some amazement. If this was a fair sample the family wasn't anything at all like my expectation. I wondered how on earth I would get on with Fred, who had picked Amabel; and what Maeve would be like, who had such a dead hand at interior decoration—or at least such a complete disregard for Max's personality.

I met them all over drinks before dinner that evening. It was an awkward hour for all of us except Max, who had such a firm conviction that we ought to get on well that it never occurred to him that we might not. My half-brothers and I

189

had eighteen years of unshared life between us, I was under twenty and they were married men ten years older. We eyed each other from different worlds of experience. It was quite simply too late in the day for us to be suddenly presented with the obligation of being fond and affectionate. It was heavy going, even though it was Christmas Eve.

Fred made a point of coming over to me to be friendly as soon as the introductions were over. He was curiously disconcerting to me; he had most of Max's mannerisms, and he looked exactly like him, but at the same time he wasn't like him in the least. As he probed, kindly, and with sincere good will for my interests, for some common ground, I realized that he was conciously playing the role of a serious, sober, and responsible Max; he was quite enormously on guard. Maeve came and sat beside us, a soft honey-colored girl with friendly eyes, who was determinedly affable and very uneasy. Amabel sat on the sofa across from us with her two children sitting each side of her, alert and watchful. John hovered at the far end of the room talking to Max, and now and then throwing a glance at me out of the corner of his eye.

I don't remember what we all found to talk about, but I remember one or two of the little conversational rocks and sandbars on which we bumped at various stages. Max asked me what I wanted to drink, and as I was saying that I'd like a glass of sherry Amabel asked crisply in her slightly Scotch burr if I were allowed to drink at home. I said, with a little warmth, that of course I was. "Of course," said Amabel, "how foolish of me." She cast down her eyes and smiled, raising her eyebrows the barest shade. It was quite beautiful to see the way in which she managed to imply that I had been reared in Bohemia, and could be expected to be inured to vicious courses. I drank at home.

Fred did something of the same kind, though purely inadvertently and without malice. Drawn on by Maeve's friendliness I had begun talking about the kind of plays I wanted to write, and saying why I thought the poetic dramas that Eliot and Auden and Isherwood were writing in those days were a dead end that wouldn't in the long run shape the future of the theatre. I was saying just what I thought would be the new kind of play, and the problems I faced in trying to write it, when Fred guffawed.

"Good Lord," he said, "at your age I was worrying about my backhand. . . ."

"Oh, Fred," said Maeve, "I'm sure Dick plays games just like anyone else. . . ."

I was isolated again as a queer fish from a queer pool, and I wasn't able to say anything about the games I liked without putting on a self-conscious act as an open-air boy. If I wasn't, at that stage, worrying about my backhand it was because I had a pretty good one. But that explanation was one that nobody who had been to a British public school could possibly give: to say you were good at a game was almost as unthinkable as saying that you were a gentleman, it was a claim that you couldn't with decency make on your own behalf.

"And besides," said Maeve, covering up for me with all the well meant kindness in the world, "I think Dick's perfectly right . . . poetry and all that is much more important than tennis, really, when you think about it."

"Oh, yes, of course," said Fred kindly.

"I'd rather be Wimbledon Champion than a poet, any day," said his son from beside Amabel on the sofa, "wouldn't you, if you could be I mean?"

"Nobody asked your opinion," said Amabel.

Fred suddenly got to his feet.

"Look here, if we're going to get these Christmas decorations up we'd better get busy—I don't know about you others, but we've got to be home for dinner at eight."

Amabel produced a step ladder, John and Maeve brought in armfuls of holly, laurel and fir that they had brought up from the country, and within a few minutes we were scattered through the downstairs rooms. Half of us were perched up high, on the steps and on dining room chairs, and the other half were handing up sprays of evergreen and making suggestions. In the middle of it all, after a certain amount of whispering with John, Fred began nodding and winking at me in a mysterious manner. When I'd smiled back at him without understanding what he was after a couple of times he beckoned to me, and led me out of the room. We slipped away through the momentarily empty hall, and out at the front door.

Shadows of bare winter trees cast by the street lamps danced on the white painted stucco fronts of the nearby houses, a couple of blocks down the street buses and heavy traffic rumbled by in a cheerful blaze of light. It had turned colder and the air had a sharp bite to it. Fred took my arm as he led me down the front steps.

"This is a great occasion," he said, "you're taking part in an old family ritual, fetching in the tree—it's down here at the side of the house, or it should be if someone hasn't pinched it."

The tree was leaning against the sooty side wall of the house, round in the narrow service passage leading to the back garden, breathing out a sweet resinous breath into the dark shadow.

"We started it years ago, when John and I were kids. Max decided we were too old for Christmas trees any more. John and I found out, at the last minute, and we went and got a tree on our own. We brought it into the house, and dragged out the ornaments and set it up all on our own. Max laughed at us, but he really liked it. So every year after that Max staged a mock rebellion against the Christmas things and we forced it on him, it became a sort of game to see how elaborate we could be in spite of him. It got to be pretty good fun. So now whenever the family is together at Christmas we stage the surprise, and bring in the tree just before dinner on Christmas Eve. I see to the tree, John and Maeve bring the glass fruits and the candles—I expect they smuggled them into the house a couple of days ago when Father wasn't looking. It's all very silly, but it's rather nice too, and I hope you'll be in on it from now on."

The tree was firmly anchored in a big copper cauldron with two handles, and we carried it in between us. It nodded and swayed and brushed our cheeks with its softly scratchy needles. As we came back into the drawing room everyone gathered round, exclaiming, "My word, it's a beauty, it must be the tallest ever. . . ." Maeve brought the boxes of ornaments out of a cupboard, and for a few minutes she and Fred and John were busy taking the treasures of their childhood out of their tissue-paper wrappings and wiring them to the branches. John uncoiled some wiring, and soon a silver star was glowing quietly at the head of the tree. We all stood back a few feet, and looked up at the gleaming pyramid of silver, red and gold.

"I think it's the loveliest ever," said Maeve, quietly.

Max came up between Fred and me and put his arms over our shoulders, smiling at Maeve. John looked up at the silver star. It was a shock to meet Amabel's cold hostile glare. Out of the corner of my eye I saw Fred frown and shake his head at her, and then her glare was replaced by a forced smile but not at me.

John looked quickly at his wrist watch. "Good grief, Maeve," he said, "it's ten to eight. If we don't get moving directly the Fenwicks will be wanting to murder us for ruining their dinner."

In a few minutes Max and I were alone among the greenery and the empty glasses. He turned out all the lights except a table lamp by the tree.

"They're not a bad lot," he said, "are they?"

"They're very nice," I said.

Max picked up a sherry glass and sniffed its faint Spanish scent of a hot dry country.

"It's a good thing for a man to have a family behind him,"

he said. "It's all very well, this being on your own, and being independent, that people of your age want so badly, but you want to belong somewhere, and you need something more than friendship to rely on when troubles come, you know. Fred and John are good fellows when you get to know them. I hope you'll get on."

"I got on with Fred," I said. "I found John a little difficult, though. . . ."

"Yes, I thought you would. John's Gwen's boy, he looks like her, and he thinks like her. Fred's more like me. . . ."

He paused and looked at me with an unfamiliar expression of self-doubt on his face.

"At first I thought I knew all about Gwen, when we were first married. I thought she knew all about me. And then I found there were all sorts of things I'd never told her and couldn't tell her, because I should have told her about them right away." He sketched a circle in the air with his hand. "There was that little secret enclosure inside me that she'd never entered. And then I found she had one too. She had a delicate, sensitive side to her that I was too coarse for, and that she kept from me. We came to terms in a funny way, without ever saying anything about it. I respected her secret life, and she respected mine, and we never spoke about it, ever. In the end we had taken what was really important to us both in the relationship and screened it off. I started looking for the complete understanding I wanted from other women, in a lot of little affairs; and she took refuge in a dream world in which I had less and less part. Children see much more than they're supposed to. John somehow knew all about that dream world of Gwen's and tried to make himself part of it. It's made him, well, complicated . . . you'll find him pretty easy to get on with, but hard to get to know."

He turned from me and stared for a moment at the portrait of himself as he altogether wasn't, and went on.

"I don't know why I should tell you that, I just meant to warn you not to be upset by finding John . . . elusive."

His expression changed.

"Now let's go out and have some fun."

We went and had dinner at Scott's Lobster House at Piccadilly, among the looking glasses, engraved glass, marble, and curly brass ornaments. When we'd eaten we strolled for a time among the theatres and the movie houses looking for a show that might be worth dropping in on. We took in the second act of a disappointing farce, and presently walked homewards. The streets were filled with people strolling as quietly as we were, talking and occasionally laughing. Max moved among them with a rotund universal benevolence, beaming at them all as if he were Father Christmas himself.

"You've no idea how decent the London crowd is, compared with what it was when I was a youngster," he said. "It was a vile town when I came to it as a boy. The streets were just as jammed as they are now, but it was all horse-drawn traffic, drays, carts, delivery vans, and buses. We lived in the reek of a dirty stable all the time. The streets were covered with an unspeakable slime. You don't know how lucky you are to live in a motor age. The smell of burnt oil and gas isn't nice, but you've no idea of the smells we had to live with. People smelt then, in a way they don't now. Nice people had baths, but the poor just didn't. They washed their faces and hands and they went to bed in their underclothes. I don't know when pyjamas, cheap pyjamas, came in, but they didn't exist when I was a boy. Not for my sort anyway. On a holiday night like this the streets were filled with a crowd that stank of stale sweat. And we all wore such horrible clothes, made of cheap serges and ugly materials, and we had to put up with such beastly clumsy boots. You don't realize what a liberation cheap shoes have meant . . . and all these cheap amusements. There was nothing to do if you wanted a bit of fun except going to the pub, the boozer. People drank themselves silly. If we'd walked through the streets like this on Christmas Eve when I was your age half the people we met would have been staggering drunk. We would have seen a dozen men and women throwing up in the gutters. And fights—you've no idea how disgustingly they used to fight, full of cheap gin and beer, you'd see women fighting each other in a circle of laughing louts."

He mused, and we walked on in silence for a time.

"I'll never forget dropping into all that when I ran away from home. I thought I was coming to a place where I could get clean, decent work—nothing like the farm drudgery. I thought I'd find some employer who would teach me a job and give me a chance to get on. I found a place in some stables off the Marylebone Road, mucking out, and they let me sleep in the hayloft over the stamping horses. Then I'd pick up a penny or two here and there running errands; and all the time I got dirtier and dirtier, and smellier, and less and less qualified for a decent place. After a couple of months I didn't even try to get work in the West End, my country clothes had too much dirt on them. I was drifting east into the slums, going downhill before I'd grown up. I nearly gave up. I'd actually started to go home, when the tide turned. I was walking through Richmond on the way out of London, looking for an odd job when I saw a ticket in a chemist's window. I forget the exact words —it began Smart Lad Wanted . . . they wanted a boy to live in, so that if they had night calls for medicine he could be sent round . . . I went in, and I hadn't even asked for the job before I was turned down. The chemist wasn't there. His wife —Queenie Hodges, bless her—was behind the counter sealing packets with red wax. I don't suppose you've ever seen a chemist's packet like that—they've gone into limbo along with the alchemist's stuffed alligators. 'Don't tell me you're going to try pass yourself off as a smart lad,' she said, 'we couldn't take on a ragamuffin like you.' I burst into tears. I hadn't any pride or guts left. I was hungry and dirty and tired. I hadn't even enough spunk left to turn away. I just slid down to the floor beside the counter, and leaned my head against the wood and cried. Queenie darted round the counter and stood over me. 'Don't you dare carry on like this,' she said, 'suppose a customer was to come in. . . .' And then she knelt down and touched my face and said, 'You poor little tomtit, you really are in trouble. . . .'

"She talked Mr. Hodges into taking me on. She took my old clothes away and burned them. She got me a town boy's blue serge suit off the peg at a draper's a few doors away, and a bowler hat to go with it. They gave me a little room over their back kitchen, the first room I ever had all to myself, and Mrs. Hodges gave me clean sheets every second week. I ate with them at mealtimes. You've no idea how glorious all that was, and to have found it in the middle of that dirty drunken world, that clean and friendly place. I'd walk through Richmond with Mr. Hodges's packets, my bowler on my head and my neatly polished boots on my feet, and I'd pity the little urchins I passed in the street who had found no way of escape.

"Mr. Hodges was very good to me. He saw I was quick with figures, and quick to understand what he told me, so I began to help him in the dispensary, measuring out drugs and mixing pills and medicines. Before long I was his assistant, and he was coaching me in Latin and Math in the evenings. Mrs. Hodges mothered me, and fed me up. Her cooking was good, and I shot up and filled out. Then suddenly there was a crisis. There was too much sock between the top of my boots and my trouser cuffs, and too much wrist at the ends of my sleeves. I began to feel self-conscious about it, and I hoped nobody else was aware of what was happening. I was paying for the suit I was wearing, so much every week out of my pay— and I knew I hadn't anything like covered it by the time it stopped covering me. I knew I couldn't ask the Hodges for another suit, and I knew I couldn't do without one. Richmond had seemed such a sunny cheerful place and now it seemed dark. I slunk around hoping nobody would notice me, in an agony at the thought of having to ask for more charity. You're too young still to know what an ass you can be when you're young. Oh Lord, I was so miserable over that suit. . . .

"Then one day Mr. Hodges left Queenie to mind the shop and took me for a walk along the towing path above Richmond Bridge. 'Me and Queenie have been talking you over,' Mr. Hodges said, 'and we think you're wasting your time in the shop.' My heart gave a jump, I thought he was finding a nice way of saying that he was going to throw me out. 'You ought to have a proper eddication with your brains, you're quicker than I am with your books, and I've come to the end of what I can teach you, not that it's been much. Me and Queenie think you should have some schooling. I've been speaking to Mr. Quinby at the Grammar School, and we've come to an arrangement. He'll cram you for the examinations you have to take, and if you pass 'em you'll get a scholarship—a guinea a week Quinby says, and a fine chance up at some new college they're setting up in London. Me and Queenie would be ever so pleased if you'd have a go. We'd both like to see you get on. You will have a try, won't you?'

"I stammered out my thanks and said I would, but in the back of my mind there was nothing but black misery. How could I go up to the grammar school in that wretched suit? The street boys were already jeering at me because of it—I dreaded the thought of facing anyone new, dressed as I was. And if Mr. Hodges was doing this much for me how could I ask him for anything more? 'Well, that's settled then,' said Mr. Hodges, and we pottered on along the river bank. We looked at some ducks swimming in the water. 'There's something about them birds I can't but like,' he said, 'they look so humorous and friendly. It's their fat little cheeks, and them brown eyes. They put me in mind of Queenie, in one of her joky moods. I dunno where I'd be without Queenie. . . .

Lord, I was forgetting, she was telling me we had to come home by way of Hickson's and get you a new suit so you'd make a good impression when we go round to see Quinby this evening. . . .' And then a look of embarrassment came over his face. 'You know when I spoke about you to Quinby I told him a tarradiddle. I told him you were Queenie's cousin. I didn't mean any harm, you understand, only I didn't want Quinby thinking I was soft. You don't mind, do you? . . . ' I wanted to say a great deal more than that I didn't mind a bit. . . .

"So you see that's how I got my start in life. I wouldn't have amounted to anything if it hadn't been for Queenie and Alf Hodges, and I wouldn't have had that if I hadn't had every bit of pride and self-respect knocked out of me before I met them. I sweat now when I think what would have happened to me if I'd had an ounce of manliness and backbone left in me when I went to their shop. I would have backed out, and gone on home to become a day laborer. I wonder how often it happened to bright boys and girls of my generation, how many of them were wasted and chucked away in those days, as I so nearly was. . . ."

We crossed Oxford Street in silence, and went on up Baker Street. Max's chin was down, and he was thinking thoughts that seemed a long way from me. I didn't like to break in on him.

"You've no idea how long it took me to get over that suit business, to work it out that there were people in the world who were ready to take you as you were, and who wouldn't condemn you out of hand on the strength of what you looked like and sounded like. I'd learned—or so it seemed then— that it didn't matter in the least what you were if you had the marks of the lower orders on you. If you looked like a ragamuffin you had a ragamuffin's chances, and nothing more. And when I'd been set up by the Hodgeses I learned it all over again. When I got to college in London I was flung in among a new kind of people altogether. My suit was funny to them, so was my bowler, and my accent. They'd draw me out to get me to use particular words that I pronounced wrong, and they'd imitate me. And there were little things. I was living on that guinea scholarship, and three shillings a day wasn't much, even in those times. I used to take lunch to classes with me—the lunch I'd learned as a country boy, bread, a slab of yellow cheese, and an apple. You've probably never seen a farmhand eating bread and cheese under the hedge—there's a trick to the way it used to be done, you cut the cheese and the bread with a clasp knife and took the hunks up to your mouth on the knife blade. It wasn't elegant, but I hadn't thought about it—it seemed the natural way to do it. It shocked my classmates. I've never forgotten looking up once with the loaded blade halfway up to my mouth, and catching two of the girl students watching me with fascinated disgust. They looked away, flushing, as if they'd been caught spying on some indecency. I always took sandwiches after that. And then I got myself a topper instead of my bowler hat, I was great on self-improvement in those days. That's when I met Gwen . . . she was a fellow student."

He was silent again for several paces, and then went on.

"I met Gwen through Miss Beckenham. Miss Beckenham took me up. I think she was in on the tail end of Charles Kingsley's Christian socialism, and teaching me manners was her contribution to the noble work of saving the working classes from themselves. She had a program. I was to be led, gently, to a higher sphere. We went to art museums on Sunday afternoons, and to concerts. "A friend has given me some tickets, I wonder if you'd care to come, Mr. Town." And we'd eat at tea shops afterwards—there was a chain of them then, the A.B.C. tea shops, the Aerated Bread Company. . . . I'd look for the cheapest and most filling thing on the bill of fare, and Miss Beckenham would steer me away from my choice to something more suitable, lighter. It wasn't nice to eat shepherd's pie after a concert, a little toasted tea cake was more appropriate. Gwen used to come along to chaperone us, and she'd sit rather silently while Miss Beckenham talked along improving lines. I found myself reading desperately to keep my end up in these refined bookish conversations, Swinburne, Tennyson, Jane Austen. And then I began finding books for myself, poets who seemed to say things that were more about life and less poetic, and writers who wrote more directly and plainly about what seemed to matter to me. I remember throwing Meredith's *Modern Love* at poor Miss Beckenham, and then I discovered Swift. 'Oh, but Mr. Town, nice people aren't like that,' Miss Beckenham would say, and her cheeks would go a little pink. 'I think they are.' 'But Mr. Town they shouldn't be, and we're all trying to make a better world, aren't we?'

"Miss Beckenham lived in lodgings in a bed-sitting-room where she couldn't entertain a man, so when we became more friendly we started going to Gwen's home in Putney. It seemed such a large house after the Hodgeses' little shop and upper part, and Gwen's mother was so very much the Lady. She served tea off a folding table, and there was a cake stand. I learned to put my hat under my chair, to hold my teacup in the right way, and to take three or four bites at a little sandwich I could have managed in one. I learned not to jump to my feet with an offer to help when the maid came into the room with a tray. Oh, I learned fast. I learned that Miss Beckenham was, just a little bit, common. Her parents were quite nice people, but they kept a shop in Reading. They didn't serve behind the counter, in fact they employed twenty or thirty people, but her father went to the store every day. Now Gwen's father was a soldier, and the younger son of a clergyman who had married the cousin of a peer. That put them a cut, or rather several cuts, above shopkeepers. It put them even further above the dirty boot farmer my father had worked for, up on a level with the Vicar, as gentry. It all became a challenge, like the scholarship examinations. If I could get Gwen and her parents to accept me I'd really have climbed up the ladder, I'd be a gentleman too."

He paused and we listened to a burst of carol singing which came to us from somewhere out of sight. As it died away he went on.

"It was a shock to me to find out after I'd married Gwen that there was still a long way to go on the ladder. When I started to have a success with my first novels we began to be asked out to dinners, and for weekends. We got on fast, and I was surprised to find that Gwen was as much out of her depth as I was. It hurt her pride in a funny way. At first she was buoyed up by a feeling that she was helping me to live up to her level, and then she found herself being patronized by people who thought they were just as much her superiors as mine. She'd given me little hints on forms of speech in the beginning, told me how to ask for things at table without giving offense, generally polished me up for decent company. And there we were being taken up by people who took things much more freely and easily—they had natural manners that weren't in the least constrained and deliberate. They clearly thought of us as a sweet little middle-class couple.

"We made a joke of it at first. We lived in rooms in Euston, north of the Euston Road in very much the wrong part of town. We called the West End the Other World, and we'd talk of our nights out and our weekends as Other Worlding. I got a dinner jacket, and we called it my Other World suit. And then it stopped being a joke. We weren't shabby genteel adventurers any more, poor in the week when I didn't sell an article or story, and rich in the week when we did. I began to earn more than we spent, regularly. We moved into a little street of stucco houses in Queens Gate, and we had a whole house to ourselves and a maid of our own. We made our first ventures abroad, and saw Paris, and Switzerland. We moved into the Other World, and Gwen saw that I'd taken her up with me.

"Her family let her down. Her father used to come in now and then in a bluff, hearty, soldierly sort of way to make a little touch, as man to man . . . there was a little temporary difficulty, an unexpected bill, and if I could just see him through to the end of the month or the quarter. And then her brother used to drop round with money-making schemes— he heard things at the bank where he worked in the City and he wanted to let me in on the ground floor. We were to go in arm in arm, in an equal partnership, his brains and my money. I remember once we were to buy a bankrupt canal and to convert it into a speedway for the new motor cars that were just coming in—he was full of sure-fire projects like that. And when I turned him down he was always quite affable about it and ready to go away with a friendly loan of a fiver and no hard feelings. They had the grace to try not to let Gwen know what they were up to, but she found out. It hurt her and it brought a sort of poison into the Other World game, we'd shown her people up by playing it.

"And then it didn't show up the Hodgeses. We'd go to Richmond to see them and take them out for little jaunts, up the River to Eel Pie Island for a picnic in an electric launch —it was the height of elegance on the river then—and they'd be brightly and cheerfully proud of me. Queenie kept a scrapbook with all my journalism in it, and all the little paragraphs in the papers that recorded my successes. They were very proud of my dear Gwen too, she was everything fine from their idea of the Other World. We were young and successful and full of ourselves, and we didn't notice how dusty and dreary the little shop was getting, and we didn't notice the smart new druggist round the corner on the High Street. Queenie never said a word, and Mr. Hodges never said a word to let us know they were in trouble. It was only by chance we found out—we met Quinby's son on the train going down to Richmond one day and he told us there was talk of the Hodgeses being sold up. They were right on the edge of bankruptcy. We had to force them to let us help them. And even then Mr. Hodges wouldn't accept a gift or a friendly loan. He insisted on the formality of a mortgage deed, and he kept up the payments till the day he died.

"And Mother was the same. Father died just as I was having my first success. I wanted to set up Mother in a little house of her own, and to buy her an annuity—but she wouldn't have it. She let me help her buy the village shop, 'I don't want to be a burden, Maxie,' she said, 'if I can take over Mrs. Marsh's grocery business I can manage and be independent.' Gwen had had a little streak of Miss Beckenham in her, she was so sure she was lifting me up to better things that it was a horrid shock to her to find that my people could behave better than hers. . . ."

An Underground train rumbled beneath us, and as the sound died away a church clock some way off told us that it was midnight. Max cocked his ear to the faint sound and smiled.

"Well, Merry Christmas, old son . . . we're keeping late hours, and tomorrow, today, we have to go through all that Christmas business."

"It's always fun when it comes to it, however much you may pretend not to like it beforehand."

"I suppose so, but it's a funny idea—having a special day for people to be nice to each other. If they lived from their hearts all the time it wouldn't be necessary; and then that good will towards men stuff doesn't really work—there's no way of being as generalized as all that—you can only feel good will towards those you feel warmly about. An official feeling of warmth put on as a social duty is a fraud—you only have it in you to love so very few people when it comes down to it. You want to concentrate real feeling when you have it, you can't disperse it in a fine spray like something coming out of a garden hose. . . ."

"But Max, you've written so much about Mankind being one family, and all that, about the League of Nations and the World State, doesn't it all, all that, depend on having generalized feelings?"

"Gaw, no, that's not what I'm talking about at all. That's just common sense, that's to do with rational arrangements to keep you from hiding in ditches from other men with guns, to see you get enough to eat, to make living more comfortable. It's got nothing to do with love. That's something very special, and very private."

He bowed his head and gave me a quick sideways look.

"That's a hard thing to talk about, between father and son —I don't know why. But you can mistake all sorts of feelings for love, you know. Hunger, for instance, you may just want sex very badly, or you may not want to be alone, or you may want something out of reach—just to prove you can get it, or even you may just want to experience something that other people talk about and seem to have. . . . There was a queer chap, a journalist who wanted to be a writer, who admired me at one time . . . he used to follow me round trying to have affairs with women I'd had affairs with. He even tried to have an affair with Gwen. . . . You want to watch out for that sort of thing." He took a few strides, considering it. "I'm an old man now, and I often try to get back the feelings that I had when I was your age when I'm thinking about you. But I don't believe I can do it." He linked his arm with mine. "Please don't resent what I'm going to say. That girl Ermine wasn't a girl for you. I think she wanted to have an affair with you—I'm not sure—I have an idea you wanted an affair with her. I'm probably wrong to tell you about it, it may give you the idea that you've missed something—and then perhaps you'll resent what I'm going to say. You were younger then, and more dazzled by me. I think you wanted

Ermine because she was like Lolotte, like your mother in a way, and you wanted the sort of affair you think I've had with women. That sort of affair sounds exciting, but it stands between you and life when you have it, and I don't want you to get into that sort of thing . . . those affairs kept me from love for a long time. . . ." His voice changed, and took on a dreaming, unreal quality. "It's hard to say how the right thing happens. I've given it a lot of thought. You belong in a family, your family belongs in a set of families, you go out and make a career and a web of associations of your own. Somehow love flows naturally out of it—the flow of living inside the web of normal associations brings you up against someone. You can't go out and look for them. . . . I went out looking for something, desperately, in a hurry. You want to take it slow—find out where you belong first, and then let the flow bring you what you want . . . that's an old man's advice. You're young, every night alone is a lost night for you. You don't know yet how many nights there are. I know how much time you've got, because I've seen so much time go by. That's the gulf between us. . . . I've wanted you to have a normal pattern of associations for a long time, I feel badly because I've never brought you into the family before . . . but things were difficult. Fred and John weren't ready for it . . . and I don't think Naomi wanted you to see too much of them. She hated Gwen, naturally enough I suppose, and she discouraged my attempts to bring you close to Gwen's children—she said I was planning to take you from her . . . and then when you were a child they were young men and the age difference was a difficulty—it ought to be easier now you are all young men together. . . ."

I was hardly listening to this tissue of unreality, and was deep in a dream of Ermine. Somehow I had to see her again, and soon. She was the only thing in life. It became an effort to give Max any attention at all, he was a stranger who hardly

knew me. I realized that I had missed what he had been saying for more than a hundred yards. His monologue was flowing on, imperturbably, along its own channel.

"Lolotte is very fond of you. She's been worrying me about
you. I'd forgotten how defenseless and dependent one is at
your age. She reminded me of it and made me see it. That's
why I've been going over my own early years tonight, I suppose. Naomi's brought you up with some pretty queer ideas
about money—she couldn't help having them, poor thing—
you get odd ideas about a great many things if you live from
hand to mouth among the rich. You'll find it rougher than
you think if you go out into the world to live on what you can
earn after the way you've lived in the past few years. Naomi's
given you no sort of preparation for reality—you're liable to
get cornered. You won't get into any jam of the kind I had
to deal with, but psychologically it'll be the same jam—and
then you'll be tempted to go all out for money instead of stick-
ing to the things that are really worth doing. I've prepared a
sort of cushion for you, a safety net, so you won't have too
far to fall. I've settled some money on you. It's a sort of
Christmas present—it sounds like a lot, but it isn't really very
much, just enough on a reasonable calculation. You won't ever
have to worry about square meals or clean shirts, it's bread
and butter and a bed for the rest of your life. The jam, and
the champagne, and the clean sheets will be up to you. It's a
trust fund, you won't be able to touch the capital till you're
thirty, but you'll get a steady seven hundred and fifty a year
or so. They'll give you your first dividends at the beginning
of the year, and after that there'll be something coming in
every quarter day. It's solid ground under your feet, so you
can pick what career you want without being forced to think
about the dull things, and if you pick wrong you'll be able to
pull out and make a fresh start. Lolotte's got the idea that
you might turn into a sort of hanger-on of that fellow of

Naomi's if you're dependent on his good will for everything—it was stupid of me not to think of it before—but now you're independent, and you'll be able to work out your own line."

"That's magnificent of you, Max, I'm bowled over. But you shouldn't have worried. Naomi's Colonel has been very good to me about money—there isn't any kind of pressure on me so far as he's concerned—in fact the reverse. I've never had to ask him for money, and the other day he told me he was making me his heir—when he dies I'll come into Marshwood and all the farms—he's really been awfully decent. . . ."

There was a moment of silence, and then Max laughed.

"I wish I'd known that. . . . What sort of a place is Marshwood?"

"It's a beautiful place, everything's perfect, the way the beech woods lie in the folds of the hills, and the house seems to grow out of the ground. It has about seven thousand acres, and it's all good land."

"And I suppose there's plenty of money to keep it all up . . . and you'll come into that, too."

"Jack, Colonel Arthur says so. He wants me to learn about farming and estate management so that I'll know how to run the place properly."

"And you like the idea?"

"I love Marshwood—it's really a wonderful place."

"And what about those plays you were going to write, eh," he was smiling sourly, "do you still mean to write them?"

"Yes, of course." Something in his voice was a challenge to me. "They're more important than anything."

"I wonder if you'll find them very easy to write in a country drawing room . . . still, estate management isn't such very demanding work, and the plays may come."

We walked on again without speaking, and turned in at the end of our street. When we were nearly at the foot of his front steps he spoke again as he reached in his waistcoat pocket for his doorkey.

"I don't really know what makes a man write. I began for the odd guinea—it was just after I'd left college and married Gwen. I was making what was supposed to be a living teaching a class of young louts of fifteen in a secondary school and the odd guinea was a powerful factor in our affairs. I discovered that the cheap weekly papers bought sketches—little fifteen-hundred-word vignettes on anything—so I began turning everything we did into guineas—if Gwen burned the joint when her mother came to dinner, if we took a walk in the park on Saturday afternoon and hired a skiff, if it came on to rain on a day when I'd gone to work without an umbrella I'd turn it into a sketch, about ovens and mothers-in-law, about cockney yachtsmen, about the meanness of the weather to umbrella carriers . . . anything. I doubled my salary, and soon I was making more at writing than teaching . . . and then I found I didn't have to wait for an incident to write about—I could invent one—and after that I found I had something to say, and I gave up teaching so as to get it said. I have an idea a drawing room is a harder place to get out of than a schoolroom . . . but there's always the example of dear Henry James, and I suppose I may as well wish you luck."

There was a chill in his manner, and for a moment I felt a stranger to him. I made small talk to try to bring him back.

"You knew James, didn't you?"

"Yes—we met—I thought we got on well. We gave each other dinners. I had a country place by then, he weekended with us, and asked us back—we corresponded, about writing— How one did it, How one ought to do it. How far one had succeeded with what one had done. . . ."

He turned the key in the door and opened it.

"It was a refined form of Other Worlding. Henry lived in a world of aesthetic motives, I lived in a world of practical purposes—I got my ideas from Swift and Voltaire—I tried to write like them, cleanly, vividly, and for a purpose. By accident I brought off aesthetic effects. . . . He praised me for them, outrageously, in letters and to my face. I trusted his sincerity and thought he was a friend who was really interested in showing me how to deepen and widen the range of my writing. I was interested in doing it, and I declared myself to him —openly, without any kind of reserve. . . . I found he was sniggering at my vulgarity behind my back, all his friendliness was just curiosity, leading me on so that I'd expose my lack of education and refinement. He said . . . oh, little waspish stinging things that got back to me—they have odd ways in drawing rooms. They stung, even at third hand, and I got my own back with a parody that was printed in one of the magazines. He affected to be bitterly hurt. We quarreled—I was supposed to have done something underhand, and everyone has said ever since that I treated James like a vulgar bounder . . . I suppose by his lights I was fair game. . . ."

The front door swung open, and we walked into the warmer air in the lighted hallway. We stood for a moment looking at each other, dazzled. The coldness in his voice was in his face too, he surveyed me as if he had not really seen me before.

"It gives me an odd feeling to think that a son of mine is going to be a country gentleman, it's the last thing I would have expected." He laughed shortly. "Well, it can't be helped —I suppose I ought to be glad for you. Let's have a nightcap before we turn in."

There was a mink coat lying on a chest against the wall behind him, and while he was speaking I caught sight of it and wondered what it was doing there. If it was a Christmas present for Amabel or Maeve it was being very casually treated—it looked as if someone had slid out of it and let it fall there on their way through the hall. It had been thrown down as Lolotte would throw down a coat. My heart leapt— perhaps Lolotte was sitting in the drawing room waiting for us—she would have news of Ermine. . . . I ran into the room.

The one lamp beside the Christmas tree was still burning, and a woman was sitting outside its pool of light beside the dying fire. She turned her head slowly, smiling across the shadowed room, as I came in, and then her smile vanished.

"Who are you? . . ." she said, standing up.

"I'm sorry, I'm Richard Savage, I didn't expect . . ."

"Let's have some more light," said Max, coming in behind me and snapping the switches. He took in the situation and his voice rose in pitch. "Oh, damn it, Alice, what confounded foolery is this? . . ."

"I just terribly couldn't bear not seeing you tonight, Max," she said. "Don't be cross, please."

"You shouldn't have come. You had absolutely no right . . . oh, damn and blast, and blast again. . . ."

Max stamped, and shook his head with exasperation. Alice tucked her lower lip under her teeth and for a moment looked like a guilty child. Her face was a delicate oval above a slender neck, and diamond clips on the lobes of her ears shone against her dark brown hair. She had long legs and arms, and she was lovely in an elegant, finely bred way. She looked at me, and smiled gently and appealingly.

"I'm sleepy, Max," I said. "I think I'll forget about that nightcap, and get off to bed. Good night."

"Yes, you'd better get along." Max glowered at me under his eyebrows, and then smiled. "You'll meet Alice another time. She's the nicest creature and the biggest damn fool in the world. We'll pretend this meeting never happened—good night, old man."

As the door shut behind me I heard him saying, "Now, look here, Alice . . ." But his voice was no longer shrill with fury.

I fell asleep and dreamed of Marshwood. The house was empty and sunlit, filled with an early-morning lightness. I heard Ermine talking, and laughing her bubbling secret lover's laugh close by, but though I went from room to room I couldn't find her. Her voice was always in the next room. I woke in an agony of grief and despair and found myself alone in a strange place. A wind had sprung up and the wooden acorn at the end of the blind cord was tapping the windowpane. I lay for a moment or two wondering where I was, and then remembered that I was in my father's house.

5

Alice had vanished by morning, leaving no trace but an occasional conspiratorial gleam in Max's eye when it met mine,
and Christmas passed off as a genial family affair. We all got
on well together round the table and round the tree. Even
Amabel forgot that I was an offense against common decency.
By the time lunch and tea were over and the party began to
break up I had come to terms with my brothers to some extent. I was to have lunch with Fred at his club the following
Wednesday, and to spend that weekend with Maeve and John
down at Datchford.

The lunch with Fred in the brown and gold Louis Quatorze
dining room of the Helicon Club was a success and it was
soon followed by another. The Helicon excluded women as
guests and even as servants, and Fred was at his best in its
hearty, Philistine, all-male atmosphere. The men who belonged
to it were mostly drawn from the professions. There were a
great many civil servants, a sprinkling of younger Members
of Parliament, a few gentlemen actors, publishers, and a number of lawyers like Fred, men who had taken silk and were

doing well at the bar. Fred pointed out two high court judges to me and I was very much impressed to find myself sitting at table with such people. It was an old fashioned lunch, of soup, brown soup, a roast, well done with brown gravy, and a good solid pudding. The thing to drink was beer in a tankard of pewter. I disliked beer in the first place, and with the taste of metal added to it I disliked it even more, but in the name of clubmanship I drank it down and did my level best to enjoy it. I was very eager to fit in, and felt oddly proud each time Fred introduced me to anyone as "my brother Richard." The members I spoke to were affable and relaxed and I was enchanted with this first glimpse of the company of men who did the world's serious work. I began to believe that there might be a level of existence at which men lived reasonably, and not in a continuous storm of emotional stress. I didn't then see the point of the club's rule excluding women, or realize what a deliberately planned and carefully preserved place of refuge it was. I simply enjoyed the sight of a number of men who had come together to take pleasure in each other's company, and I envied them their ease of manner.

My weekend with Maeve and John was more disturbing. I changed trains halfway to Datchford and completed the journey on a little ambling branchline that ran from village to village through a gentle countryside of water meadows and small pastures. When I got out at Datchford Halt and looked at a stumpy gray church tower of stone and flint through a screen of elm branches and saw the guard and a porter taking empty milk cans out of the van at the back end of the train I was powerfully reminded of my old journeys down to Minster. John and Maeve coming smiling down the platform even looked, momentarily, like the Willinghams. John whisked us off in his big white sports car down twisting lanes while Maeve warned me not to expect anything special.

"It's just going to be a cozy family weekend, just us, and then the gang will come by to dinner—Tishy and Jock Aiken, and Mike and Poppy Hughes, and there'll be Molly Higgins for you to flirt with. We might go dancing, or we may just stay at home and roast chestnuts and sing if it's a filthy night —we'll see how the weather turns out—oh, John, did you remember the beer?"

"I thought we'd pick up a case at the Golden Ball—that's why I'm taking the long way round."

"Oh." Maeve turned back to me. "The Golden Ball's our local . . . it's run by a character, Tom Duckett. It's not bad in its way."

The Golden Ball was by the river, and its garden was full of punts and skiffs wintering under green tarpaulin covers. The lawns running down to the gray sluicing floodwater looked greasy and cold, but you could see that it would be a pleasant place in summer. The tiny bars inside were very snug, lined with stuffed fish and photographs of Tom Duckett in his cavalry days riding polo ponies or with groups of troopers standing and sitting in front of British and Indian barracks. We sat on settles beside a log fire drinking pints of brown ale until John over a second pint showed me how to play shove halfpenny while Maeve gossipped with Tom. Then two of the pub's regulars came in and Maeve and John played them a game of darts for drinks while a rambling discussion of the cricket club's program for the next season began. Presently we loaded a couple of cases of beer into the back of the car and drove on to lunch.

"Here we are," said Maeve, "it's a silly place to live, but it's rather a dream."

It had once been a water mill, and it stood on the edge of a swiftly flowing stream lined with willows and alders. One heard the water talking under the old millwheel in all its rooms, and light reflected from the mill race danced on the living room ceiling. Inside and outside everything was a perfection of neatness and order. There was a skillfully laid out garden, which consisted of one secret close after another, hedged in with box and yew, beautiful even in its winter bareness. There was a collection of ship models in the drawing room, a collection of Meissen china, and a garage workshop in the old coach house, gleaming with every kind of machine tool, where a racing car and a racing dinghy waited to be played with. John had made the garden out of the mill's old vegetable plot. John had made the ship models. John had the collector's eye that could spot Meissen in forgotten corners of junk shops, and he had bought the racing car after an accident for nothing and rebuilt it. He had won cups with the racing dinghy. The floor of the garage behind the sheeted racing car was occupied by the frames of two slender boats, standing upside down on trestles, above a litter of shavings. John showed them to me with quiet pride.

"I'm building a couple of kayaks—those Eskimo hunter's boats," he said, "if they turn out right we ought to have some fun with them this summer—or any time after Easter, if I get them finished by then."

Tishy and Jock and Mike and Poppy and Molly all drove up to the house in sports cars during a fifteen-minute stretch at about seven o'clock. John threw a couple of logs on the fire as they all stood round peeling off long tweed scarves and leather coats, and Maeve lit candles and turned out the lights. The maid in her neat apron and white cap brought in a tray loaded with bottled beer and half-pint tankards with glass bottoms. There was a general outcry of "Ah, that's the stuff," "This is what we came for," and "Get weaving with the bottle opener, chaps." And in a few moments these remarks gave way to "Cheerio," and "Down the hatch." Molly Higgins had a husky voice and a lock of hair that fell down across her eyes. She had a trick of throwing it back with a gesture that threw her face up appealingly, and showed you her strong healthy neck.

"I can never really make out what beer really tastes like," she said, "can you?"

"Oh, of malt and hops and things, I suppose."

"Oh, that's a dull answer," she said, "you have to do better than that. Maeve told me you were frightfully brainy. If you ask Jock what beer tastes like he says squashed wasps and gym shoes after they've been put away for the winter. Jock says things like that all the time, he's fun—you'll try to be fun—won't you."

"I'll try."

"Well p'r'aps you'd better not try—keep pouring with the beer and maybe it'll come natural." She lay back on the sofa and her breasts pushed out against her canary-yellow sweater. She followed the movement of my eyes. "Oooh," she said, "naughty thoughts."

Maeve came by and filled up our little tankards.

"John says I'm to tell you he'll pour a bucket of cold water over you if you don't behave, Molly," she said.

"I'm not behaving, am I," said Molly.

"I think you're behaving beautifully," I said.

"Another victim for the old treatment," said Jock. "You watch out, Richard old chap, Molly's deadly when she's on the make."

"Actually I rather go for your baby brother, John," said Molly.

Tishy and Poppy gave each other meaning looks while Jock and Mike and John laughed and drank great gulps out of their tankards.

Before dinner the talk was about cars, and during dinner it turned to politics. Taxes were too high, and the Labor Party was no good. The Labor men hadn't the background. But you shouldn't vote for the party, you should vote for the man. Jock was Labor, "I mean I'm sympathetic generally speaking with them," but he always voted Conservative because Jebb was a better man than Blackstone. Everyone agreed that you couldn't vote for Blackstone against Jebb. After dinner there was a pause while we argued about dancing or staying at home. It was settled for dancing. The women went upstairs to do their faces and the men went outside. We stood discreetly spaced along the edge of the lawn, pissing, and looking up at the moon playing tag among the racing clouds overhead. The bare willow branches threshed in the wind and the night air was full of the earthy smell of the watermeadows.

I rode with Molly as we raced to the roadhouse where we were to dance. She sat up very straight as she drove and gave her mind altogether to the machine and the road. Her lips were slightly parted and her head was tilted back at a proud intent angle. The air tore round the windshield and bit at our cheekbones and foreheads. The gang traveled in a tight bunch passing each other and repassing, sometimes racing down the straightaways nose to tail at from eighty to ninety miles an hour. Molly hardly spoke until we were dancing in the Ace of Clubs.

"You were scared coming here, weren't you?"

"Yes I was, badly scared."

"It feels marvelous now, sort of unknotting, doesn't it?"

"Is that the point?"

"Mmm, and being ahead of the odds. I mean by rights we should have been killed a couple of times on the way. We would have been if we hadn't been bloody good. Being ahead of the odds makes me feel extra alive." She flung her hair back. "It's better than booze, better than anything except a wriggle."

"Is a wriggle what I think it is?"

"I expect so—it's marvelous for unknotting. . . ."

We went out into the parking lot, and made love on the air-filled leatherette cushions of the back seat of the M.G. in the red glow of the Ace of Clubs' on-and-off sign. Molly was innocently greedy, and it was all very quick and easy, and nothing but the thing itself. In no time at all she was scrubbing my mouth with her handkerchief to get off any stain of lipstick.

"Tell me I'm a wizard wriggle, won't you?"

"You're a divine wriggle."

"The best you ever had?"

"The best I ever had." I crossed my fingers in the dark.

"What's a wriggle like?"

"Like being swallowed by an oyster."

"Maeve was right. You are brainy. That's much better than anything of Jock's. I do like you."

We went back inside and danced, and presently the whole gang raced down the wide main road, swinging in and out of the trucks, to the Old Barn where there were suits of phony armor against the walls and the band was supposed to be better. We ate scrambled eggs and bacon and danced until the Old Barn closed on us. The party broke up on the desolate tarmac of the parking lot. The neon signs were all out. Trucks passed on the road, dark sheeted shapes frantically pursuing the glare of their own lights.

"Well, good night all, good night."

"Cheerybye, chaps."

"Take care, Molly."

"Be seeing you."

"God bless, chaps."

"Good night all."

In the car going home with John and Maeve I fell into a beery doze of physical exhaustion.

"Is the missing heir asleep?" said John.

"Worn out, poor lamb."

"I thought he was fading in the last hour. I suppose Molly gave him a treatment."

"We shouldn't have let him in for it, it was rather awful of us."

"I don't see what's awful about it. He probably liked it. Molly loves it. A lot of men like it her way, with no production, no fuss, no bother, and no hangover."

"I suppose that's what makes it seem so awful, the meaninglessness of it."

"You know, I sometimes wonder if women don't like trouble for trouble's sake."

The remark produced an uneasy silence. I waited for Maeve to answer it, but no answer came. I was hoping that her reply would be an important revelation of what she profoundly felt, and that it would give me my first clue to the inner mechanism of either of them. But the engine roared, the tires hissed, and the wind blustered round us, and nothing was said.

"That was rather a divine dress Poppy was wearing," Maeve said.

Something in her tone made me think that this point of disclosure had been reached and passed before, that there was some tacit agreement between them that it always would be passed. It might be rather pleasant to have such an agreement with those around one, to be always warmly wrapped up and never to be naked with one's vitals exposed. It might not be really necessary to be either earnest or intense about what one felt or thought, outwardly; life would be much easier if one never put any opinion or belief on the line. There would be no disputes and no frictions that way, it would be like living in Fred's club all the time.

I woke late the next morning and hurried downstairs, afraid that I might have disorganized the household routine. But I found Maeve and John quietly going through the Sunday papers over a late breakfast. Coffee and bacon and eggs were keeping warm over spirit lamps and it was clear that the routine was proof against an oversleeping guest. As I drank my coffee and read the Sunday *Express* I noticed that John was rather surprisingly dressed up. His Saturday sports clothes had given place to a trim blue suit and a dark tie. Maeve was in a dressing gown, making up a book list from the review pages.

"The new Arthur Bryant looks interesting, John, shall I put it down?"

"My paper's pretty lukewarm about it."

"Then I'll lay off."

"Oh, I don't know, I'm mad keen on anything to do with Pepys. We'd better have it."

"Righty ho, and the new Stella Gibbons for me."

John looked at his wrist watch and got up.

"I'll be off in about fifteen minutes. I think I'll take a turn in the garden till then."

He went out lighting his pipe. I thought that I had never smoked one and would try.

"John goes to church," said Maeve. "You don't have to. He'll be back before lunch, unless we arrange to walk over to the Golden Ball and then he'll pick us up there."

"I don't think church is my line."

"Well, don't go then." She smiled. "John won't mind, though he does take it terribly seriously. He always says how you feel about God is something quite private."

The morning sun twinkled on the dozens of horse brasses and the collection of pewter in the dining room. There were no pictures on the walls, their place was taken by a number of framed ballads and broadsheets. Two small settles stood each side of the fireplace. The room had been made to look as much like a public-house bar as possible. I looked up and saw my brother in his blue suit solemnly walking up and down in the garden, and presently, missing him, heard his car pobbling in its sports-carish manner as he drove off.

"I suppose you're wondering how last night adds up to this morning," said Maeve suddenly, putting down her paper.

I said not, with rather self-conscious politeness.

"Well you should, it doesn't add up."

A sort of frozen embarrassment possessed me. There was always the inner longing to know what people were really thinking, and the hope that they would declare themselves, and then when self-revelation came I shrank from it. Maeve looked at me, rumpling her hair with one hand, supporting her chin in the other, her elbow planted on the table. Her dark blue quilted dressing gown was loosely about her, and her eyes were frankly on mine. It was a moment of complete intimacy on equal terms, such as I had only once before enjoyed with a human being, with Ermine. It had come about then through sex. For a moment I recoiled from Maeve, thinking it could only come about through sex, and then suddenly became aware that this time it had come about through sympathy. We liked each other. My embarrassment passed.

"Last night wasn't really your thing, was it?"

I nodded, and she went on.

"I could see you were trying desperately to fit in. I wish almost that you hadn't tried so hard. It might have been better if you'd just been stuffy, and ruined our evening. The word has gone round the gang that The Missing Heir is all right. I wish it hadn't." She lit a cigarette.

"I don't know why you should wish that. I'd like to get on with John. . . ."

"Why? . . ." She pushed it through a blue cloud of smoke.

"Why—because he's my brother, I suppose. . . ."

"And because Max has some crazy idea . . . it's ridiculous. You aren't John's brother. You're his half-brother . . . and not in a very nice way. Your mothers hated each other, and your being born at all was a sort of outrage to his mother. . . . I'm sorry if that hurts you, but you know it's true, don't you?"

"As a matter of fact I do. It's what we're trying to put behind us."

"Well, why?" She looked at me with the same absolute frankness. "Don't you see what an impossibility it is? It's a sort of sick idea. You're natural enemies. . . ."

"I don't see that. As a matter of fact I'm rather overwhelmed by John. He's pretty much what I'd like to be. He does what he wants when he wants. He's marvelous at doing all the things I'd like to be able to do, making gardens, and boats, and being able to do anything he wants with his body, sailing well, driving well, playing games . . . he's got the ease of living I'd like to have. . . ."

She stubbed out her quarter-smoked cigarette abruptly and viciously.

"That's because you're still adolescent. John's sick. I'm his nurse . . . all this, the house, the boats, the cars . . . it's all occupational therapy. If I didn't love him I wouldn't be able to bear it." She lit another cigarette. "It's sometimes more than I can bear to see people falling for him, the way you're falling for him, without realizing what a waste of a man he is. . . . all because of loving Max against the grain of his hatred. I'm always hoping that it'll break out one day, and wash away in a torrent of bitter words. I long for him to throw off his beastly self-control, scream with pain, and show his loathsome hidden wounds, so that the air will get at them and they'll heal—and then he'll grow up at last. I've begun to believe in the last year or two that it isn't ever going to happen. . . ." She ran her hand through her hair again. "I've known John all my life, since I was five, I think, it might have been when I was six. I don't know. We lived almost next door. We were always in and out of each other's houses. We got engaged secretly when we were sixteen and seventeen. John's mother began to die that year. She'd never been ill before, she was one of those fragile little gossamer women who are made of leather inside. Everyone was taken by surprise. John and Fred found her one day lying on the sofa in the drawing room with her face covered with sweat. She was in pain, and she'd never had that kind of pain before. . . . She didn't believe there was anything the matter with her, wouldn't believe it. She tried diets to cure her indigestion, as she called it. She wouldn't go to the doctor. She thought doctors and medicines were all silliness, for weak people. She disregarded the pain, though it came back again and again. She lost weight, and her face shrank.

"We were at the age when we'd just caught onto things. We weren't supposed to know that Max was away in Spain with a woman called Carol Blake. We weren't supposed to be able to tell that Gwen was dying. But we knew. Fred and John and I would have awful endless, helpless, circular conversations sitting in the summer house, or in the old schoolroom at my home, about what we ought to do. And then we got my father into it. Somebody found out where Max was, and made him come back. He came back angry. The house was full of his irritation—he thought it was just some trick to get him to come home. And then there was a great coming and going of doctors, and consultants, and Max was suddenly quite different—upset and guilty. There was an operation, and it wasn't any use. We weren't supposed to know, still, but what the surgeons found meant that there wasn't any hope—Gwen had three or four months to live. So Max put off Carol and settled down to be terribly nice to Gwen for the time she had left. But Gwen was strong, horribly strong, and she let go of life inch by inch. Six months went by, and then seven, and she was still there, drugged, emaciated, and helpless, but alive.

"You know what Max is like, the bounce and energy there is in him. He got bored, bored . . . bored stiff. He made up his mind that as the doctors had been wrong about the time they were wrong about the disease. So he went back to Carol. Carol had a lovely place in the South of France and amusing people went there. Being entertained and flattered by Carol and her friends was much more fun than waiting at the death bed of a woman who wouldn't die. Max said he was going for a week, and he stayed. Gwen's will began to break in the eighth month. Nothing else was keeping her alive. She began to sink and Max was sent for—but he wouldn't come. He wrote back, a letter about false alarms, and he accused the doctors of playing up to what he called Gwen's dramatics. The doctors wrote him, everybody wrote him, but he wouldn't come. He came the day after she died, after they'd sent him telegrams."

Maeve's cigarette burned her fingers, and she dropped it into her coffee cup. She lit another.

"I don't blame John for being hurt. I was hurt, devastated by it all for the time being. I can see it's hurt you to hear about it . . . it was awful, and unbelievable while it was happening. But you have to put these things behind you. John never could. He never recovered. He's never faced anything serious since. He's spent his life trying to wipe out that summer and autumn, trying to remake a carefree adolescence for himself. We haven't had a marriage. We've played house together. What you admire in him is all the little dodges he uses to put between him and anything important. What he's bloody good at is being nobody and nothing. You've no idea how good he was before Max broke his courage. You don't know what he could have been. You can't imagine what it was like living through that time, living close to him as he found out more and more, and drank in his mother's wrongs, and shriveled up inside. I meant to help him get over it. You can't begin to know what it was like to realize that he wasn't ever going to, that he was broken. . . ."

Maeve got up and went and stood by the window looking out over the lovely garden in its bare winter neatness.

"It's rather disgusting of me to dump all this out onto you. It's none of my business what you do with your life. You've got a perfect right to hang round Max adoring him, and imitating him like Fred, or playing like John. I don't know which is worse, though, Fred with his pompousness and his dreary club, or John with his toys. . . . I suppose it's because I hate what's happened to John so much that I want to see you break out instead of being broken in. . . . I know Max wants you to see a lot of us, but I don't think you should. You can't ever be truly frank, with John, he'll evade it. And he'll never be frank with you. It won't be healthy. . . ."

She turned and faced me.

"Here I am preaching a sermon. I suppose John's is nearly over. I'd better get dressed if we're going to meet him at the Golden Ball. It's a nice walk."

She came over and took my hand, holding it gently and looking down into my face with a curious seriousness.

"I hope you haven't minded this. It's done me good, saying what I really think to someone I like. I don't often get the chance. . . . Please don't go on being Max's son, or Naomi's. . . . Try to be Richard, anyone, as long as it's someone. . . ."

She left me. At the Golden Ball it was shove halfpenny and darts and beer, and that evening we went over to Tishy and Jock's and stood round the piano with tankards in our hands and sang *The Wearing of the Green, The Lincolnshire Poacher,* and the *Foggy Foggy Dew.* The firelight glinted on copper warming pans and jugs, and Jock's collection of hunting prints hung on the walls. On the platform of Datchford Station the next morning I said that it had been a wonderful weekend and when John and Maeve urged me to come again when I felt like it I promised that I would, but I knew that I would not.

The atmosphere in the St. John's Wood house had changed during the weekend. Max had been away too, and he came back after I had settled in. He seemed surprised to find me there, and after a momentary flash of irritation became overwhelmingly agreeable. We had lunch together and he talked about politics, enlarging on a theory that the English and French politicians, with the help of American business, had made Hitler inevitable by what they had done in the twenties.

"Isn't he just a freak?" I said. It was a far-off cozy time. "A sort of General Boulanger, only a little more successful.

Won't the Germans get bored with him when the theatricals go on, and nothing much happens? All those torchlight parades, and all that hanging out banners, won't fool the Germans for long, not when they find they're just as poor and as badly off as ever. They'll kick him out."

"He won't give them a chance. He'll pitch them into some idiotic war before they get the hang of him—just the way old Kaiser William's soldiers and Junkers pushed Germany into the World War because they couldn't face admitting they'd gone bankrupt. You'll see, when Hitler's run through the petty cash that's lying round he'll go to war too. Have you ever thought about it—what you'll do when war comes? It's going to be a bigger war than anything we've ever seen—there won't be any holding it tidily down on battlefields, it's going to spread out over everything. . . ."

He launched out upon the changes that tanks and aircraft had made in warfare, and sketched what proved to be an accurate enough picture of what was coming.

"The soldiers are going to pretend they're fighting along the old lines for the old things—this ridge, that gap through the mountains, that communications center, but the real things will be factories, and mines, and oilfields. There'll be a tremendous amount of plain brutal hurting and breaking people, sickening them with the idea of going on, breaking the will to fight and the will to work. It's going to be much worse than anyone thinks. They all talk of air raids. They think of being killed dramatically and quickly, or being maimed and buried in houses—they've forgotten the thing we glimpsed in the last war on the Somme and at Verdun—the wearing down of men in the front lines, the wholesale starving of women and children behind them, the first amateurish efforts to frighten whole towns and cities, whole peoples. Everyone's afraid of a quick war, this Blitzkrieg they talk about—they don't know they're in for a long-drawn-out industrial competition. It's all as clear as daylight, but nobody's worked it out."

I sat back, watching him, leaning back in his chair making gestures with his cigar, a small, plump, neatly manicured man.

"Everybody has this idea of a few surprise attacks knocking a country out; they talk of the German air force paralyzing England in a few hours, blocking the railroads and the ports, putting the power stations out of use, bringing everything to a standstill. It's childish. They don't see the thousands of tons of bombs it would take to do it, the incessant stream of bombers coming in night after night, day after day. They haven't even the sense to see that that's what they ought to be afraid of, some bloody-minded set of fools setting out to murder big towns, rather than a dashing sort of hussar raid and a big bang. The Germans haven't got enough planes to do it yet—but they're starting to build them . . . and we're going to try to outbuild them, so that we can destroy precious things and human lives on an even bigger scale than they can. . . . It's all insane. . . ."

"Do you really believe it's going to happen?"

"Yes, the world's in the hands of fools."

I sat looking at him with two thoughts in mind; one was an amused, patronizing wonder at the arrogance that enabled him to feel so sure that he knew better than all the diplomats and statesmen of the world; the other was a prickling of greed. If the war was going to mean so much bombing it might be a good idea to buy some aircraft shares. As the allowance the Colonel was giving me was quite enough for my needs I would be able to invest the income from Max's trust as it came in, there might be quite a bit to be made that way. Or would it be more fun to buy a car?

"Beaverbrook won't let the *Express* print my articles about that sort of thing any more—he says they upset people and scare off advertisers. He had me to lunch the other day to tell me so. He said I was sinking into a senile pessimism. He had his Foreign News man there to prove to me that Hitler wanted peace. He'd just come back from Germany and he knew . . .

there was no shaking them. They told me I was getting out of touch. I told them how the old editor of the *Express* suppressed an article I wrote when Bleriot flew the channel for the first time. I said there'd soon be airplanes carrying twenty or more passengers between Paris and London as regularly as buses ran between Hammersmith and the Bank. The editor said he'd seen Bleriot's plane, a thing as convincing as a wicker chair, and he said he wouldn't print the article—because I was too valuable a contributor and he wasn't going to let me turn myself into a laughing stock. Oh, I was wrong about that, by twenty years or so . . . maybe you'll have twenty years to enjoy yourself before it all goes wrong. I hope so."

"You didn't think the first war was going to happen."

"Not then. I thought it would come later. I wrote a book about it, all about a big European war in which London and Paris and Berlin were all smashed up. I'd been seeing a lot of a man called Professor Soddy then, and talking about the new ideas that were coming out just then about radio-activity, and splitting the atom. It was a new thing, this idea that matter could rot, and decay, poisonously. It made me think of bombs that would start this rotting of atoms and burn out whole cities with radiations. I gave the scientists till the thirties to work out how to do it . . . that was in 1914, when the book came out everyone was thinking of the battle of Mons. The battle made my speculations seem very unreal, and when the war was over London and Paris and Berlin were still there, a few bombs had been dropped and a few people had been frightened, but it hadn't amounted to very much. It looked as if I were wrong . . . there still aren't any atomic bombs, thank goodness. . . . Perhaps I was wrong. I've been teased about it since. There was a clever-clever article in one of the weeklies a month or two back claiming that my science was all wrong—he showed that I'd lost my gift for seeing ahead somewhere about nineteen hundred and ten. He made some very funny joke about my atomic bomb, he called it the modern semi-literate's equivalent of the philosopher's stone that the old alchemists searched for. I had the pilot of an airplane dropping the bomb from an open two-seater monoplane—I forget the details—there was a hand-set fuse that the pilot had to operate before he dropped the thing overboard. The bright young man who wrote the article said that my mind hadn't been able to take in anything more elaborate than a hand grenade—he said my military horizons were limited by what I'd read about the Boer War. . . . It's funny how things like that get under your skin. I've arrived I suppose as well as you can arrive—they're going to give me a banquet with speeches when my sixtieth birthday comes along, it's going to be an orgy of respectful boredom and I'm formally going to be declared a Grand Old Man of English letters—they keep that sort of thing until everyone's bored with you and nobody young respects you any more. All the young chaps like the man who wrote that article will be sneering in the background. . . . How he annoyed me. I spent a whole night arguing with him and flattening him out for his ignorance . . . and at the end of it he was right I suppose. Those physicists, Rutherford and his boys, have been working ever since those early days to get at the power in the atom and they're using bigger and bigger machines. I suppose I was pretty silly to think of an atomic bomb no bigger than a suitcase . . . but it's hard to admit being wrong over a thing like that. . . ."

He mused, leaning back, sucking at his cigar.

"Someday they'll do it. . . ." He looked suddenly and disconcertingly into my eyes. "The really good men are in the laboratories these days . . . when you read history you get a queer picture of concentrations of greatness—there are periods when it seems to be concentrated on plays, on paintings, on music, on international law, or civil law, on business, for a time on novels . . . but the great men are all in the sciences now—Einstein, Freud, the physicists and the chemists—they're the world-shapers these days—they make the other voices sing small. . . ."

The little whitened tube of ash on his cigar fell and rolled down his waistcoat.

"You've got a good mind. Are you sure you want a few plays—and a little estate management—to be the big thing in your life? Are you going to be content, pottering on the margin of things?"

"That and poetry—poetry is the biggest thing there is," I said, "everything feeds poetry . . . it says everything men know."

"If it does, then you're right. But knowledge takes new forms, and the new forms mean new ways of expression. All, all, the constructive thinking in physics and chemistry, the new explorations of what the universe is, of what place life has in the universe, is being done by mathematicians . . . perhaps if you can make that mathematical language into verbal language you can make poetry out of it . . . but you'll have to understand a great deal you don't even think about now . . . the sort of intuitive responses to things that poets used to be able to get by with are almost worked out. . . ." He eyed me. "It's a challenge . . . you know up to a point the history of religion is the history of human knowledge . . . every new discovery about life and the human situation was turned into rite and ritual. The old religions dealt with everything men knew in a compressed language of symbol . . . and they developed as men learned. Until they suddenly closed the books—the crystallization of the Bible, the development of sacred books, like the Koran . . . they were religious disasters. When the great expansion of knowledge came in our chapter of history it all took place outside the field of religious belief . . . the religions couldn't admit the new knowledge . . . their patterns of symbol were closed. They fought against opening them . . . they fought the new knowledge and tried to suppress it. They lost their unversality . . . they

231

were left with only a section of the human mind. . . . I've an idea that something like that is happening to poetry . . . the poets don't speak for their time any more, they speak the language of refined bystanders. They're educated out of the common run of new ideas, they speak to only a section of the educated world, a section devoted to old books and old familiar ideas . . . the only part of the new knowledge they touch is psychology—because the psychoanalyst's couch is cozy, and the relationship between the analyst and the patient is direct and personal . . . it lends itself to mystifications and personal aggrandizement . . . Coleridge is the first modern poet, with that fake German scholarship, and that portentous claim to a private revelation of universal importance . . . and then there's his ability to communicate, and then only partially, inside a tiny circle of friends . . . he's a sort of Ezra Pound born before his time . . . you don't want to get into anything like that. . . ."

"No." I felt my ears burning with hot anger. Max had no streak of poetry, of the artist in him. A silence spread between us over the polished table. How could I talk to someone so remote, about what I truly wanted to do? Max took a grape from the silver fruit-basket in front of him and cut it free from the bunch with a pair of fruit scissors with mother-of-pearl handles. When he had popped it into his mouth and eaten it, he looked at me again.

" 'Find in the middle air, an eagle on the wing, recognize the five that make the muses sing. . . .' It isn't as easy as it was. . . ." he said.

"I didn't know that you . . ." I said, startled to recognize the lines from Yeats.

"It's always a surprise to find what people are carrying round in their heads. . . . I'm not against poetry, you know. It's just that I want you to take it seriously . . . not just yourself, that's not enough. But the thing itself . . ." He broke off, and made the familiar hurdy-gurdy movement with

232

his hand. "It can't be a safe little corner where you crawl away to play with your own feelings. It's got to be the big thing, or it won't be worth a damn. I've nearly managed to say the big thing I had to say . . . but I don't know how many people have heard it. It's very grim when you get to my age and you still don't know that . . . even if they do give you banquets."

The maid came in to clear the coffee things and the fruit plates away. Max's mood changed.

"I haven't been to a circus for years. I saw the posters the other day, and I got some tickets for tonight. Alice is coming along—it's time you met her properly. What do you say?"

He had become once again the friendly uncle arranging an outing for a child he didn't know very well.

We had a ringside box, and we had a very pleasant evening. Somebody to do with the circus recognized Max and tipped off the leading clown of that year, a tramp romeo who made a specialty of pleasing the cheap seats by paying embarrassing visits to boxholders. As he bore down on us I suffered a moment of the panic that had sometimes come upon me in the old days when I was out with Max and Lolotte, but this was Alice, and she handled the thing beautifully. When the clown after staring at her in a moonstruck fashion for some time suddenly opened his vest and released a large bright red heart on the end of a spring she blew him kisses with both hands. Everybody seemed to love it and laughed without malice. When he came to the edge of the box and went into his tramp romeo routine with his erectile heart quivering in front of him she played up to him with cool good humor, and without any trace of embarrassment. While she was writing I love you on the heart with a white crayon he had given her, a flash lamp went off, and we discovered that a photographer had crept up on us. We all turned towards him, still smiling, Alice with one hand on the clown's shoulder and the other on his huge paper heart. The flash went off a second time in our faces.

"Damn," said Max furiously. "Oh . . ."

"Don't worry, my pet," said Alice, "you never see that kind of picture again, ever. I've had them do it to me hundreds of times in nightclubs and places, and nobody ever prints them."

The rout of clowns flowed out of the ring, taking the tramp romeo with them, and the spotlights lifted onto the Wallendas, brightly white on their silver trapezes up near the roof, and as they swung into their act we forgot the whole episode.

While I was having breakfast the next morning the pretty little maid brought in the *Daily Sketch*, a paper which, taken for the kitchen, didn't usually appear above stairs.

"I thought you might like to see the paper," she said. "There's ever such a nice photo of you and Mrs. Carver and Mr. Town at the circus, on the center page."

There we were, next to the new leopard cubs at the zoo, and alongside a ship aground on the Goodwin Sands, Max, Alice, myself and the clown. We all had happy faces, and Alice, leaning forward to write on the heart, looked very attractive in a healthy animal way. There is a warm glow about a sexually contented woman which is liable to come out very powerfully in a photograph. It hit me in the face as I looked at Alice's picture. It was something to do with the set of her shoulders, of her head on her neck, with an all-over physical ease.

"It's very nice, Rose," I said, "but I think you'd better put it away before Mr. Town sees it."

"It's ever so like. I'd think he'd be pleased."

"He'd like it, if only it wasn't in the paper."

"It's funny, him being so important, and not liking to be in the paper . . . and it's a sweet picture of Mrs. Carver, too."

I took a last look at Alice and folded the paper.

"Thank you very much for letting me see it, Rose, but I think you'd better get it out of sight before Mr. Town comes down," I said.

I thought it could be disposed of and forgotten as easily as that. I didn't realize that the photograph was being distributed by an agency that had subscribers in every country where Max's name was known, and I'd forgotten that he belonged to a press cutting agency. The whole thing slipped out of my mind as soon as Rose had closed the dining room door behind her.

I saw a good deal of Alice in the next couple of weeks. She would arrive at tea time and we would talk until Max came down from his study. She was honest, witty, and kind, and I grew fond of her very quickly. She was very much in love with Max, and it was pleasant to see the way she lit up with happiness when he was with her. He was as happy with her, and I benefitted by the overflow of good humor which she generated in him. Our teas were very good fun, and quite made up for the fact that I became an extra man round about six or seven. I would leave them then, and go out to have dinner with a school friend or with Fred at the club, and leaving a happy house made these evenings all the more enjoyable. When I found myself alone I would eat early at an oyster bar at the Café Royal and go to a theatre. The intoxication that came over me as I sat watching the seats fill up, the house lights going down, the footlights coming up, and the curtain rising, was better than any company. And in the mornings there were sheets of paper to be covered with more and more of my first seriously written play.

All in all I had a very good time until Amabel sought me out on one of her days. She came over from Fred's house in Belsize Park a couple of times a week in her capacity as housekeeper for Max, and, as she put it, to keep his secretary Miss Household up to the mark. I generally managed to avoid her, but this time she came into my room and stood confronting me like Eugene Aram's conscience.

"I wonder how much longer you mean to stay, Richard," she said.

"I thought the plan was for me to stay on until after Max's birthday banquet, until the beginning of next month."

"Don't you think it might be wiser to cut your visit short?"

"Have I upset Max, or anything?"

Amabel tugged downwards at the hem of her tailor-made jacket, a curiously prudish gesture.

"No, it isn't that at all. I'd have thought you would have been well aware how ambiguous your position was—particularly now that Max is a little more in the public eye than usual."

"I don't think I understand."

"People talk, you know. I thought Max was very short-sighted, asking you to stay in the first place. And then when Mrs. Carver started coming here in and out of season, well, I've heard some very unpleasant things said . . . about that photograph that was in the papers the other day. I hope your mother didn't see it. I can't think what she can have felt if she did. . . ." She wrinkled up her face with an expression of disgust . . . "You're really old enough to realize that you shouldn't be seen about with your father and Mrs. Carver."

"I'm rather proud of Max, and I like Mrs. Carver. She's a very nice woman. What's wrong with being seen with her?"

"I'm rather disappointed in you, Richard."

"Go on, Amabel." I had a queer feeling that my blood had turned black in my veins and was scalding, I was in a killing fury for the first time in my life. "Go on, tell me what's wrong with my being seen with my father and Mrs. Carver."

"If you don't know I can't possibly tell you." She cast down her eyes and smiled. "Your ill temper rather gives you away."

"That wriggles out of it nicely."

"If you can't discuss the matter reasonably perhaps we'd better not talk about it at all. When you're a little older, and you've had more experience of normal life, you'll understand why I think you'd best go home. I'm only advising you in your own interest."

She left me, poisoned with berserk rage. I did no more work that morning and I was still angry when Alice came in at tea time.

"You're looking terrible cross today, Richard?"

"I had a spat with Amabel."

"Tell."

"There isn't anything, really, to tell. She just made me mad with that Scotch self-righteousness of hers. She's horrible."

"She's very proper. I expect it's a great strain for her, putting up with Max and his bad ways. You have to make allowances—people get panicky out of their depth."

Rose brought in the tea tray. I looked under the covered dish to see if we had toasted tea cake or muffins, and Alice picked up the *Evening Standard* to see what the Low cartoon was.

"There was a letter for you in the afternoon post, Master Richard," said Rose.

I took it from her and recognized Naomi's handwriting, sprawling swiftly towards the edges of the envelope. When I opened it I saw the photograph from the *Daily Sketch* cut neatly from the page.

"Dear Dickie,

I don't know what idiocy of Max's let you in for this but I can't help feeling that you're almost old enough to know better. I suppose I should have warned you that Alice Carver was hanging round Max, and I should have told you what a dangerous woman she is. Before she married poor Henning Carver—an angel of patience poor lamb—for his money— her father ruined himself by speculating—she was in a horrible scandal with Basil Twyning—the son not the father—he left his wife for her three months before their second son was born. It was the cruelest shock for the poor girl, and a dreadful humiliation. When she'd got Basil to leave his wife she pretended she didn't want to have anything to do with him

and ran away abroad and Twyning killed himself. Alice left
Henning after they'd been married eight years—she just ran
out on him when he was ill and left him alone in his house
with no one to look after him but the servants—he nearly died.
Poor Henning spent years trying to pay off the bills she'd run
up. She was with some Greek for a year or two after that. It's
just like Max to be taken in by a little harpy like Alice, and it
doesn't surprise me in the least that she's wormed her way
into his life. I really worry sometimes at the extraordinary
mental deterioration that has overtaken him since that horrible Lolotte got hold of him. He's not the old Max at all, and
I'm afraid for his mind. But what is too bad of him is to drag
you about in public with a woman like that and I do warn you
to be more careful. You're particularly vulnerable, and you've
got to keep yourself free of any suggestion of louche behavior. Things that other people can do, you just can't. I know
you won't be able to understand what harm a photograph
like this can do, but it's these silly things that stick in people's
minds and make the sort of reputation you have. Jack saw the
picture, and although he didn't say anything I think it hurt
him terribly to see you exposing yourself to that kind of
thing. I do hope it will make you realize how utterly reckless
Max is, and I do beg you not to let him talk you into sharing
these shoddy little episodes that seem to be playing a larger
and larger part in his strange life. Humor him as much as you
can, but when it comes to going to public places with that
dreadful woman or anyone like her just wriggle out of it somehow or other. I should have put you on your guard, and I can
kick myself for not doing so before this dreadful picture found
its way into the papers, but I know how you feel about Max
and I didn't want to spoil your illusions because they seemed
to mean so much to you. But you're almost a man now and I
must speak out before you get involved in some sordid scandal
as I was. . . ."

I rolled the paper into a ball and threw it into the fire. It half uncurled as it burned, and for a moment it looked like a malevolent little face leering at me from the flames. I took the poker and knocked it into pieces.

"Something horrid?"

"Beastly, I don't know why people want to make so much beastliness. . . ."

"Oh, lovey, not everybody does. You just don't have to let the ones that do bother you, they don't matter, not really."

"But they get under your skin so frightfully."

"They can't unless you let them. You don't have to let them. You just have to find out what you really want to do and do it. If you worry about people approving of what you do they can get at you all the time."

"You don't mind what people say about you?" I looked at her sitting so calmly opposite me, wondering if she would be as placid if she had known what was in Naomi's letter. "No matter what they say?"

"But lovey, if what they say isn't true it can't matter—and if it is true, well you've done it, and you have to live with it even if they don't talk about it. There's no getting round what you've done, you know." She looked at me with absolutely clear eyes. "We all do pretty frightful things sooner or later, even if we don't mean to . . . and sometimes things look awful that really aren't." Her eyes dropped and she studied the paper. "They say this new play at the Court is very good, have you seen it yet?"

"Not yet, I thought of going tonight."

"Isn't it terrible dull for you, going to plays and movies alone so much? You ought to have a girl."

"I'm not lonely."

"That's not what I meant, really. I mean you ought to be starting to make some life for yourself that hasn't anything to do with Max or Naomi." She folded the paper. "You mustn't stick around getting hurt and ingrown."

"Maeve said that. Amabel was trying to get me to go away this morning. Why does everyone want to drive me away from Max? . . ."

"Because he's careless, and cruel without meaning to be, and he hurts everyone sooner or later, and because it's time you found something solid for yourself somewhere else."

"I've heard all that, before, thank you."

I picked up the paper she had put down and began to read it, trying to prevent my hands from trembling with anger. I knew she was sitting watching me, and with undiminished friendliness. But her warmth had for the moment the aspect of treachery. I couldn't bear to accept her good will. When she spoke again I pretended not to be listening.

"Your father's a Victorian. He's out of another time. He learned everything he knows in another world. It's all irrelevant to yours. You've got to learn something quite different."

I thought I saw an opening, and a chance to hurt her.

"I don't see, then, why you bother."

"Oh, Richard, I'm a woman. I'm twice your age, perhaps a year or two more than that. And it's a fair exchange. I get something from him, and he gets something from me. I don't beg him to give me something readymade just in return for being his woman . . . you expect an awful lot just for being his son. And he doesn't know what you want—he can't know, because, poor pet, he knows all about things and nothing about people—that's why he goes from one woman to another. It isn't in him to be any more use to you."

"I don't believe you. He understands more about . . . oh, everything, than anyone else I've ever known. He . . ."

"But you can't, or at least you don't, ever tell him anything that's really important . . . like about being in love."

"Suppose I'm not in love . . ."

"Oh, my poor baby, it's with you night and day. I can't look at you without wishing I could do something for you that would make it all right. You're having a horrid time."

"What do you know about it? How do you know?"

"Max told me about Ermine, when we were talking about you one time. I'd said how odd you hadn't a girl friend when you were so warm and emotional. He said I had you all wrong, and that you weren't ready for that sort of thing. He told me about Lolotte's plot to get you into bed with Ermine, and how you hadn't the least idea what was going on. He told me about it as if it was funny, and how he'd managed to prevent you from being seduced. I knew at once that that was it. . . ."

I told her all about Ermine, with my heart lifting as each word of it came out.

"There you are. That's the important thing. And you've never been able to say a word to him about it. You won't be able to now, or ever. It's your thing. He doesn't come into it. You're on your own. That's how it ought to be. You're all wrong to think he ought to come into it."

"I suppose I am."

She studied my face.

"Do you still love her, very much, in spite of her off putting letters?"

"I don't believe the letters . . . she's something else. I know. . . ."

"Poor Richard, I hope you see her again soon."

"I've got to."

Alice smiled and turned to look into the firelight.

"Perhaps you will." She reached out and touched the fluted silver Georgian teapot. "The tea's nearly cold. Ring for Rose so that she can make some fresh before Max comes down."

"I don't think I'll wait any longer. I feel like a walk." I went over and pressed the bell. "You've given me a lot to think about."

"Promise not to be cross with Max. You mustn't blame him for being locked up in his things—it's not his fault. It's just the way he is. . . ."

241

I walked downtown, beyond Piccadilly, into Carlton House Terrace, past the German Embassy, and then back into the brightly lit domain of the theatres and the movie houses. Nothing attracted me until I came to a little theatre where a girlie revue was in the tenth month of its run. I went in and spent an hour looking at thighs and breasts and navels. It was vulgar, cheerful, and amusing but I left the show before the final curtain and walked home to lie awake for a long time wondering where Ermine was and what she was doing.

A few days later the house was all bustle as Amabel and Miss Household fussed and telephoned, approving and revising the arrangements made by the organizers of Max's birthday banquet. Max was busy in his study hammering out an article commissioned by one of the daily papers, to be called "Sixty Years of Triumph—or Disaster?" The atmosphere was unfavorable for writing my kind of play, and after listening to the hurrying footsteps and the shrilling telephone for a time I left my in any case rather uninspiring bedroom writing desk and took a long bus ride over to Dulwich to look at the Rembrandts that I had heard about but never seen. When I came back it was late afternoon and the light was going, fading into a greenish dusk. It was colder than when I set out, and as I got off the bus the conductor said that it looked like snow to him.

I turned out of the main road into our street snuggling down inside my coat collar and almost ran into Rose. She came towards me, running with the awkwardness of an unathletic girl, swinging her feet out sideways, and she stopped at the corner, looking up and down. Her cheeks were flushed and a lock of her brown hair hung down over one eyebrow.

"Whatever is the matter, Rose? . . ."

"Oh Master Richard, sir, we must find a policeman. . . ."

"A policeman?"

"Oh yes, sir, please . . . there's a foreign lady at the house

—carrying on something awful . . . you wouldn't credit the things she's been shouting at Mr. Town and Mrs. Amabel . . . I was frightened someone would get hurt, and I slipped out for the police. . . ." Some of the confusion left Rose's face, and was replaced by a grin. "She's got Mrs. Amabel locked in the little closet under the hall stairs."

Lolotte! I thought.

"We'd better keep the police out of it, Rose, at any rate until everything else fails."

When we got to the house the front door was standing wide open and two small boys were standing at the foot of the steps peering into the hallway with wide eyes and open mouths. I heard a muffled drumming which I took to be Amabel beating on the closet door, and I heard the unforgettable voice of Lolotte, more highly pitched than I had ever heard it before, and rather louder. I distinguished the phrase "randy old lecher. . . ." I encouraged the little boys to be on their way and to think about something else by banging their heads together briskly, and hustled Rose into the house.

"You'd better go down to the kitchen, and wait," I said. "I'll see what I can do."

I stood in the empty hallway listening to the pounding on the closet door and wondered what on earth was the best way to handle the situation. I thought that Amabel would be very little help in calming Lolotte down, so she would be better where she was for the time being. She could be smuggled out of the house later. My eyes fell on Lolotte's handbag, lying on the chest where I had once seen Alice's coat sprawled in glossy splendor. It had been flung down, too, and it had spilled out a variety of passports, lipstick holders, key rings, and small wallets. Among the ruck I saw a piece of paper torn from the *Paris-Soir.* . . . I turned it over and saw myself, Max, Alice, and the clown, and read the caption: "Who will win the heart of the charming lady, the clown or the savant? An alert photographer seized this delightful moment at the Olympia

Circus in London in which the great English man of letters Max Town and his épatant companion good-humoredly played their sufficiently embarrassing parts." So that had brought Lolotte down upon us.

I looked up, and saw Lolotte glaring at me from the upper landing with eyes luminous with fury. Her appearance was more shocking to me than her state of wild anger. She was terribly thin, and she had aged. Her neck, which I remembered as a smooth column, was now an affair of tense sinews. Her hands gripped the baluster rail like talons. She raised one hand, and pointed at me with arm and index finger fully extended.

"Ah, there he is, the bastard! The little jackal sniffing round the trail of the old beast his father. . . ."

She folded her arms and nodded her head, drawing herself up to her full height and inhaling deeply, filling her lungs for a further outburst of denunciation. When it came it was a good two minutes' worth of polemic about treachery and betrayal. I recognized in the middle of it a sequence of phrases of a distinctly Racine-ish flavor. Had she been speaking in French she would probably have fallen into Alexandrines. It struck me when my first tendency to cower in panic had passed that she was having a thoroughly enjoyable time and giving a bravura performance modeled fairly closely on some French actress's interpretation of a melodramatic role. When she paused to take new breath I clapped with enthusiasm, and cried, *bis, bis,* with genuine admiration. Lolotte looked startled for one second, and then profoundly shocked.

"Richard, you ill-mannered brute, you are making fun of me."

"Of course I am. You're being magnificent, but you're overdoing it."

"How dare you say that? This is tragic for me. I love that old tomcat your father, and now he is discarding me. I am a woman of a certain age—I am tired, worn out, my time to

244

charm and appeal is over. I am used up by submitting to his whims and his wickedness, and now he is tossing me aside, like all his other women. I have refused other relationships for his sake, marriage offers, he is all I have. Well, I am not one to be lied to and abandoned. I have pride. . . ." Her voice began to rise in volume as she inflated her chest. "I have self respect. I am *hochwohlegeborn,* I am not a woman of the people. I am no plaything. He cannot. . . ."

"Look, Lolotte, come down to my level, or I'll come up to yours. Then you can tell me what it's all about. But don't shout at me, and don't try to make your voice carry to the back of the gallery."

"You dare to try to bully me, you wretched waif?"

"Somebody has to. Come off it now, do, you've made your big scene, and I'm getting a crick in the neck talking to you up the stairs."

Lolotte glared at me for a full second, and then walked down the curved stair. We went into the drawing room together and I fetched her a glass of brandy. She drank a little of it and looked round her with a wondering expression.

"And all this beige, and bourgeois coziness . . . is this the taste of the new woman?"

"What new woman?" I lit a cigarette as casually as I could. "The house was decorated by his daughter-in-law, John's wife, as a matter of fact."

"Richard, you are being tricky. You were in this picture at the circus that has driven me frantic, you too, your father like a smug booby grinning, and you grinning, and this sleek sexual football of a creature with the pretty arms. You know this woman, don't pretend to me that you don't. I know, and my instinct tells me what she is. I looked at this picture, and I knew at once. The old fox, the old billygoat, this woman is at the bottom of it—this is why he told me he must come to England, to get in touch with the English public again, to gather material for new articles, to see his sons, to have medical

treatment, to receive testimonials on his seventieth birthday
. . . it is all rubbish, it is all a new woman. . . ."

"You've got it all wrong, Lolotte. This house is the setting
for a polite family comedy called Max's boys, or something of
the kind. He came back to England to do all the things he told
you, but mainly to bring his sons together. He suddenly felt
guilty about our not being a united family, and he bought this
place to give us a rallying point. Partly for that, partly to be
a façade for this birthday affair. He's been around as a writer
for nearly forty years, and now he's graduating as a Grand
Old Man of English letters. It's nothing to do with any
woman."

"No? Then this *poule* in the photograph, this creature dripping with sex, what explanation of her do you give me?"

"Oh, Alice, Alice Carver is a friend of mine. Max was taking us out. That's all."

"Your mistress, *hein?*"

"Er, yes, my mistress."

Lolotte threw her head back and laughed.

"Oh, Richard, forgive me. You tried that hard, but you're
a hopeless liar. You blush . . . to the tips of your ears. . . ."
She deepened her voice to imitate mine. " 'Errr Yerse, my
mistress.' Besides it only makes the picture uglier if you think
of it. First the poor little boy trailing round with his father's
mistresses, then the father trailing round with the son and his
mistresses. . . . You should have had more self respect. . . .
It wasn't a good lie."

"No, I suppose it wasn't."

"Tell me the truth." She swallowed some more brandy.
"You owe it me. We're old friends."

"I'm not sure that I can. I'm not sure that I know it." I
groped in my mind for obscure suspicions that I hadn't altogether faced, and found them taking shape in my mouth as
words. "Max did come here with some idea of uniting his
family, with putting together the pieces that lay scattered

about. I suppose he thought they'd be lying where he left them when he walked out. Then he found the pieces of the family had changed. We've all become used to being fragments, we've fitted ourselves into other patterns. We've got our own lives, we aren't just notions in his head. He's interested in his notions, and not in us. At Christmas time when he got us all into a room together he saw it. We aren't as interesting or as pliable as his notions were, we bored him. When he saw what we were like he dropped us, and called the comedy off. The woman you saw in the picture was there, and he took up with her to fill in the blank. That's the truth . . . it's what he does to everybody, all the time."

"And you don't mind?"

"No. He's Max. How can one mind?"

"You've grown up, Richard, it amazes me how you've grown up. And I've grown old."

Lolotte finished her glass of brandy, and fingered the empty glass.

"I'll get the bottle."

As I went through the hall I heard Amabel beating on the door of the closet, and I turned aside to set her free.

"You must have heard me before." She stepped angrily out from among the brooms and the tins of floor polish.

"I did. But I couldn't let you out till she'd calmed down."

"It's an outrage. I've never been treated so vilely, or spoken to in such a fashion. I'd like to give her a piece of my mind."

"I shouldn't, Amabel," I said. "It'll only lead to more trouble and unpleasantness." I put my hand on her shoulder. "Why don't you . . ."

"Take your hands off me." Her eyes were blazing with anger and filled with tears. "You're all birds of a feather. Poor Max . . . you've all battened on his weaknesses. You're all hateful, and shameless, and he's far, far, too good for you."

"You too? . . ." I was amazed.

247

"Oh," she said, "oh . . ." and slapped my face as hard as she could. We faced each other, aghast at the moment of revelation, until she went blindly past me and began fumbling for a coat in the little room alongside the front door.

"I'm going to fetch a policeman. I'm going to charge that woman with common assault. I'll make her sorry she ever came here. . . ." She was sobbing as she pulled on her shapeless nanny's overcoat.

"I shouldn't do that."

"Somebody's got to teach her she can't just trample all over decent people. I've got some backbone, if no one else has."

"But think how it will look in the papers . . . much worse than the circus photograph . . . and the birthday banquet's only a week off. You can't do it."

"She'll do Max an injury."

"Oh, I don't think so . . . they've been through this sort of thing before. . . . You'd best just go off home and forget about it."

"I can't bear to leave poor Max in the hands of such dreadful people. . . ."

I shrugged my shoulders and went and got Lolotte her bottle of brandy. When I came through the hall again Amabel had gone.

"That woman you let out of the closet," Lolotte said, "who is she? She is a most uncouth, rude person for Max to have about him, even as a secretary. She makes a very bad impression."

"That was Fred's wife. I don't think you were very tactful with her."

"She ordered me out of the house. She was very ill bred. It is incredible that Max should have let one of his sons marry such a woman. What can he have been thinking of? He is so careless about his children's future. You mustn't allow yourself to drift into marriage with such a nonentity—with the kind of girl one can push into a closet—it's ignoble to be married to an inferior."

"She's not the kind of woman I'm thinking of, no."

Lolotte took a sip of brandy and rolled it round her mouth before swallowing it, looking at me thoughtfully.

"So you're thinking of marriage, at your age? Perhaps you need Ermine again to teach you not to be English and heavy and serious. She came to England with me . . . you'll find her at Murray's Hotel, she's waiting to hear from me. Perhaps you'd be a nice surprise for her, who knows?"

I got to my feet.

"Promise you won't start shouting at Max again . . . it didn't do any harm in France, they understand scenes—but they aren't understood in St. John's Wood . . . you are going to be good, aren't you? . . ."

"I'll give him a little torment, for hurting me. But I won't shock any more people, tonight anyway, now I've got Max to myself."

"Well, I'll run along and see if I can find Ermine."

When I came out into the hall Max was leaning over the stair rail peering downwards and listening to the restored silence of the house.

"Where is she? . . ." he whispered. "Have you talked to her?"

"Yes. She's in the drawing room, in a pretty reasonable frame of mind."

Max came to the foot of the stairs and put his hand on my shoulder.

"Yes?"

"Oh, nothing. There's nothing to say, is there?" He gave a twisted smile. "I'm sorry about all this . . . well, it can't be helped. Lolotte is Lolotte. . . ."

"What about Alice? Should I try to warn her or anything? . . ."

"I spoke to her on the upstairs telephone. . . ." He mopped his forehead with his handkerchief. "That's all right for the time being. . . ."

"I'll be getting along. I'll be in late, I expect . . . so good night, Father."

"I think that's best . . . good night, Old Son."

I stood and watched him walking warily up to the drawing room door and going in with his head cocked a little on one side, and after I had listened to the murmur of voices for a minute I went off to find Ermine.

6

When I came out of my father's house and the heavy front
door shut behind me, the open air, washed clean by a shower
that had fallen a little while before, smelt fresh and cool. I
sucked in a few breaths and realized that it was just the anti-
dote I needed. I had intended to jump into a taxi, the first that
came along, and to go as fast as I could to Ermine, or to her
hotel. But I saw now that it would be a mistake to go to her
fresh from Max's turmoil. A walk would clear my head, and
give my heart time to stop racing. So I set out on foot.

Murray's Hotel stands on the corner of Iwerne and Porte-
sham streets at a point halfway between Piccadilly and Oxford
Street on the northern frontiers of Mayfair and quite a considerable way from St. John's Wood. I had plenty of time to
think as I walked down past Lord's Cricket Ground and
through down-at-heels Paddington towards Ermine. It was
very hard to imagine her at Murray's. The place had been
"smart" in the eighties—South African millionaires and
American bachelors with good social connections had often
stayed there for the season when embarking on penetrations

of London society. It had gone down very quickly after that, and an Edwardian redecoration had failed to make it come back. It had become a headquarters in town for retired people from places like Cheltenham and Bournemouth who had come up for the Chelsea Flower Show, or who were seeing a medical specialist or their lawyers. When they got back to their provincial retreats they recommended Murray's to their friends, because the rates were so very reasonable, and it was so pleasantly quiet. I tried to think of Ermine among the drifts of gray ladies, and gray gentlemen, military and clerical, who incessantly whispered or wrote letters in the public rooms among the potted palms, the spidery tables, and the Louis Seize chairs, and I squirmed at the thought. I dawdled. It was going to be hell meeting Ermine in London, her place was in the South of France, in my dreams. Passing through Dorset Square I realized an awful thing, Ermine was a dodge, a refined way of thinking about sex. I wasn't in love with her at all, and never had been. But I had pretended to be in love with her and I had written love letters to her. And she had come to England trusting in my word, she would certainly be expecting me to marry her. I would have to go through with it, unless I was going to behave frightfully badly. Men didn't, after telling them they loved them, let women down.

As I walked on I followed this gloomy line of thought to various ends, making a loveless marriage and never, until she died, a radiantly happy silver-haired old lady, letting Ermine even suspect the truth in one rapid fantasy and in another going out to British East Africa with a shadow on my name: "That's Savage, been out here twenty-five years—he's never been home on leave—they say he can't . . . some scandal about a woman." Then it occurred to me that Ermine, if I didn't marry her, might commit suicide. This would make me grim and a little bitter, tragedy would lend me a romantic aura that would fascinate women, they would come to me, with their lips slightly parted, eager to be wronged. I had read somewhere that Byron's success was of that nature. There would be a coroner's inquest; searching questions would be put to me and I would answer them with cool insolence. "I believe she was fond of me, I really don't know." My evidence would be reported in full in the evening papers, and there would be photographs. Naomi would be desperate, I would read her frantic letters to some beautiful girl who would laugh nervously. I would look into her eyes and see that she was a little afraid of me, but powerless to resist. I snapped out of it with difficulty and came to earth feeling so notorious that I should be attracting hostile or envious attention, from the passersby, and saw the gray monotony of Gloucester Place stretching away before me. It was not empty, there was a little light traffic, and the usual scatter of walkers, some of whom were turning their heads briefly to give Sergeant-Major Rumbold a second look.

I had seen the Sergeant once or twice before, in the Strand from the top of a bus, at Hyde Park among the crowds, but I had never come face to face with him. He marched towards me at a steady, even, regimental parade step slowly twirling his white oilcloth umbrella. Written round it were the words A FLAGRANT INJUSTICE, A CRYING SHAME. The lettering was neat, and he twirled it slowly so that his message could be read as he walked along. His suit was made of white oilcloth too and the front and back of the jacket were covered with more neatly lettered inscriptions: *Sergeant-Major Rumbold victim of a war office clique! Parliamentary Enquiry demanded* AND REFUSED! *What Price* MAGNA CHARTA. *An Innocent Man* WRONGED. *My fight for* JUSTICE *has lasted* A LIFETIME. I was transfixed by this sudden encounter with one of the old familar sights of the London streets and stood staring at him. He drew level with me and stopped. For a moment I was afraid I was going to hear his tale of grievance, but he quietly took a cigarette from a packet of Woodbines and in a gentle voice that went surprisingly with his burliness and his scarlet punchinello face he asked me for a light. "Oh, certainly," I said. "Perhaps you'd care for a weed, sir?" "No, thank you," I said. "You'd be surprised how good the tobacco is," he went on gently, "quite as good as some of the more expensive brands made by the same company. The thing is that they're a *smaller* cigarette." He gave me a searching look and blew the smoke from his first puff out through his nostrils. "But for the iniquity of these nonconformist-inspired licensing laws I would ask you to join me in a beer round the corner, to repay the hospitality of your match," he said, "but I'm afraid they're not open just now. Some other time, perhaps." "That would be very pleasant." His tranquil air of detachment made me curious. "What did they do to you?" I said. A rather puzzled look came over his face. "It was a great many years ago," he said, "I find it difficult to remember. I have pamphlets which explain the whole question, I used to sell them for a penny, but I have been out of copies for some time, I really don't remember all the details. There was some misunderstanding about regimental funds. They said dreadful things at the time. They used the word embezzlement. But most of it is beyond me now." I hesitated for a moment, but he seemed so calm and his manner was so quiet that there seemed no harm in asking the question: "In that case why do you bother with all this?" He drew himself up. "As an educated man you should understand that, sir, it's a matter of principle. I must fight on to the end." He paused. "I must be getting along now, sir, if you'll excuse me. This has been a most enjoyable little break." His umbrella began to twirl slowly and he stepped out smartly again at his measured pace.

I stood watching him for a moment or two and then caught the eye of an elderly woman standing on a nearby doorstep. "Poor old chap," she said, "still I daresay he's happier than most, if the truth be told." "I daresay he is," I said. We smiled at each other, and she went in at the door and I hailed a taxi and told the driver to take me to Murray's, to Ermine.

I waited for her in the palm lounge, sitting stiffly on a brocaded unsociable in the middle of the room, behind me a gray-haired lady knitted while her companion read out the names of the movies playing at the local theatres, and of the actors playing in them. They discussed the movies, and the casts. "Oh, I like her, ever so much, she has such a sweet face." "But I think we've seen that movie, dear." "Oh, I don't think so, no, I'm sure you're mistaken. At least I've never seen it." "But dear, you must remember. It's the one where she was the daughter of that unfortunate Colonel and she was going to have to marry the unsuitable man, and there was this nice young man she'd known since she was a little girl." "You mean on the ranch in California?" "I fancy it was in Virginia, the Old South, you know, the Colonel had those sideburns." "I believe I begin to remember. . . ." The conversation addled on until I suddenly looked up feeling stared at and there was Ermine. She was wearing a Garboish hat that framed her entirely unmade-up face, and her hands were jammed mannishly into the pockets of a coat of extremely Berlin cut, with excessively padded shoulders. Her expression was severe, a little scornful and a little apprehensive. I saw that she had changed. The glow of youth had left her and without it I could see that she was not pretty; for a second, because she was wearing no make-up, I thought that my first impression in the South of France had proved right and that she was on the edge of being plain. I stood up with a social smile as she said, "So there you are— I expected to find you in the lobby."

"It's good to see you."

It was clear that I was not to kiss her, and we shook hands. We walked in silence, and in a curious agony of awkwardness, out of the palm lounge and into the lobby.

"What brings you to London?"

"Lolotte."

"You didn't want to come."

"No, Lolotte insisted." She looked about her with distaste. "I told her it would be no good."

"That sounds odd."

"It is, rather. Lolotte and I aren't getting on any more. We've been quarreling all year. I gave way to her in this out of loyalty to our old friendship. But it's the parting of the ways—definitely."

"What have you been fighting about?"

"Oh, all sorts of things—my engagement, and fundamentals. How one should live, how one should not live." She looked about her. "Isn't there some café we could go to . . . we can't talk in this morgue."

"I don't know . . . there aren't any cafés . . . not in London, there are pubs, and tea shops, but not what you have in mind."

"Well then we'll just have to walk, I suppose."

We went out through the slowly spinning door onto the street.

"It's all so mournful and drab," she said, "the atmosphere is so dead. I have the impression that England is rotten, finished. Lolotte told me I had to come to think things out in a healthier atmosphere. She's a tragic figure, in a way, she represents something pathetic Germany has outgrown. I am for the New Germany."

We walked on for a few paces.

"You've changed a good deal," I said, "you sound much more serious."

"I'm glad you can see that. My whole life has changed. I was futile and disgraceful but now I live a sane life. I've grown up. A great many of us in Germany have discovered sanity, my whole generation has grown up. A wonderful new life is beginning."

"What's happened, Ermine, have you got religion or something?"

"No, I haven't—well, it's not religion. It's a matter of faith, in myself, in my country." She pulled off her hat and shook out her hair, dazzling in its cleanness and vitality. "It's a matter of having a purpose in life. I am engaged to a wonderful man and we have a glorious life planned together, not just for ourselves but for our country and our children's happiness. Lolotte can't see it. She has these old bohemian ideas of personal happiness. We argue in circles. She said I had to come here to see—something, I don't know what . . . there's a marvelous togetherness in Germany now, we're all going towards the same goal together as comrades, setting our petty little selves on one side. It's marvelous. I'm not lost any more. Here I see nothing but lost people, and an empty life. I shan't come back. Lolotte hoped I'd stay."

"Do you mean you're going in for all that Hitler stuff?"

"He is a very great man, until you have heard the Leader you don't know what greatness there is in the human heart waiting to be called forth."

"I don't believe it's any good, you know."

"I don't suppose you would."

"This chap you're going to marry, is he a nice chap?"

"He is a young officer, a fine young man."

"Then you're falling in with the destiny you told me about once."

"No, it's not like that any more. It's nothing automatic and dead. He will be one of the makers of a new Germany and a new world, and I will give him support with my love and help create the new order by giving him strong and beautiful children. We will bury and forget the horrible past."

Her words had, along with their brisk certainty, a curious effect of disengagement from the figure walking along beside me. I watched her as she spoke, with sidelong glances, and realized that she was far from plain. I had looked at her first expecting to see the pretty, sexy girl who had given herself to me so freely, and seeing that she had changed had assumed that she had changed for the worse. But I saw now that she had grown away from me, from that kind of irrelevant contact, and that there was in her face something larger than there had been. She had grown up and she was, simply, beautiful. She was speaking these empty phrases from no great depth in her mind, they had as little to do with her as I had. The realization was wounding and I tried to assert myself.

"The horrible past of which I am part? I don't remember anything degraded or low."

"No . . ." her voice changed slightly, "I don't mean that."

She let me take her hand, and we walked on with linked fingers.

"Was it a help?" she said gently.

"The greatest possible help."

"Even worth the pain of thinking you were in love with me for so long?"

"Yes—and in a way that's been a help, too."

"I'm glad." It was a very small smile, no more than a slight softening at the corner of her mouth, that signified the extent of her gladness; I was still irrelevant. "That shows as much as anything how far we've been forced apart," she went on, "you still inhabit Lolotte's world."

"What on earth do you mean?"

"She's old-fashioned—you are too—most English still are." She had rolled up her felt hat and tapped it on her thigh down near her knee with her free hand, as if it were a riding crop. She thought. "You see, you're still living in a personal world where a thing like that matters tremendously. Lolotte's like that. You're liberals, you believe that everything revolves round private happiness, you can still believe it."

"Don't you?"

She held my fingers tightly.

"Not any more. One can't—not there, anyway."

"What's different there? What can be different?"

She shook her head.

"Everything's different. It feels different, all the time, even the air we breath. Coming here makes me feel like a fish—as if I'd been taken out of my pool and laid down on the grass. You don't know how different."

"But what's changed . . . I don't mean about us—we've grown up. . . ."

She laughed.

". . . I don't mean altogether. I just mean we've grown on beyond that kind of playing with our bodies." I was a little angered with her laughter.

"I wasn't laughing at that," she frowned, "but that you should say that just shows how great the difference is."

"It's idiotic trying to talk like this," I said, "I've just thought of a place over by the park—it's a skating rink, actually in a sort of club—you have to be a member to get in —there's a café in a gallery upstairs where you can sit and watch. . . ."

We sat over a pot of tea in the gallery while the skaters swirled in their dreamlike swooping below us, endlessly circling the outer oval of the converted hotel ballroom. Every now and then two or three people would detach themselves from the procession to cut figures in the open central space. Ermine put an elbow on the table and cupped her chin in her hand, looking down over the parapet.

"I dreaded meeting you." She didn't turn towards me.

"I did too, or at least from the minute I knew you were in London. I thought I'd been longing for it."

"I thought you were going to be—you know—frantic for bed, and sentimental about it. You write terrible letters—forced—they didn't sound true. Well, that's putting it mildly. They were dishonest, really—they meant bed, bed, bed, and they said love, love, love. You mustn't ever write to anyone that way again."

"I don't believe I will."

"Lolotte thought—she had the greatest hopes—that you'd be passionate, irresistible, and that you'd break me down—so that I wouldn't go back."

"I thought you'd believed me, my letters I mean, and that you were going to deliver yourself like a due bill on my door-step."

"It's wonderful to find that we're friends. I haven't talked, really talked, to anyone for, oh, I don't know how long. . . ." Her eyes were following a girl in a red dress on the floor. "That one's going to fall . . . there . . . now. . . ." The girl wobbled, fell, and slid diagonally across the open space on her behind, her back stiff with protest against her humiliation, her face agonized. There was a little flurry while she was helped to her feet. Ermine turned her eyes on me.

"When I laughed on the street I was going to say something that I know—and now I'm here with you, in this atmosphere, although I still know it it's hard to put it into words. But there's no question for me of not going back, there's no question of my not marrying Wieland . . . it's not a question of what I want or don't want . . . my world isn't like that any more. We all talk like that—the way I was talking about the new life—because there doesn't seem to be any point holding out—it's not any use what one person does as a person—something else is in charge, a force—not him, although he rides it, and seems to be it—the Leader, I mean—but, it sounds silly, it's so different here—but history, something flowing, something stronger than any person, the shape of the time, I don't know what. I've settled for what seems the least bad thing my time has to offer, Wieland, babies, a place of refuge that doesn't mark me out as a fugitive—I can't explain."

"It doesn't offer happiness."

"No—well, not *no* altogether—I wish I were a word-spinner—but happiness isn't possible—what's coming isn't going to be a happy time, not for anyone."

"I'd almost rather you'd gone on talking to me about the new life."

"I know. But you've got to listen all the same . . . in my place, where I belong, it's not possible to go on pretending. Life isn't the sort of private adventure it's been for Lolotte, not any more. Not there."

"Then why on earth go back?"

"Because it's decided—history has decided—the force I was talking about. It's no use running—it will come after me . . . do you understand. . . ."

She had laid her hand down on the table cloth, reaching towards me, and I placed a hand on hers. We sat in silence for a minute in which I tried to look her in the face and failed.

There have been many occasions in my life since then when I have felt that time has gone by the hour only to find when I looked at the clock that the period covered has been no longer than ten or fifteen minutes, but out of them all I remember this one with Ermine most vividly. We said nothing and understood a great deal. I knew that she was appealing to me, to destroy her belief in what she had come to accept, to give her instead reasons to believe in an uncontaminated happiness. I wanted to be able to do that. But I had worked nothing out. All my life I had lived alone, inside a wall of my own desires, inside the ghetto of my own demands for happiness. I had never seen anyone else's actions, or interpreted their words, unless it was through the veil of their effect on me. Now I was being asked to give Ermine something and I was powerless to do it. Until that minute I had never thought of her as anything but a complement to my life supplied by fate. For the first time I really became aware of a need greater than my own, of the identity of another person. I had, it abruptly dawned on me, no experience of life at all beyond my own desire for it, and no conception of how to enter into a human relationship. When I talked I discussed my own necessities, I had never had a conversation in which gifts of understanding and recognitions had been exchanged.

"We are a sad pair, aren't we?" Ermine murmured. She slipped her hand from under mine, patted it, and then withdrew. She picked up her teaspoon and began to rearrange the tea leaves in her cup.

"Tell me about Wieland."

"Wieland? . . . Wieland has come to terms—it's an enviable thing to be able to do. He has given himself up as a person to the new army—it isn't just a matter of deciding on a career—he would say he was a professional soldier, a regular army man, and saying that answers—but it's more than that. He has *joined*." She gave the word a lingering emphasis. "It's like entering the priesthood, making a surrender of yourself to an organization with a purpose—in this case the purposes are political, social, I can't say what exactly—I know the slogans —I told you what they were when I was pretending to you that I'd come to terms . . ."

"You mean simply that he's a Hitlerite, a Nazi?"

"No . . . he actually despises Hitler as a vulgarian . . . it's hard to say. . . ." for a moment she seemed to concentrate on her tea leaves. "You could say he has simply surrendered to the force that has brought Hitler to the top as its agent. He conceives himself as wedded to another instrument of the same destiny . . . it's to be the German century, perhaps the beginning of a German period like that of the Roman Empire. . . . The destiny of the nation is Wieland's life; either it's taken him over, or he's given himself up to creating it. Everyone in his generation has . . . even the ones that seem to be fighting it, Wieland's cousin Albericht calls himself a Communist but when you ask him how a man of his class, with his background, can be a Communist he says that Germany, with its capacity for organization and its industrial skill, would take the lead in a Communist Europe in ten years—it's the only hope for a civilized Europe, he says. . . ." She paused, and then went on. "You see they all think all the time in terms of mass movements, social forces, the historical process—then they think of where they belong in the scheme of things. . . ."

"And you, can you swallow it all?"

"I am a German, I belong with my people. I can't do anything else."

"But you can come here, you can make a fresh start . . . leave all that behind."

"I can't leave it behind. You know, it's terrible, how completely German I am. Since I've been in London I haven't seen anything that doesn't make me feel impatient . . . all the narrow streets, the dinginess, the smallness. I think a dozen times a day that if we had won the war we wouldn't have made so little out of our victory. Every day I find myself thinking this isn't a great people, there's been a mistake, they have somehow stolen something from us . . . our destiny."

"So you're joining, too."

"Yes, I suppose so, simply because it's easier. . . ."

"You've changed enormously . . . horribly."

"That's not fair."

"It's the truth."

"No, it's not. It's you who have changed." She looked up and we faced each other. She went on.

"Lolotte wanted to change me. I behaved as she wanted me to, it was fun. But it didn't change me. I remained a girl of my class, my time, and my place. We've all had our sexual adventures and played at being free, now we're all settling down to be what we have to be. You've no right to be cross about it. Unless you've something better to offer."

"Now you're being unfair."

"It's not a question of fairness or unfairness, it's just the way things are."

The skaters were thinning out, and the waiter in his brass-buttoned white coat and scarlet trousers was hovering with our bill. The place was nearly empty. Everyone was going home to dinner. I paid, and we moved off. It was one of those shapeless evenings that are inflicted on the young who have no places of their own. We went to a cocktail bar and talked until dinner time, we moved on to a restaurant and ate, and from there to a club and danced, talking in circles at each place, always conscious of the attendant waiters, the people at other tables, the stir and movement round us. At the dance club we became a little tipsy, grew heated, and quarreled. The club had a low ceiling and its walls were covered with small squares of looking glass except for one large section where a painting by Matisse was hung. The ceiling height seemed to force the buzz of talk and the bumping music down into our laps and the squares of glass, deliberately placed slightly out of alignment, gave the effect of flutter and discontinuity that seemed to be desired. Unlike most nightclubs this one had a club atmosphere, the crowd was homogeneous—and that evening as usual I could put names to nearly half the people there; a few were writers who wrote for the magazines I read, painters who exhibited at the galleries that I went to; all of them were men and women who had been to the same kind of schools, the same universities, and who were, in fact, almost of one large family in that if you went back for six generations or so they would all, or almost all, turn out to be cousins, linked—discernibly however loosely—to those houses whose names occur again and again in English history. I had taken Ermine there because of this family party atmosphere, I had joined the club with great excitement because I had longed to be admitted to the set, which seemed to me enormously cultured, civilized, and humane—now, sitting beside her, with both our chins high with temper, each staring straight ahead, so as to avoid the concession of admitting that we had snapped, I saw the white band playing second-hand jazz and with a sort of pathetic earnestness imitating movements that were natural and spontaneous in the bodies of another race in the life of another country. To their music the dancers waggled round, carrying their thin intellectual faces and fine heads distantly above bodies and legs that jerkily applied for entry to a dark and thoughtless heaven. When they were sitting out dances they sat down to a parody of the food of another country and chattered like birds in a bush. The Matisse, seen over their shoulders and between their heads, looked unhappily appropriate, as if it had been painted by a man desperately fighting to forge the innocence of childhood. These were the pleasures of the adult world that I had fought to get into . . . what could Ermine think of them? I could almost see with my mind's eye a gleamingly blond Wieland striding through a pine wood, open-necked and briefly shorted, sneering at the "Afro-Saxons," pretenders to mastery who had been unmasked by the *Zeitgeist*. I experienced the pain that one suffers when one's family reveals itself as good-hearted, rompish, and irretrievably mediocre to that selected, intellectual, sensitive friend one has after much inner debate brought home for the first time—the friend turns out to be a prig, the family vulgarians, neither can be explained to the other, both let one resoundingly down. My country was, somehow, exposing itself, or being exposed; on the other hand Ermine was being an idiot, dishing up all those political bromides. . . . It occurred to me that it would be clever to say that I thought she ought to be very happy with Wieland, and that she'd chosen the life she was made for. And then I looked at her and saw that she was nearly in tears.

"I'm sorry, Ermine, I've been so stupid. . . ."

"No you haven't, I'm in a state, that's all. You must take me home—back to the hotel."

In the taxi her tears came, and with tears the need for sheltering arms and a shoulder to cry on. I stroked her soft sweet-smelling hair. Sympathy created tenderness and one emotion passed insensibly into another. Presently she turned up her blind tear-wet face and we kissed mouth to mouth. When the taxi slowed up in front of the hotel she murmured, "Don't leave me now," and pulled on her hat so that her tear-stained face would be shadowed in the lobby.

In the morning she seemed completely happy, and when I woke I heard her singing to herself as she ran a bath. I called to her and she came through from the bathroom humming and still brushing her hair with long sweeping strokes, to sit down on the bed beside me holding the brush in her lap with one hand and touching my bare shoulder with the other.

"I wish I was in love with you," she said. "You're really very nice."

"Yes, it's a great pity we aren't in love."

"Well, facts have to be faced—I think I shall go back to Germany today." She began brushing her hair again.

"Do you always brush your hair before you have a bath. . . . I mean, don't you have to do it all over again? Afterwards . . ."

"I've had my bath—this is going to be yours. It's the first stage in throwing you out."

She bent down and kissed me, a peck on the forehead. I tried to take her by the shoulders but she wriggled free and stood back.

"Be good . . . and when you see Lolotte at Max's tell her I'm going—" She went over and looked at some papers beside her handbag on top of the bureau. "The boat train leaves Liverpool Street at six—tonight I'll be being seasick, and tomorrow I'll have breakfast in Holland."

"It's decided."

"Yes, it's decided." She put her arms behind her and stood in the attitude of a schoolgirl reciting a lesson learned by rote in class. " 'When he came to the river Rubicon, which parts Gaul within the Alps from the rest of Italy, his thoughts began to work, now he was just entering upon the danger, and he wavered much in his mind when he considered the greatness of the enterprise into which he was throwing himself. He checked his course and ordered a halt, while he revolved with himself, and often changed his opinion one way and the other, without speaking a word. This was when his purposes fluctuated most; presently he also discussed the matter with his friends who were about him, (of which number Asinius Pollio was one), computing how many calamities his passing that river would bring upon mankind, and what relation of it would be transmitted to posterity. At last, in a sort of passion, casting aside calculation, and abandoning himself to what might come, and using the proverb frequently in the mouths of those who enter upon dangerous and bold attempts, "The Die Is Cast" he rode across the river.' There you see I am not altogether a scatterbrain. I know scads of Plutarch by heart."

"I wish you weren't going, all the same."

"Well, I am, and it's no use crying over spilt milk." She grinned. "When Wieland has won his wars I'll see that he has you brought over to be a slave on his family estate in Bavaria, and we'll be very kind to you. It won't be too bad—if you work hard and do what you're told."

"Your lot won't win—it's impossible. . . ."

"Now don't argue—and get up and have your bath and dress. . . ."

I walked home between eleven and twelve in brilliant sunshine which glittered with a warm promise that the winter was not going to last much longer and that it would soon be spring. Perhaps Ermine was right, one should decide what to do and do it, and happiness would look after itself. I felt an immense sense of well-being. London, the world, life, was an enormous cake from which I could cut myself as large or as small a slice as I chose, and if I cut firmly enough and sharply enough it would have the flavor I wanted. A night with the warmth and beauty of Ermine's body close to me had made me forget her altogether, and to forget that she was going back to eat whatever dish should be put in front of her.

All thought of her was banished from my mind soon after

I got back to Max's house. I let myself in, and when I had hung up my coat I went into the living room to say something to the portrait that I would never be able to say to Max himself. I looked up at it, and said, "Thank you, I am very glad to be alive." The portrait seemed to look back at me with the hint of a friendly humorous glint in its eye, as if it were saying, "What, no reservations?" "None at all. Thick or thin, the whole shooting match is worth it." The faintly satirical look remained, and for some reason it made me stroke my jaw and realize that I was unshaven. "What a night with a pretty girl won't do for a chap," I seemed to hear him say, and I shook my head. "No, I'm serious—it is all worth it." And I started upstairs to get myself a shave. As I reached the head of the stairs the door of Max's study flew open and Lolotte appeared in the opening. She spun right about as she opened it, without apparently seeing me, and gave vent to a passionate cry of "Never, never, never!" on a rising scale. It was as dramatic and as alarming as the unexpected striking of a cuckoo clock. I stood frozen and heard Max's voice from inside the room speaking in tones of exasperated, martyred reasonableness.

"But she's indispensable, she's the best secretary I've ever had, I can't face breaking in another . . . you must apologize to her . . . please, Lolotte. . . ."

"Ah, secretary. I know you old men and your secretaries . . . the shut doors, and the 'taking dictation' after luncheon . . . I know what all this means. I am no simpleton, you cannot make a fool of me so easily. I will not lend myself to your degradation. . . ."

"Lolotte, I won't listen to any more of this. . . ."

"So now I touch you on the raw, now I begin to see the nigger in the woodpile—this is the big thing for which you will fight—it is not the simple foolish Alice I should keep my eye on—she is just a pastime, a diversion, a blind, behind her skirts I see the big thing—Amabel is the serious threat. You are an artful old villain, but I am not deceived. I will have things out with this slyboots, so plainly dressed and so demure, who has used the son as a stalking horse for the father. This we will settle, once and for all. I will talk to your woman, face to face, the whole squalid machinery of this fantastic ménage will be unveiled. . . ."

"I forbid it. . . ."

"You, you monster, it no longer lies in your power. . . ."

Lolotte swung round again and started towards the head of the stairs, with Max behind her desperately grabbing at her and being shaken off.

"Listen to me, Lolotte, for heaven's sake stop and listen."

"The time for talking and listening has gone by, unless I should speak to some purpose to the *police des moeurs* if such a thing exists in this country of hypocrisy and vice. . . ."

I made an unsuccessful attempt to withdraw backwards into the wall, and then found myself involved in the scene, as a piece of driftwood is swept up into a breaking wave. Lolotte paused, and fixing me with an outstretched pointing arm, launched into a denunciation of Amabel while Max stood behind her holding the sides of his head with his hands. His eyes met mine and I read in them pain, unhappiness, and an appeal which I did not wholly understand, but which I realized was not so much for him as for her. While this silent exchange took place her tirade flowed over me and round me, filling the whole stairwell as an aria fills an opera house. I had a sense that the walls were bulging with the pent-up torrent of sound, and that jets of slander must be spurting out through the letter-box opening, through the keyholes, through the cracks of the window frames, that a pane of glass or a door might blow out at any moment under the remorseless pressure. When at last she paused to draw breath I found myself weakly putting forward the claims of reason.

"But, Lolotte, all this is unbelievable—after all, you know Amabel. . . ."

"Yes! That is it—precisely—I know Amabel—and I know this monster about whom nothing is unbelievable. They make a fine pair, the hypocrite Protestant woman, gray and mouse-like outside—within a flaming crucible of obscene distorted passions. You are too young to know lechery, Dickie, until you have had to do with one of these meek mouse-like women. . . ."

As I listened to her expanding on the bizarre thesis I was faintly conscious that I had heard a bell ringing somewhere in the depths of the house. I had seen too, out of the corner of my eye, the maid coming into the hall, hesitating, withdrawing, and then, as the bell rang again, reappearing and vanishing in the direction of the front door. But I hadn't paid this sequence of events enough attention to think what it might mean because its possible significance had been crowded out of my mind by the sudden realization that I was faced with someone whose imaginings in certain departments had a greater reality than any facts. As this dawned on me I met Max's eyes again and understood the nature of the appeal he was making. To say that Lolotte was mad was the one perfect defense against her that he had, and the one that no amount of humiliation and distress could force him to adopt. A loyalty to what she had been, to what they had shared, prevented him from making the declaration that would take the sting out of all her inventions and reduce them to the level of ravings; and he was afraid, terribly afraid, now that Lolotte was no longer armed with her beauty, that some victim like Amabel would stumble on the key, and by uttering the words mad or madness, push her over the edge of the world of realities and into the abyss of her private illusions. I flinched from this sight of the depths over which we were poised, and looked helplessly down into the hall. For a moment I could not quite believe what I was seeing. Under the stress of the unfamiliar circumstances the young maidservant's social defenses had broken down and she had ushered a little knot of Japanese gentlemen into the house. There were as a matter of fact only four of them, but they gave the impression of a crowd as they stood gleaming with embarrassed smiles and flashing spectacles, bowing rapidly and uneasily, and darting glances upwards, away, and at each other. Lolotte broke off in the middle of a sentence describing the burning sexual hunger of a plain woman feeling that youth has gone and that age is approaching, while Max moaned. With an access of superhuman strength he grabbed her round the waist and rushed her, backwards, into his study. The door slammed behind them. I found it necessary to mop my face with my handkerchief, and as I did so, feeling horribly weak at the knees, the bowing below became frantic as if a lot of mechanical toys had been set off. It was accompanied by a great deal of nervous hissing, which I took to be apologetic in intention. It was too much for the maid who, reverting to some atavistic pattern of behavior that I had read about in Victorian novels but had never hoped to see, flung her apron up over her head and scuttled away through the service door. I took a firm grip on myself and went down, smiling a smile that must have been fully as Japanese as any of theirs, and groping for a suitable remark. I found myself at last on their level, still with nothing to say, bowing automatically in response to the bows that were being offered to me.

"Perhaps you'd care to take off your coats, and put down your parcels . . ." I said, barely knowing what I was saying.

"You are most kind."

They whispered rapidly to each other, and took off their coats, helping each other, and passing their parcels from hand to hand in a frenzy of polite movement. I saw with dismay that I had got them to stay when I should have invented a pretext for asking them to leave.

"I'm afraid," I muttered, "that you'll have to excuse Mr. Town. . . ."

"Oh, no—surely not." The spokesman's eyes seemed enormously enlarged behind his thick-lensed spectacles. I found the effect hypnotic. "We are luncheon guests. The arrangement is of long standing. The engagement was, indeed, made in the course of correspondence conducted by myself on behalf of these gentlemen from Tokyo. . . ."

He broke into a rattle of translated explanation, interrupted by hissings and ejaculations, from his companions who stared at me, rather with apprehension than annoyance. Over their heads I saw that the dining room door was slightly open and through it I saw a table set with an unusually large number of covers. We were, clearly, in for lunch.

"Well, then, I am sure everything will turn out all right. . . ." I was conscious that the phrase had gone a little wrong, and bowed slightly to cover up my impoliteness. It set them all off again, but beaming this time.

"I am neglecting the introductions. I am myself Professor of English Teminoku of Osaka University, this is Professor of English Hyatami of Nara University, this is Professor of Natural Science Suzaku of Jikoyen University, this is Professor of Sociology Nakamura of Osaka University. You, no doubt, are employed in some secretarial capacity by Mr. Town?"

"Well, no, not exactly, actually my name is Richard Savage —I'm just a guest, well, you could say a relative . . . anyway I'm staying with Mr. Town for the time being."

While I floundered I observed that Professor Hyatami removed his spectacles, polished them, and put them back on again in order to stare at me like a bird dog. When I stopped he spoke rapidly out of the corner of his mouth in Japanese broken twice by the word Savage. Professor Teminoku smiled, a less automatic smile than before, and the Natural Science man giggled.

"Professor Hyatami," said Teminoku, "has made a distinguished study of Bohemianism in Western cultural life."

He did not enlarge on this cryptic utterance.

"'Cynala, I have been fait'ful to you in my fashion,'" said Nakamura, blushed horribly and was overwhelmed with giggles.

"The poet Dowson," said Hyatami with something like severity, "belongs to a period with which Mr. Savage is likely to be unfamiliar. I do not imagine your generation is excessively familiar with the literature of the nineties?"

"Well, no. Though I suppose everybody knows that tag line about Cynara. It was in the title of a play last year, I think. But let's go into the drawing room and have a glass of sherry."

Sherry and biscuits had been put out and the formal business of pouring glasses and handing round cheese crackers helped us through the next few minutes. And then when an awkward silence developed it was time for second glasses all round. The dry Amontillado, a delicately pale yellow, had something of the flavor of sake and the visitors drank it rather as if it were that familiar drink, putting back their glasses as if they were the little china thimbles in which the rice wine is usually served. They were fairly large sherry glasses. I noticed after a while that Hyatami, Suzaku, and Nakamura had quite rosy complexions and was intrigued because I had never thought of Japanese as having that kind of color. The phrase "little yellow chaps," or possibly "plucky little yellow chaps," had stolen into my mind at some stage—I tried to think when, and decided it was probably something that I recalled from Mr. Willingham's account of what he had spoken of as "a trip out East." Another phrase that had surely come from the same source was "believe me, it's a case of 'never the twain shall meet,' as the poem says." But they seemed friendly and rather forthcoming in the flesh, certainly very easy to get on with considering the daunting circumstances of their arrival. I noticed that the decanter was empty and rang. When I asked the maid for more sherry she looked at me with a hint of desperation.

"It's gone half past, sir."

"Oh, yes?" I didn't quite see the point.

"Luncheon was for quarter past, sir."

"Oh dear, well I daresay Mr. Town will be down directly."

"Very good, sir." She looked quickly at the Japanese, who were murmuring among themselves, and then rather doubtfully at me. "Cook's terribly upset, she says everything is spoiling."

When she came back with the refilled decanter I was involved in an almost acrimonious discussion which had sprung up between Hyatami and Nakamura on the question of Dowson. Nakamura's theory was that the disorder of the poet's personal life was a deliberate protest against the mechanization and regimentation of industrial society, something on a par with the Nihilism of the Russian intellectuals. Hyatami would have it that a purely Freudian motive lay behind his rather dingy adventures, and that he had become a poet because in Western society the man of letters was allowed by tradition to behave in an antisocial way. This sounds like a dull conversation but Hyatami had an inexhaustible fund of anecdotes about the domestic irregularities of Western writers which he drew on freely, introducing each new record of impropriety with the phrase: "Purely for purposes of illustration . . ." His mind was a fascinating distorting mirror which gave everything familiar a hitherto unimagined aspect.

"Take, purely for purposes of illustration, the case of Lady Caroline Lamb. . . ." said Hyatami, and plunged delightedly into the scandals of Whig society. "When this woman realized that she had forfeited her place in society she resorted to the only possible means of self protection available to her. No personal reform would have been adequate, no demonstration of contrition she could have made would have redeemed her. There was only one thing for her to do, and this she did, she wrapped about her the mantle of literary tradition and wrote a novel. To the lady novelist everything is forgiven.

This point is proven by the case of George Eliot who was entertained as a luncheon guest by the daughters of Queen Victoria even though it was known that she had committed adultery not in a passing episode but in a long continued cohabitation. It was unthinkable that any ordinary woman should have been so received by royalty but to a literary lady anything was permitted. . . ."

"I don't believe you're right, Hyatami," I said.

"The facts are all on my side."

"But still . . ."

"Now, purely for purposes of illustration, take the case of the non-literary Sir Charles Dilke. . . ."

Hyatami gave a racy account of this surprising politician's divorce and of its effect on his career. I noticed that everybody had finished their drinks and that there was barely enough sherry left in the decanter to fill two glasses. Nakamura clearly wanted more and sensed my embarrassment. A broad grin covered his face as he realized what the situation was. He clapped his hands.

"We will initiate our young friend into the Chinese game of guessing fingers and play a round with the last of the sherry as prizes."

The game was explained in a babble of talk in which I am afraid I failed to grasp what the finer points of it were. At any rate we were all soon excitedly calling numbers to each other in an apparently random fashion. Something went wrong and we began again with an enormous amount of giggling that grew in volume as Suzaku and Nakamura began to come out as winners. As they rattled numbers at each other Teminoku heckled them with jokes about the utility of statistics in the practical field, and when Nakamura had finally beaten the Natural Sciences man it was discovered that Hyatami and Teminoku had quietly filled their glasses with the last of the sherry and were ready to toast the winner and the runner-up. There were good-natured outcries of protest and there was a little tussle between Suzaku and Hyatami over the charged glass in the course of which the sherry was spilt down Hyatami's shirt front and a small vase of flowers on an occasional table was upset. Handkerchiefs appeared on all sides and there was a frenzy of mopping, apology and wild giggling. We none of us noticed for quite some time that Max had come into the room and was standing in silent astonishment just inside the door.

The introductions were difficult. The shock of suddenly finding Max with us confused me and I found it surprisingly hard to remember which Japanese was which and what his post and university was. There were a number of corrections, made with polite hissings that indicated that my mistakes were not resented but that the record should be kept straight. These on top of the several outbreaks of uncontrollable giggling drew the proceedings out for longer than seemed necessary or desirable. I felt weak and a little scared when it was all over and the social initiative had passed into Max's hands.

"I think we might go in to lunch straight away," he said, somewhat coldly.

"We would prefer it if you were to receive our gifts first," said Professor Teminoku, bowing, losing his balance, and recovering by grabbing a chair back. "Then with the formalities completed we could take luncheon in a more relaxed atmosphere."

The proposal was apparently agreeable to everyone except Max, and he assented to it with a gesture that was more one of surrender than of consent. His head was on one side and inclined forwards, his hands clenched by his side as he listened to Teminoku running through a speech, evidently learned by heart, which expressed the admiration and esteem in which Max Town was held by liberal Japan in general and the friends of English culture in Osaka University in particular. While he was speaking the hall clock struck two with firmness. Hyatami made a similar speech that was rather longer.

Suzaku spoke for scientific Japan, progressive Japan, the scientists of his faculty, disclosed the fact that he had written a novel, compared Max with Zola and, to his evident surprise, with Ruskin and Carlyle, and went on to speak for an association of Japanese writers who had charged him with a message of congratulation which he proceeded to read. This message was signed by forty-two members of the association whose names he read out. There was a strange music to the list, and the reading had something of the effect of those chapters of the Old Testament which give the names of the tribes and their leading members and which sound like the spells of a forgotten magic. It was then Nakamura's turn. He began by giving a brief outline of the history of sociology in Japan. Before nineteen hundred Japanese sociology had been influenced by various persons like Bentham and Mill whose ideas, though good, seemed to Nakamura and men of his generation to be fundamentally cold and inhuman. Between nineteen hundred and nineteen hundred and twenty there had been much heart-searching among Japanese workers in this field, in the course of which it was often said that Western thinkers were too inhuman to provide inspiration for Japanese, they had too alien an approach. Then in the work of Max Town Nakamura and his colleagues had discovered a warmth of spirit, an emotional kinship, that bridged the gulf of racial difference. At this point Nakamura forgot altogether how his prepared speech was to continue, and stood for a few seconds in an uneasy silence. He blurted out another half-sentence and once more dried up. He began to sweat profusely.

"And now on behalf of . . ." prompted Teminoku.

"And now on behalf of . . ." Nakamura took it up and rattled off the names of three societies of sociologists and statisticians and of a literary association. "We offer our profoundest congratulations and good wishes on the occasion of your seventieth birthday." He came to an end and bowed three times, all smiles.

Max made a short reply, at first uncertain, and then abruptly exceedingly graceful and deft.

"And now," he said, "lunch. Lead the way, Richard. . . ."

"The gifts, the gifts, please," cried Teminoku.

"Yes, oh yes, certainly, the gifts," said Max faintly.

The room filled with wrapping paper as brocaded boxes were unveiled, then the boxes were opened and a snow of tissue papers fell everywhere, then silk bags with heavy silk cords and tassels appeared, and these at last yielded up the presents: a hideous netsuke, intricate and a dirty brown; a dark green jade disk carved with the symbols of the Japanese zodiac; a very early cast-iron duck of great beauty and simplicity that looked more Chinese than Japanese to me; and a dark purple coat of a richer silk than I had ever seen or touched before. Max was deeply moved by the story which these objects told; they were, even the remarkably ugly netsuke, precious things of the kind that collectors and museums compete for—even the coat was a precious thing, a garment that a very wealthy and distinguished Japanese would wear on a formal occasion at home—and they were all paid for by writers, schoolteachers, and university professors and lecturers who lived, as he knew, lives of the narrowest poverty. He touched the jade disk with his fingertips and, as he enjoyed the patina which it had acquired in its six hundred years of life, fought for words.

"I don't believe I deserve these magnificent gifts. . . ." he said in a low tone, and looked up.

It was apparent that the shock of his sudden appearance was wearing off. Nakamura swayed slightly and hiccupped loudly.

"I think we really should go through to luncheon," said Max, this time with authority.

As we walked through the hall I saw that the hands of the clock were announcing that it was ten minutes to three. I heard Hyatami speaking to Max in front of me.

"This has been a most enjoyable introduction to the informality of Western literary life. In future I will think of you beside Lawrence as one whose burning spirit rises superior to all rigid conventions. . . ."

They left in a happy daze at half past four, climbing into a taxicab in fits of giggles like so many schoolgirls.

"If there's much more of that sort of thing I shall really feel seventy by the time these celebrations are all over. . . ." He looked thoughtful. "I think you made a mistake in letting them have all that sherry, you know. I hope they don't get into some sort of scrape. . . ."

"I'm sorry. It just happened somehow."

"Things do happen—they can't be helped." He paused. "Look, I want you to take a note round to Alice. I haven't written it yet, it'll take five minutes or so—could you be ready to go out thenabouts?"

"Yes, of course—and that reminds me. I've got a message for Lolotte from Ermine—it had clean gone out of my head. I'd better go up."

"I don't know if she'll be awake. I gave her a sleeping tablet. Don't wake her if she is asleep . . . won't it keep?"

"Ermine's going back to Germany tonight."

Max balanced the iron duck in the palm of his hand, and let a second pass.

"What a beautiful thing this is . . . I suppose I was very stupid about you and Ermine."

"I don't think so. As it was I had the terrific sense of a score. . . ."

"That was worth a good deal, eh?"

"As much as giving Harry the slip."

"Funny that you should remember that. I can see that it wouldn't have been nearly such a tremendous thing if Harry had put me on the train and sent me off with his good wishes."

"As it was it all came to nothing because Lolotte set it up."

"You're not blaming her, I hope," he said sharply.

"No, of course not. But we were made for each other—I don't know—there's a complete sympathy, everything. But because it wasn't an accidental discovery, because the whole thing was ready-made, contrived, because it didn't flow naturally out of our own lives it didn't flow into it. You can't force these things."

"What a lot you know about life, Dickie."

"Now you're laughing at me."

"Yes, but in the friendliest possible way." He patted my shoulder. "Run along and freshen up while I write that note."

I went to my room and when I had dipped my head in cold water and swallowed several glasses of it I swore that I would never drink sherry before lunch again. With a clean shirt on I felt a great deal better and quite ready to face Lolotte. I opened the door of the dressing room where she lay resting and peered into the darkness to see if she were awake. There was no sound. For a moment I thought she must be sleeping very quietly but almost at once I recognized the unmistakable sensation that tells one that a room or a house in which one expects to find someone is empty. The tension of another presence was not there. I snapped on the light and looked over to the bed. I had never seen a dead body before but I had no doubt of what I was looking at. I went slowly downstairs, feeling a greensick emptiness.

"I'll be with you in a minute," said Max.

"No, you must telephone for a doctor at once."

"You're looking very white," Max said looking up from the little rolltop desk in the drawing room and staring at me. "It could be just the sherry, couldn't it? Perhaps you'd better go upstairs and lie down. I'll call the doctor if you're still feeling badly at dinner time."

"It's not me, it's Lolotte."

"Lolotte!" He started to his feet.

"Don't go up. There's nothing you can do."

We faced each other for an age.

"Are you quite sure?"

I nodded. I watched him bend over and tear the note to Alice across and across. Then he went over to the telephone and I heard him asking his doctor to come round. I stood empty-minded until he had finished, and remained empty-minded until Max came and put an arm round my shoulder.

"Don't take it too hard. Remember, Lolotte would have hated to get old. . . ."

It made me think of Ermine. She would want to know. I went down to her hotel and found that she had already left for the station. Getting another cab outside Murray's took several minutes, and the traffic as we went eastwards across London was heavy. The minutes lagged away in one jam after another and just before we reached Liverpool Street I heard a clock striking six. When I got inside a railwayman was taking down the indicator at the end of the platform that said 6 P.M. Harwich—Hook of Holland, Continental Boat Train, and replacing it with another that said 6.25 P.M. All Stations, Bishops Stortford and Norwich. I looked at the bare rails beside the platform until a small tank engine came in towing the empty coaches of the 6.25 in backwards. The driver of the engine got out, wiping his hands on a piece of cotton waste, and stood watching the homeward bound office-workers streaming past him with their little attaché cases and their folded evening papers. I stood there realizing that there were things in life that could come to a definite and final end. Ermine was really gone.

7

It was Alice who took charge of our lives in the next few days. When my trance of self-pity lifted at last in Liverpool station I went to a phone booth and called her. It had occurred to me that Max was alone in the house with Lolotte's body and that he might need the support of Alice's gentleness and understanding to see him through the strain and unhappiness that I felt sure Amabel would manage to create in dealing with the practical side of death. I could imagine her coming back to the house radiating a Calvinist confidence that the Almighty had personally intervened in this case, as he had when the Assyrian came down like a wolf on the fold, his cohorts all gleaming in purple and gold. She would feel that Lolotte had met no more than her just reward for locking up one of the elect in a cupboard, and I felt that Max would find her tight-lipped triumph very hard to bear. It is easy to be wrong about these things. Lolotte's death somehow punctured Amabel's self-confidence entirely, perhaps she was appalled to see that energy and will power as great or greater than her own could wither like the grass in an hour, perhaps some obscurer sense told her that her hatred, which was really jealousy, had killed Lolotte and she felt guilty. It would be hard to say, but, knowing Amabel, I would favor the first theory; at any rate she collapsed into tearfulness and inefficiency almost at once and had to be taken home within a few hours of her being sent for. There she wept in a darkened room, to her husband's intense bewilderment, until exhaustion supervened, and the following day she was prostrate as if she had just passed the crisis of a serious illness. It took her nearly a week to recover. In that time Alice had handled everything, getting in touch with the Essling-Sterlinghovens by telegram, finding out in a telephone conversation conducted in perfect German what they wanted done, and then making all the funeral arrangements. Lolotte was cremated at their request, and a representative of the family, the Freiherr Geyr von Essling-Sterlinghoven and Erlencamp, flew over to attend the ceremony and to take the ashes home. I expected him to be a tall thin Prussian Junker but he was a round-faced tubby little man who found a naturally jolly temperament hard to suppress for the occasion. At lunch after the cremation Max was evidently surprised to find both how unlike Lolotte he was, and how little he corresponded with his mental picture of her background. Alice drew him out in conversation and discovered that he had three passions, for racehorses, for English tweeds, and for briar pipes. He confessed, shyly, that he could hardly bear to leave England without either visiting some stables or doing some shopping. "This has happened," he said, "at a very unfortunate time of year." So Alice arranged that he should go down the next morning to see Johnny Massinberd's stables at Lambourn. As the trains weren't convenient she lent me her car and asked me to drive him down. "It'll be good for you to get away from all this for a few hours," she said, "you're looking very peaky, and sad too, poor lamb, a drive'll be just the thing."

I was a little surprised when we set out early the next day to see that the Freiherr had with him not only a large pair of binoculars but also the urn which contained Lolotte's ashes. I supposed that he, for some reason, didn't like to leave them in his hotel room. The urn was placed, without explanation, in the back seat of the car, and I presently forgot it as the Freiherr prattled away about German race meetings, stables, and breeders. Johnny Massinberd's stables were something to see, and we arrived in time to catch the rugged horses being brought in from their morning exercise by the whole retinue of tiny stable boys, handlers, Massinberd, and his trainer Jock Wilcox. The Freiherr loved every minute of it and everything about it all, relishing the rolling downland country, with its clumps of beech trees, the village with its brick and flint cottages, the old gray church, and the splendid beasts. He was very happy and nothing seemed to cloud his pleasure until we set out for London again after lunch. He sat beside me in silence while we drove for a few miles, evidently turning something over in his mind.

"I wonder if I could ask you to do me a great favor," he said in the end. "Rather an unusual one."

"I'd be glad to do anything I can."

"Well, this involves your becoming a confederate in what may seem like an act of blasphemy. You see, this urn, which I have with me . . . it will be taken home and placed in the family vault of the Essling-Sterlinghovens in the Pomorze. I don't know if Lolotte ever spoke to you of the Schloss Essling —if she did you'd be well aware that she detested it—she was unhappy there as a child—she was never happy there later on —it's a medieval barrack on a crag in the middle of a pine wood that always seems to be dripping wet . . . the chapel to tell the truth is the least attractive part of it—it's on the north side of the castle and it seems to be in, well, perpetual shadow, you might say, it's dank, it's horridly cold—I always have to put on a double thickness of woollen underclothes when I attend a wedding or a funeral there . . . when my sister was married there she had to wear long woollen combinations—

she was advised to by our mother—although it was June
. . . the place smells of damp . . . you see what I'm driving
at? . . ."

"Well, no, not exactly."

"You must see that such a place is nowhere for Lolotte
. . . with her love of sunshine . . . of everything foreign
. . . Schloss Essling is the essential Germanic place . . .
You see I don't want to have it on my conscience that I took
her back."

"I see."

"I was wondering if there was some hilltop known to you
where we could set her free, so to say. . . ."

"I believe that's a very good idea."

"I'm glad you see it."

We stopped and looked at road maps, and presently the car
bumped up along a grass track and we came out on that stretch
of the Ridgeway where Max and I and Lolotte had walked
together long before. We found a clump of barrows, those soft
round turf-covered prehistoric burial mounds that show by
their occurrence on high and open places how closely our
pagan ancestors identified the beautiful with the divine, and
without a word spoken we agreed that it was the place. For all
its winter bareness the width of the Thames Valley below still
looked gentle and kindly. The Freiherr climbed to the top of
a barrow and shook out the contents of the urn. The light ash
smoked away in a gray veil that drifted for a hundred yards
or more before it disappeared, and a few heavier pellets of
calcined bone fell among the grasses at his feet. He stood for
a little while taking in the large prospect, and then came down
to me where I was standing watching him from a distance.

"Now she will always be free as she wanted to be," he said.

A mile or so away we came on a field where some men
were at work hedge-trimming and burning the cut branches
on the edge of the plowed land. The trash fires had burned out
at the far end of the hedge where the men had been working

on the previous day and the Freiherr refilled the urn with the cold wood ash from one of these heaps.

"English hawthorn will deputize for Lolotte until the last trump sounds," he said, "when it does I shall have to make my explanations to the family. Well, I imagine I shall have long enough to think of something . . . and I think Lolotte will be happier waking up among a Celtic war band than she would if she were to find herself surrounded by the Essling-Sterlinghovens she detested. Better affront family pride than her, when all's said and done."

He screwed the cap back on the urn.

"I shall have it soldered on before I leave," he said. "I'll tell them back home that the customs authorities required it . . . then there'll be nothing to worry about till judgment day."

I was sorry to see him go when he left the next day with three suit-lengths of Scotch tweed and half a dozen Dunhill pipes. At tea time I told Max what an awfully nice chap I had thought he was, and he snorted.

"You don't know what he is, I've looked him up."

"Oh? Isn't he just a racing man?"

"He's a lieutenant-colonel, one of the brains of their new army, a fanatic for mechanization. He's even crazier about tanks than this fellow Fuller, or Liddell Hart."

"Isn't that sensible enough? If he is a soldier, I mean, isn't that the line he'd have to take?"

"All right, but don't tell me what a decent fellow he is. He's busy making a meat-axe that's going to bust everything up one of these days." He got to his feet. "I've got to go and work on that birthday speech of mine some more," he said, "I'll see you later."

"The old man seems rather on edge," I said to Alice when he'd gone.

"Well, it's been a hard day. There were some Spaniards

and two Czechs for lunch and they didn't speak awfully good English. And there are some American professors for dinner —if they're like their letters they're going to be rather heavy going. Poor pet, it's hard work for him being a public monument on top of the other thing."

"It must have been horrible for him to find that she'd suddenly burnt out like a match. I don't suppose he'll really feel it until the rush of this next week lets up and lets him down."

"You're not to patronize him." Alice spoke unusually sharply, but her voice immediately softened. "What he hasn't yet realized, and what will hurt him when he does, is how much he has longed for just that."

"But," I tried to put my discovery on the day of her death into words, "the enormous tenderness he put into trying to shield her from other people . . . he must have loved her."

"Of course he had loved her, and loved her for having loved him. But there aren't any greater burdens than those one takes up out of a sense of pity. And when one has shouldered them it's more than angelic not to want sooner or later to be relieved of them. You'll find that out, sooner or later. Lolotte became a dead weight that prevented him from living with any kind of ease years ago, he couldn't help wanting a simpler happiness. He had no chance of having it while she was alive. And his being her victim was the only thing that kept her alive."

"I can't think of her as a sort of vampire."

"You only had the wild fun of her. You could, perhaps, glimpse the horrors of her private remorse, but you never had to help her to put it aside. There was no one else to do it. Max had undertaken that. Now he begins to see how much he gave up, and to what little purpose. Your description of how the little round soldier man threw her away on a hilltop brought that home to him. The next stage, and the worst, is when he faces up to admitting how much he longed to throw her away himself, oh, ages ago, and what a blessed relief it is to know that he won't ever have to worry again about what is going to come into her head to think or to do."

"But he didn't find it very hard to throw other people away, when it suited him."

"I don't know. I think you'd be surprised to find that he's been chucked more often than not. Women aren't, you know, really as maternal as they're made out to be. That's a warning."

"You mean that women want men to be as interested in them as they are in themselves?"

"Something like that." She smiled. "I can see in your eye that you're on the verge of asking what draws me to him—well it's my business and his, and none of yours. That's not a snub—and you're not to pretend that it is. It's just that I won't have you being as tremendously absorbed in me as you were in Lolotte. That's all. I've spoken about it to you before. I'm going to take Max away after this shindig is over. I've never seen the East and he hasn't either, I'm taking him to India, and the places beyond. We'll be gone for a year, perhaps longer. You will be on your own feet when we get back, won't you?"

"I should think so."

"We'll find you absolutely wrapped up in something that has nothing to do with Max—and in some girl who isn't a bit like Lolotte, or me, or even like Naomi, and you'll scarcely have time to do more than say hello to us . . . it'll be wonderful."

"It sounds as if you're awfully keen to get rid of me."

"It's what anyone who was really fond of you would want," she said. "Dear Richard, do try and make a go of it."

It was the last talk we had of that kind. When we were alone together after that she kept things on a cheerful, easy, social level of inconsequence which was always pleasant and friendly but which didn't in the least encourage emotional dependence.

I found it wounding at first and I wished very much that Lolotte were alive again. But after a day or two of being at a loose end and feeling like a lost dog I started to look up school friends who lived in London and one or two young people I had met down in Wiltshire through Naomi's colonel and I found that there was a surprising amount to do and to talk about with them. And then all of a sudden the night of the birthday banquet had gone by.

There were no more distinguished or undistinguished foreign visitors at the house, and what coming and going that there was had to do with preparations for Max's departure for the Far East.

Life seemed strangely quiet in the next two years, and although I was doing a great deal and having a very good time, I felt the absence of Max and I could not get used to the idea that from now on Lolotte's behavior would be altogether predictable. I drove down one afternoon from Oxford to visit her hilltop, hoping to feel a sense of her presence, but she had blown away with her ashes and had melted into the general assurance of long habitation that the whole landscape gently offered. I looked down at the church spires and towers that dotted the valley and heard them say that they had been there through the thick and thin of up to eight hundred years, and I found at the scuffed-up entry to a rabbit's burrow not far from the grave mound where Geyr had stood with the empty urn a flint skin scraper that had been there for two thousand years or more. I went back to New College with a sense that the University was right after all to disregard the inky blue political storm cloud that was building up so ominously beyond the Channel and to stick resolutely to its program of preparing us for life in a continuing and indestructible civilization. Every now and then the mounting tension, very like that preceding a bad thunderstorm, made me and many of us feel that the occasion for learning the kind of things that we were learning had gone by, it was time to beat the alarm through streets, to raise recruits, hand out arms, and do something. Some of us impelled by these feelings joined the Communist Party, others put on black shirts—those were the Romantics—the realists joined the Royal Air Force Volunteer Reserve or the Territorials. It was hard to bring oneself back from the passionate night-long arguments about the ethics of war, the possibility of civil disobedience at the level of international politics, the political necessities that would shape our lives, to those cold daylight discussions with tutors about the definable meanings of the words that we were using with such heat and certainty.

There were the pleasures of learning to think and there were other grounds for enjoying Oxford. Stetson, my best friend, was a keen poker player and a temperate drinker—these bald facts conjure up for me the curious beauty of a green baize table covered with brilliant cards, the fascinating tensions of the game, a window curtain flapping gently as a soft air steals in from the Garden Quad which is filled with the scent of a warm June evening, and the flavor of hock and seltzer. There were winter delights too, nicely combined of worldly and intellectual elements. Stetson, myself, Frank Jowett, the grandson of Irving's great rival, and a dozen others had a little private drama society that read plays and listened to critical papers. The suggestions of this are highbrow and austere, but the society called itself The Burgundian, and its ritual demanded that at each meeting a member elected at the previous meeting should produce a ripe Stilton cheese and half a dozen bottles of a Burgundy never before tasted by any of the members. We met in each other's rooms, and read and tasted the dark red wines, close-packed in a semicircle round an open fireplace where a coal fire glowed and crackled. When it was a paper night, the reader would stand by the single lamp placed on the mantelpiece and all the other lights would be put out, the circle of listening faces would reflect the red glow from the grate, and here and there a glass would send back a ruby gleam.

There were good summers too. One year Stetson and I, with two of the girls who had been at the dance on the night of the banquet, and who had come up to Lady Margaret Hall, drove through the Poitevin and the Dordogne searching for good food and Romanesque architecture; the next year we idled across northern Italy from Milan to Venice, looking at the lakes and the Dolomites, paintings and Palladian villas, unaccompanied that time, and on bicycles.

And behind it all there was Marshwood and its solid peace, with the dead clock silent in the stable turret, and the stream running quietly through the watermeadows. When I was there I felt even more strongly the sensation that I had experienced at Lolotte's resting place, that the itching, nagging crisis that was building up in the newspapers was an ephemeral thing and that here was the solid enduring fabric of reality. Colonel Arthur ministered to it and cherished it, so that it was easy to think of him not simply as a property owner doing what he would with his own, but as a contributor to a mystique, almost as the holder of a priestly office. Naomi seemed to be wholeheartedly his assistant and I began to feel every time I went back that we had always been there, and that we would always be there. Walking across the fields on a Sunday morning to the ritual eleven-o'clock service with the Colonel, Naomi, and those of our weekend guests who chose to go, and listening to the faint pealing of Teffont's bells down the valley traveling to us under the louder, closer ring of our Chilmark chime it was hard to think anything else. Finding my place in the hymn book for the first hymn I would take in the triple lancet window behind the altar which was a memorial to the Colonel's grandfather, the marble plaque on the wall of the north aisle that had been put up to his father's memory, and a brass to his sister who had died young, and I could see among them memorials to come, to the Colonel, to Naomi, to myself, and to my son, each engraved in its turn with the phrase "of Marshwood House in this parish." The future seemed to stretch away solidly beyond any mere incident of foreign politics, so certainly that it was impossible to imagine any shift of circumstances that could destroy it. At the center, there was Naomi's happiness in her absorption in the routine of the house and the life of the place. Her face was tranquil and although I sometimes looked for them I never saw those gleams from behind her face, slipping out through her eyes, of the old Naomi quickly gauging my reactions to her performance and judging if I were a friendly or a hostile critic. I tested her to the limit once by mentioning Lolotte, and received a placid answer.

"It must have been horrid for you, when she died so unexpectedly. You were very fond of her, weren't you?" She barely looked up from her embroidery.

"Yes . . . she was very likable in her strange way," I said, guardedly, and wondering how she would go on.

"I wonder that Max never married her." Her needle went in and out of the canvas without any change of pace. "She was very much the right woman for him. She had hardly any life apart from his. He really needs someone, always needed a woman, with that gift for self-abnegation."

"It always seemed to me that she lived entirely to herself. . . ."

"Ah, that's because you're a man. It would take a woman to see how altogether devoted to him she was. . . ."

"I always thought she just wanted to take possession of him, to sweep him up into her own life. . . ."

"That was only her way of presenting herself to him, as something obdurate that had to be overcome." She sighed. "Some men still like that sort of thing, you know." She got up. "Let's go and look at the peonies before lunch."

We strolled out to the square space enclosed by box hedges

292

beyond the cedars which had once been a bowling lawn, and which Naomi had had transformed into a peony garden.

"MacGregor hated doing this," she said, "and now he's enormously proud of it, bless his heart. He told me this morning that he's asked the head gardeners from Chillingham and Godestone to come over to see it tomorrow. I think it's a success, don't you?"

"It looks as if it had always been here, already."

"It's nice to think I've given the place something. . . ." She slipped her arm under mine. "And it's nice for me to see you growing up to be at home here, and so sure of yourself. I've worried a lot about you, but I don't any more."

MacGregor came into the garden with a look of alarm barely concealed under the wide brim of his Panama hat.

"It's all right, MacGregor, we're not cutting any. I wouldn't dream of it until after tomorrow," Naomi called to him across the bright beds.

MacGregor took off his hat awkwardly and mumbled something as he approached us.

"I've had a letter from Kelway's, madam, they have a new bloom that I think we should have. It has a purple cup with a double center of cream tinged with rose. They're only offering it privately this year. May I tell them we're interested?"

"Oh, do, it sounds very promising."

MacGregor smiled and left us.

And yet . . . there was one day after I had been hunting with the Colonel, a glorious day that had produced a hard unchecked run from find to kill halfway across the county. We had come home after dark in that delightful physically sated state when all one wants is a long soak in a hot bath, dinner, a glass or two of port in front of a fire, and bed. We had been up since five and out in the open all day making history that the hunt would cherish in its annals for a generation. After my bath I came downstairs in slippers looking forward to a doze and a glass of sherry beside the fire in the white drawing room. I opened the door quietly and saw Naomi standing at one of the windows with one hand holding back the curtains so close to the panes that I knew she was resting her cheek against the cold glass. She stood there without moving, staring into the darkness outside, and when I spoke turned towards me so slowly, letting the curtain fall into place behind her, that it seemed almost as if she were sleepwalking. She moved over to the fire without any expression on her face, and only when she felt its warmth looked at me and smiled and asked if I had had a good day. Whatever dream she had been immersed in remained with her as an indefinable bloom for the rest of the short evening; she was with us, but her mind was somewhere else.

I never caught her out like this again, and the few hints that were given to me during my second year at Oxford only became recognizable for what they were in the light of later events. There was a letter from the Colonel that mentioned in passing that Naomi was very much taken up with helping the local Women's Institute put on a comedy for a national competition, and then months later another, saying, "Your mother is very cock a hoop with her triumphs as a producer. I daresay she'll tell you all about it when we come up to see you on Thursday." When I saw them the following week the matter had gone out of my head and I forgot to ask how the village actresses had made out in their competition. They had, apparently, won and had very much enjoyed their excursion to London for the finals. It was the Colonel who brought the subject up, and who described the victory with beaming pride. While he talked Naomi smiled indulgently and seemed to concentrate on her cold salmon. When he'd finished she looked up almost absently and asked me a question.

"Is this boy Frank Jowett as good as they say?"

"I think he's going to be." I looked across the restaurant where we were eating and saw him, with his big actor's face, deep in conversation with another undergraduate who was taking part in the University Dramatic Society's *Coriolanus.* "Would you like to meet him?"

I brought him over to be introduced and Naomi gave him a businesslike, oddly penetrating look as he shook her hand.

"You have your grandfather's looks," she said, "if you've half his talent you should have a great future."

"I'm surprised that you should know who my grandfather was," Jowett said, looking flattered, and Naomi shook her head, deprecatingly.

"Oh, I'd recognize that strain anywhere," she said. "There's no difficulty in recognizing one of your clan."

They talked for a minute and then Jowett went back to his table, obviously pleased that Naomi had heard that great things were expected of him. We went off after lunch to see some boat races and I thought no more of the matter until the next day when Frank came up from behind me on a bicycle near the Martyr's Memorial and then zigzagged slowly to keep pace with me, talking rather aimlessly. This and that came up and was dropped, and then the meeting at lunch.

"It was a funny thing your mother knowing I was taking the lead in *Coriolanus,* after all we've only been in rehearsal a week."

"I suppose that is odd." It hadn't struck me.

"Ah, well, it's one of these mysteries," he said. "Drop in at my place tonight, Stetson and one or two others are going to be there, Betty and the Swedes . . . it might be fun."

On this tentative note he pedaled off. I didn't think twice about what he had said, as there seemed to be nothing in his words to think about.

Nearer the production date of *Coriolanus* Larry Brook came up to Oxford to coach the producer who'd asked his professional advice. While he was there Larry asked me to lunch with him. I was glad to see him and I found him a little grayer, plumper, and a great deal happier. He'd given up, he told me, trying to be Chekhov, and he was finding it much simpler to be busily and successfully Larry Brook.

"It's middle age, or worse perhaps," he said, "this settling down to a modest acceptance of the fact that I am the best thing going in my middlebrow line, but it's very restful. I'm up here doing my duty to culture, a bout or two of that in the year keeps my conscience clear and then I can get on with this cozy business of being dazzlingly successful at my own branch of commerce. I feel very fatherly now when I see you young fellows setting out to prove you're geniuses."

"What are you really up to?" I asked.

"Oh, plotting as usual. Scheming to pull youthful genius down to my level."

"How you harp on that theme."

"Well, I'm after Frank Jowett, really. He's full of notions about playing in art-theatre versions of *Crime and Punishment*, Kafka, and all that, and I've got a wonderful part for him in a thing of mine that's going to run for years and make him a matinee idol. . . . I do think the food in Oxford is really quite unbelievable—how you educated young men can stand it I can't think . . . what was I saying . . . oh, yes, about Jowett, poor fellow—he's dreaming of regenerating the English stage with discipline and goodness what, integrity I think, lifting the curse of Du Maurier and the gentleman amateurs from our native boards. I've been breaking it to him gently that we commercial men having been using the Stanislavski approach for years and that he'll have to learn our job before he can teach us how to do it. I tell him that he'll be able to make us eat out of his hands when he's got a huge reputation and a following—showing him the kingdoms of the world from a high place, in short. He is damn good, and I've got to have him for my play when it comes down to it."

"Is it going to be a really good play, Larry?"

"The best I can manufacture . . ." Larry suddenly looked

at me with an almost indecent curiosity and said deliberately, "It's got a wonderful part for an older woman in it."

"Whom are you thinking of?" I asked.

"Oh . . ." Larry's look of curiosity was replaced by one of amusement. "I have my ideas. I don't think I'll have any difficulty casting it." He sat back in his chair and pulled out a cigar case. "That question is pretty well settled, as a matter of fact—the only problem is this young man's part. He has to be convincingly, breathtakingly, young and incomplete, and he has to be a born actor. It has to be young Jowett, in short. And once I've got him we can fix the date of the New York opening. . . ."

"You don't usually open in New York, do you? I thought you liked to go there with an established hit."

Larry looked vastly amused by some secret joke again.

"Oh, there are special circumstances in this case . . . partly it's a question of the nature of the play—there are the two English characters and the others are Americans. I've rather fallen in love with America, as a matter of fact, head over heels . . . there's nothing in the world like autumn over there . . . nothing." He looked at me as if he expected me to see a joke and then his expression became almost contrite. "Forgive me," he said, "I've been being very tiresome, talking about myself so much. Tell me about your plans. . . ."

I was a little bewildered by his obvious embarrassment, and for some reason I felt awkward about talking to him about what I had decided that I had to do for the next few years.

"When I go down, when I leave the University, I shall be going into the Brigade, into the Colonel's old regiment."

"Oh my dear boy, my dear, dear boy . . ." Larry stared at me for a moment and then began to laugh almost uncontrollably. The tears streamed down his cheeks. I thought he was laughing at me because he assumed that I was going for a soldier to please the Colonel, that this was evidence of a final capitulation to Marshwood and its spirit. I thought of trying to explain to him that my decision had nothing to do with that at all, that it was simply a matter as Ermine had put it of coming to terms. That there was going to be a war now seemed beyond any question, every day's papers, every night's news report on the radio pointed to the inescapable fact. Whatever plans I made I would soon be a conscript, it seemed best to go into a crack regiment of my own choosing rather than to wait for my time to sweep me up. It would be soon enough to make private plans when the war had been fought and a private world returned. But it was useless to try to say anything of what was in my mind, there was no penetrating the wall of hysterical laughter which stood between us. For a moment I sat looking at him and then I got up and left him. As I walked angrily out of the restaurant I was conscious that there must be some reason for his outburst that I knew nothing about, and that I might get it if I demanded an explanation. But I was too angry to think what it might be or to wish to wait for it. And so I had no warning of what was to happen.

The summer term ended and I went off, after spending an uneventful night at Marshwood, to take part in the excavation of a Bronze Age camp on the Welsh border. The camp was on a hilltop not far from Tintern Abbey in the Wye Valley and it was a spectacularly lovely place. I enjoyed every minute I was there and I liked the niggling procedures of scientific archaeology—the concentration they demanded kept my mind off the news that was getting worse and worse as the year sloped away towards the Munich crisis. There were seven other volunteers from various universities helping at the dig and we were all very conscious that this was perhaps our last free summer before uniforms were put on us. We spoke very little about the future and concentrated on our work, on poaching fish out of the Wye, and on flirtations with the dark-haired and dark-eyed border girls who had a hint of the Welsh lilt in their musical voices. In pursuit of these young women we struck up friendships on the neighboring farms that led us into a good deal of unpaid labor in the harvest fields in the evenings. We all became brown and healthy and great drinkers of perry, the pale-green pear wine of the district. It was a happy time.

It was broken halfway through the second week in August by a telegram that simply said, "Come home as soon as you can. Arthur." I said good-bye to my new friends reluctantly and set out on a long cross-country journey that involved several changes of trains and which seemed to take all day. The Colonel had signed the telegram so he couldn't be ill, and I felt sure, knowing him, that if it were Naomi who was in danger he would have found some kindly warning phrase that would have prepared me for bad news without alarming me. This abrupt summons couldn't refer to that kind of situation, it must be something else. I puzzled over it and at last reached the conclusion as far as possible from the truth: The Colonel had decided that war was so close that he had used his influence with his old regiment to get me a commission, and I was being sent for to take it up at once. But then he would have explained himself if it had been that. I puzzled myself into a daze, and dozed through the afternoon as the branch-line trains trundled through the hot summer landscape. When I got out of my fourth train at Dinton Station it was dusk, and the platform, the station buildings, and the countryside were yielding back into the cooling air all the heat that the sun had burned into them during the day. It was stifling. Even the leaves on the trees seemed to have wilted. I looked about me to see if Jempson the local taxi-owner was anywhere about, and saw instead Hilary, the Colonel's stableman and chauffeur, coming towards me touching the peak of his uniform cap. His face was just visible in the blue-gray light but I saw that he had his company face on. When he was handling the horses and at ease with me and the Colonel his face was mobile and expressive, but when he was dealing with guests in the role of chauffeur he cultivated a poker face and a remote manner that he had acquired in some earlier phase of his existence when he had been required to help at table as a footman. He wore it now like a mask and instead of smiling and saying hallo Mister Richard he said, "Good evening, sir" in a toneless voice.

"Hallo, Hilary," I said. "I'm very glad to see you. How did you know I was coming by this train?"

"I didn't, sir. The Colonel said I was to meet all incoming trains from one o'clock on."

"I'm afraid you've had a long wait."

"It's of no importance, sir. May I take your bag?"

His back was rigid as he walked off towards the car, and when we sat side by side bowling off through Teffont towards Marshwood he was stiffer than ever and sternly silent.

"You don't happen to know what the trouble is," I asked after five silent minutes.

"I'm sure I don't know, sir."

It was clear that whatever it was was very bad.

The downs lay like dark waves frozen into immobility under the sky which was indigo except for a faintly green radiance in the west and the air that blew in through the open windows of the car was rich with the harvest smell of ripe straw. Though I couldn't see them I knew that behind every hedge the crisp fresh stubbles dotted with shocked-up wheat and oats stretched away into the semi-darkness. In a few more weeks shooting would begin. It was very good to be home, even if I had come back to trouble of some kind.

The Colonel was in his study and I was shocked to find him as I did. He was sitting in front of his green leather-topped desk with his hands in his lap staring at the pigeonholes in front of him. When I came in he swiveled his head round towards me with an expression that had momentarily something hopeful in it but which then drained away leaving a woebegone blank in the place of his usual warm and hearty look. It is a case of illness, I thought, he has had a stroke, but I instantly realized that if it were so he would be in bed and under medical care.

"It's you," he said flatly. "I'm glad you've come . . . though I see, now that you're here, I was wrong to send for you. There's nothing you can do. I'm sorry, my boy. . . ." He slumped back in his chair. "I don't know what to say. . . ."

"Is there anything wrong, sir?"

"Yes, yes, there is. Everything's as wrong as it can possibly be." He raised his eyebrows and passed a hand across his forehead. "I can hardly believe that things are as wrong as they are. . . . It's your mother. She's gone . . . left me. . . . She doesn't mean to come back."

"You mean she's run away."

"Yes." He rubbed his forehead again with the same look of utter bewilderment. "It's very hard for me to credit . . . she seemed happy enough and she never complained . . . did she never say anything to you?"

"Not a word, sir."

"No hint of any kind? Nothing?" He faced me. "You had no idea of this American project?"

"American project, no . . ." A great light began to dawn upon me, I saw Larry shaking with laughter, and heard him saying, "It's got a wonderful part in it for an older woman."

"Well, I'll tell you what's happened." He stood up and began to pace the far end of the room. "About a month ago Naomi told me she was worried about one or two little symptoms, not of anything serious, but of something that ought to be looked into. Some woman's thing that she should consult a specialist about. So we made appointments in London. I was to have gone with her, but then the appointments were changed to days when I happened to have pressing things to attend to down here, quarter sessions, that sort of thing . . . so she went alone. She went up to town for a second examination three days ago. She telephoned me to say that Sir Charles Wykes, that's the doctor fella, wanted to give her a more thorough going-over than the first day's appointment allowed, night before last, and that she'd be home, last night it would have been . . . well, she didn't come. I telephoned her hotel. She wasn't there. I supposed she'd gone to stay with a friend. I called all the friends I could think of but she wasn't with any of them. I got a letter this morning . . . posted in Southampton. She sailed on the *Queen Mary* the night she was supposed to come back here. She's out at sea now on her way to New York . . . you're sure you know nothing about all this?"

"No, nothing . . . at least . . ." I tried to tell him about Larry Brook.

"I can't make head or tale of that rigmarole . . . the thing that I can't endure is what she says here. . . ." he pulled a letter out of his pocket with the immediately recognizable scrawl on it. ". . . She says she's been very happy here, begs me to forgive her, says she'll always be grateful to me, says she's not the sort of woman to make me happy, says she doesn't fit into my life, says that in all fairness she can't go on with a deception, says she's going to Reno, means divorce. . . ." He flapped the letter at me. "Can you understand all that? Do you know what she's thinking about? What she can mean? Say if you know." He stopped, staring at me. "Do you know?"

"Yes, sir. She's an actress. She's going back to the stage. She doesn't exist anywhere else. Larry Brook came to her with a perfect part, written for her. She couldn't bear not to take it. She will open in the play, I should say, towards the beginning of November in New York."

"I'll go after her. I'll contest the divorce. I'll make her see reason . . . she must be having some kind of breakdown. . . ." He stared again. "This Larry Brook . . . do you think she cares for him?"

302

"Not in that way. Don't torment yourself with thinking you've been left for anyone, a man. She's gone to the theatre, to be what she is."

There was a long silence.

"She told me she was sick of it . . . that the whole life had become horrible to her. Was she lying to me?"

"No, she believed it, absolutely, then."

"Have I been the damnedest of fools?"

"No."

"You couldn't very well have said yes. . . ."

"I would have if it had been true."

He grinned like a dog that has had poison.

"Then what in God's name has happened?"

"You offered her the perfect part, written for her, and she couldn't bear not to take it. It was a part she'd dreamed of playing all her life. . . ."

"Then I have been a damned fool."

"If you want to put it like that you can. But there's something else to be said. She was happier in the role you gave her, for longer, than anyone else ever made her."

"But in the end it wasn't a good enough part."

"She exhausted the possibilities that were in it for her."

"And now she's off to something else. . . ." He twisted his face into a grimace. "Upon my soul, you don't make her out very attractive. I can hardly bear to hear you talk this way about her."

"Tigers may not seem very attractive to goats, to see how splendid they are you have to take into account that they're tigers. She's Cleopatra to me, Shakespeare's not Shaw's, she's Nora, all kinds of people, quite different—irreconcilable. She's been a loving mother, and an absolutely indifferent one who had a child by mistake, she's been a cold-hearted bully, and a wonderful friend. I wouldn't, now I'm not demanding that she always appear in a particular role, have her any different. The price would be to destroy her. It's too high."

"You at least have a claim on her that she can't very well shake off when it suits her."

"It's the sort of claim that I have on the wind to bring me air to breathe. I count myself lucky to get it."

He considered it, and then spoke quietly in an extremely gentle voice.

"But I love her, you see, Richard."

"Then you can't want to tie her down—she has to be all the different women she has to be."

"It's very hard to see that."

"It's painful, but we have to face it."

We faced each other again for a space and then I saw that his face cleared. He touched the bell and after a minute Manson appeared, grave-faced, and electrified with an overmastering curiosity that made his eyes flicker nervously between us.

"Oh, Manson, young Richard here has been traveling all day. I can see that he's famished. What have we got for him?"

"There is the cold lamb, sir," said Manson in a sepulchral voice. "I think Cook has a cherry tart, and there would be cream—unless of course Master Richard would prefer something in the way of cheese?"

"I think the tart would be the thing."

"I expect you'd like to eat and tumble into bed," said the Colonel, "you look quite tuckered out. How about a tray in your room?"

I saw that it was his way of asking to be left alone, and said that I would like that very much.

When Manson brought up my supper he was a man clearly torn between a variety of emotions. His feelings towards me were complex; he was loyal to the house and to the Colonel, he knew that some affront had been put on it and some hurt done to the Colonel, but he was not sure of its precise nature. He did not know how far, as Naomi's son, and an interloper, I was involved, but had expected that I would be in some way against the Colonel. Having seen us together in an ambiguous situation that suggested friendliness rather than hostility he had revised his assumptions, which had been like Hilary's —had indeed been worked out with Hilary in a series of below-stairs conferences which had engaged Cook, the three housemaids, Driver, Naomi's maid, and Manson himself— and was now off balance, hesitant between the poker-face treatment that would imply that I had become an outsider, and the old friendliness. All he knew was that Naomi had vanished, and that her vanishing had left the Colonel in greater distress than he had ever seen him in before, even after his father's death. He concluded that there had been a final break, but he could not be sure. He hovered over me and the tray as if he could not bring himself to go away without extracting some clue, some clinching remark, that would enable him to go downstairs as the bearer of news. While he fiddled with the tray, unpacked my bag, and sorted the clothes I had taken off before slipping into pyjamas and a dressing gown, taking some things for the wash, the shoes for cleaning, and the jacket and trousers to be pressed, he gave me one skillfully contrived opportunity after another to be communicative. At last, throwing all discretion aside, and discarding all the ruling conventions governing relations between master and man in which he had been encasing himself for some thirty years, he took the bull by the horns.

"Do you notice anything missing from the room, Master Richard?"

I looked vaguely round taking in the Admirals, the shelf where *Jorrock's* and *The Tactical Use of the Heavy Machine Gun*—a more interesting book than I had first thought—still held their places, at the Kodiak bear, the solid desk and bed, the big comfortable armchair.

"No, nothing, I think. . . ." I wondered if he had been counting the silver.

"Might I draw your attention to the mantelpiece?"

The trophies I had collected since I had come to Marshwood, a small jar of Roman glass, a flint axe head, a few framed photographs, were all there. But the green bowls had gone.

"I've searched everywhere for your bowls, sir, but I haven't been able to find them."

"Well, don't worry. They're not in the least important. I just liked the color of them."

"I was afraid you might think that there had been some carelessness when the room was being cleaned. I made sure that the maids were not responsible. It seems, sir," he emphasized his words, "that they've gone."

"Very well, it can't be helped. I shall have to look about and see what I can find to take their place." I couldn't endure the probing any longer. "Well, thank you, Manson, I have everything I want. Good night."

When he had gone I went over to the fireplace and stood looking at the empty spaces where the two bowls had been. Their absence was startling because it undermined everything that I thought I knew about Naomi, the whole basis of our relationship. I went and sat over on the window seat. The enormous night offered all its mysteries, a chained dog down at the home farm barked furiously and I guessed that a fox was about. What new role had Naomi embarked upon? I tried to assemble what I knew like the pieces of a jigsaw puzzle. I saw her as she had played to Max, the New Woman proud of herself and her freedom going out to choose herself an equal as a partner; I saw her again, as she had created herself for me, as the innocent victim of a Byron-like seducer; I saw her again in those middle years as a woman of the theatre existing only in her roles, a woman whose personal life was a mere diversion; and then I saw her once more as the natural aristocrat who, trapped by necessity into the humiliations of the life of the theatre, had been rescued and had returned to her true level as the Lady of Marshwood House . . . and what then? I knew that, as certainly as the sun would rise in the morning, there lay ahead a scene which I would have to play with the Colonel. He would tell me that what had happened had changed nothing between us, that I was still his heir and that I was to think of Marshwood as my home. He would mean what he said and we would both in our hearts know that everything was changed at the roots, that Naomi's departure had made my position at Marshwood altogether false and that we would inevitably drift apart as the years went by. The true link between us was broken, and if he still made me his heir he would be handing his beloved house across a gulf, to one who would be as much a stranger as any other future owner that chance might bring along. Had she gone simply to bring that breach about? Could it be simply that she found that her place at center stage had been usurped by the juvenile as the result of the Colonel's action in handing me the future of his house and its properties? Had she, as the implications of this came home to her, thrown up the part and left the stage? I wondered too what had taken her so precipitately back to it. The magnitude of the challenge presented by Larry's play—it was in Larry's mind Frank Jowett's opportunity, it was a machine to lift this youth with all his natural gifts out of obscurity into a position to take the theatrical chieftanship which his great actor-manager grandfather had enjoyed—provided a motive. It was a second chance, an opportunity to re-enact the Marshwood situation. She would act Frank off the stage and make his dazzling opening a mere background sparkle in the blaze of her splendid return. Could she be as simple in her motives as all that? I turned back to look at the blank spaces where the bowls had stood. She could only have taken them because I had given them to her, because she knew that they had meant something to me, because I had given them to her in the first place as a token of love, because in the end she loved me. . . .

But then if love was in her heart why had she been so wantonly cruel to the Colonel, tearing, plucking herself out of his life, as in the old days the public hangman had torn the heart out of a quartered traitor? I caught sight of myself across the room in a looking glass, and without thinking lifted my chin a little, improved my posture, and spoke aloud: "Yes, why? . . ." And it struck me poignantly that I was acting The Colonel's Heir. I recalled my other roles. The Wronged Child, The Unrecognized Genius, The Fool for Love, the low comedy part Max's Boy. . . . It occurred to me that I had always taken the Colonel as all of one piece, a man made as one saw him. It had never occurred to me to wonder what roles he had played before I knew him, what role he had played to Naomi. I saw what had been involved in his marriage in a new light, what presented itself as at first blush a disinterested desire to love, protect and cherish an unhappy woman could also be interpreted as a grandiose project of the Svengali kind in reverse. He had taken up a spectacular public figure, dynamically engaged in exhibitionist displays of her personality, and had transformed her into his private treasure, an accessory to the life of his house. The irony of her words in the peony garden revealed themselves—"It's nice to think I've given the place something." The whole measure of her distance from the Colonel lay in the remoteness of that gift to the place from the true nature of her unique creative and interpretive genius. What a lust for power lay behind the desire to pull her down from the summit where she belonged to become a performer in the Colonel's private play in his private theatre. It was in line with the rest of him, power was the motive that would make a man wish to shape a crowd of odd lots into a regiment of troops, and having done that to keep them at the level of a first-class formation. And as I saw his desire to pull her down plainly for the first time I saw myself beside him mewling and protesting that she was not a cozy Mummy figure. What could she do but leave us . . . she was not one of those like Alice, one of the dressers of life, standing ready in the wings with the costume for the quick change, or waiting in the dressing room with all the apparatus for a new role. She was one of the leads round whom the plays of life turned. The curtain had come down on the Marshwood comedy and we, the supers, had to look for other parts. We might grumble that she had prematurely ended a long run by walking out and setting us "at liberty," as they say in the theatrical employment advertisements, but that was only because we shrank from recognizing her right to a larger theatre than we could or would provide.

The quiet dark outside the room presented itself not as a void now but as a darkened stage on which anything and everything might happen. A huge tragedy called war was in preparation, a piece with parts of every kind in it, the Colonel as a soldier already probably had his chosen for him in some file in the War Office in London. I would be able to choose my own. And when that piece was played out the whole of life would open out again before us. It was not at all a bad thing to be "at liberty" and free.